The Great Silence

The Great Silence

What Remains After Belief

DAVID W. FALLS

RESOURCE *Publications* • Eugene, Oregon

THE GREAT SILENCE
What Remains After Belief

Resource Publications
An Imprint of Wipf and Stock Publishers
199 W. 8th Ave., Suite 3
Eugene, OR 97401

www.wipfandstock.com

PAPERBACK ISBN: 979-8-3852-7492-5
HARDCOVER ISBN: 979-8-3852-7493-2
EBOOK ISBN: 979-8-3852-7494-9

VERSION NUMBER 02/12/26

Contents

Preface

I grew up surrounded by the rhythms of belief. The prayers, the hymns, the Sunday routines were simply part of daily life. What stayed with me, though, wasn't the words people spoke—it was the quiet afterward. While others seemed sure of what that silence meant, I found myself listening to it in a different way. It didn't reassure me or frighten me; it simply made me curious. Even as a kid, sitting in a pew with my legs too short to reach the floor, I wondered what filled the space everyone else called holy.

That early curiosity never quite went away. It followed me into school hallways, late-night conversations, and the long, private moments when belief is supposed to feel most certain. I didn't doubt to be difficult. I doubted because the explanations I was offered, however sincerely given, never settled. They failed to hold up the moment I examined them. I kept asking, not to tear anything down, but because I wanted whatever was true to stand on its own.

As I grew older, I found that many of the claims I had been taught were surprisingly fragile. Answers meant to resolve mystery only created new ones. The more I learned, the more I realized that honest inquiry and inherited doctrine rarely travel together for long. Reason doesn't always lead where we expect, and it certainly doesn't lead where we're told it must.

This book began with a simple question: if a perfect and personal God exists, why does the world look exactly as it would if He didn't? The question isn't theological—it's evidential. A claim that large should leave traces. And if those traces aren't there, then belief becomes a story passed down, not a truth discovered. Doubt, in that sense, isn't defiance. It's responsibility. It means holding faith to the same standard faith demands of everything else.

Along the way, I found myself in good company. Hume, Russell, Pascal, Epicurus, Camus—men separated by centuries, yet united by an insistence that honesty matters more than comfort. Their questions are still unsettled, not because they are obscure, but because belief avoids them. To read their work is to see convictions that once felt immovable begin to weaken.

This book also looks at scripture, morality, and the long human habit of calling our hopes "revelation." None of it is written in anger. It's an attempt to understand what remains when the lens of tradition is set aside. If God is real, evidence will lead us there. If God is not, then meaning must be found in what is human, not what is heavenly.

Ours is a century where old certainties confront new evidence. Science has explained what myth once guarded, and reason now ventures into spaces once considered sacred. Even artificial intelligence, something no prophet ever imagined, has begun to expose how deeply human our gods have always been. But this is not a book about technology; it is about the mind that made it. We are the first generation to watch our own questions reflected back at us, and in that reflection, much of what once felt divine looks strikingly familiar.

These pages trace a personal unlearning: the steady shift from inherited belief to earned understanding. The journey is not from faith to cynicism, but from assumption to clarity. It is what happens when the stories that shaped us are tested rather than simply repeated.

If you reach the last page with absolute certainty, you have missed the point. Certainty is what I began with, not what I found. The aim of this book is simpler: to follow evidence wherever it leads, even when it leads beyond the gods. That kind of honesty requires its own kind of courage—the courage to set aside what we wish were true in order to face what is.

I've come to believe that is the most faithful act a person can perform.

Acknowledgments

I am grateful to my brother, Gary, for the many conversations we have shared around questions of belief, and for those still to come. I have enjoyed our exchanges, and I look forward to many more.

Gratitude to my wife, Stephanie, who has listened to every theory, counterargument, and question with patience and grace. Her calm in the face of endless debate made this work possible.

Introduction

"What can be asserted without evidence can also be dismissed without evidence."

Christopher Hitchens

The question of God has never been just about existence. It's about endurance—why the idea persists even when the evidence does not. Across history, people have searched the skies for signs, listened for voices in fire and storm, and built entire civilizations around stories meant to explain uncertainty. Yet alongside every generation of believers, there have also been people who simply couldn't accept mystery as an answer. Their doubts weren't acts of rebellion; they were attempts to make sense of a world that rarely behaves the way faith says it should.

Belief survives because it meets a human need. We look for patterns when life feels chaotic, and for purpose when suffering feels senseless. Religion once provided both. It offered explanations when science was in its infancy and language struggled to describe the unknown. But as knowledge grew, the scope of the divine shrank. Not because scientists set out to destroy faith, but because the world turned out to run on reliable laws rather than hidden intentions. Explanations once attributed to gods receded; not in defeat, but in proportion to our understanding.

Today, this shift is visible not just in individuals but in entire populations. The fastest-growing religious identity in the United States is now "None of the above."[1] These so-called Nones are not defined by hostility toward faith; most are simply unconvinced. They live with uncertainty that mirrors the one I felt as a child—an intuition that inherited belief no

1. Pew Research Center, "America's Changing Religious Landscape," 2017.

longer aligns with lived reality. Their rise marks a cultural turning: doubt has moved from the margins to the mainstream. Faith is no longer the default, and the question is no longer why some people leave religion, but why others remain. In their hesitation I see a reflection of the journey this book traces—not rebellion, but an honest attempt to let conviction follow evidence rather than tradition.

What follows is not an attempt to reconcile faith and reason or to stage a debate between belief and disbelief. I am not interested in defending skepticism as an identity or attacking belief as a weakness. The goal is narrower and more demanding: to examine why religious claims are exempted from the standards we apply everywhere else, and what changes when they are not. This is an inquiry into origins, persistence, and consequence, not a manifesto.

This book follows that same movement. It does not balance belief and skepticism as equal options, because the evidence no longer treats them equally. Every serious inquiry into the origins of life, mind, morality, and the universe has favored natural explanation over supernatural intention. What earlier generations interpreted as miracles now falls within physics, biology, psychology, and history. What we once called revelation often reads like memory—human stories trying to make sense of fear, joy, suffering, and hope.

The chapters that follow take up that inquiry directly. They begin with the burden of proof and the simple but uncomfortable question of why belief demands less evidence than any other claim of similar scale. From there, the book examines arguments that once seemed persuasive—Pascal's Wager, Russell's teapot, appeals to tradition, and the notion that morality requires divine command. It looks at suffering, scripture, and the psychological pull of certainty. Later chapters turn to modern challenges to faith, including the role of technology in revealing how predictable and deeply human our patterns of belief have always been. The final chapters ask what remains when the old explanations no longer suffice, and why meaning doesn't disappear when the gods do.

That intellectual trajectory mirrors my own. My first experience of doubt didn't come from philosophers; it came from the night God fell silent, the night prayer met quiet and nothing in the room changed. The silence didn't feel hostile—it just felt honest. Years later, philosophy helped me name what I had sensed as a child: that doubt is not defiance but discipline. It's what happens when we hold religious claims to the same standard we apply to every other question about reality. And when I later encountered science and technology—fields that operate without appealing to the divine—the gap between explanation and belief widened further. Not because algorithms or microscopes "disprove" God, but because they reveal how often our gods reflect our expectations more than the world itself. At one point, that curiosity led me to build my own "God Helmet," hoping a machine might illuminate what prayer no longer could.

To doubt God is not to reject wonder. It's to refuse illusion. The earliest thinkers to disentangle nature from the divine didn't make the world smaller; they expanded it. Explaining lightning without Zeus did not drain the sky of awe. Understanding evolution did not empty life of meaning. If anything, removing supernatural explanations restored the universe to itself—vast, indifferent, and astonishing. Reverence grounded in reality carries a different kind of beauty, one that doesn't depend on being protected or promised more than the world can give.

This is not a book about reconciling faith with reason. It's about what happens when reason is allowed to speak plainly. It asks what belief becomes when miracles are replaced by evidence, when morality is understood through empathy rather than command, and when meaning is chosen rather than inherited. My aim is not to wound religion, but to outgrow the need for it—to show that clarity and compassion do not require a divine source.

My hope is that these pages offer more than critique. I want them to show disbelief as a constructive stance: a way of meeting uncertainty without surrendering to fear, a commitment to live truthfully even when truth feels incomplete. You don't need to be certain to value reality. You only need to prefer honesty over comfort.

Wherever you enter this book—whether from conviction, curiosity, or unease—the destination is the same: a recognition that mystery does not require a master, and that meaning survives perfectly well without the supernatural. This is the story of a search that began in faith and led to understanding, of how the silence I once filled with prayer became the space I no longer tried to fill.

What remains, in the end, is not God but the human mind—still questioning, still creating, and still learning to live with what it discovers.

PART I

The Case Against God

1

Silence as Evidence

"Extraordinary claims require extraordinary evidence."

CARL SAGAN

THE REPLY THAT NEVER CAME

The first time I prayed, I expected something to happen. Not a miracle—just a shift, a warmth, a presence—but the room stayed exactly as it was. I remember staring into the dark, waiting for a reply that never came. That should have been the end of it, but I kept trying. I prayed again the next night, and the next, convinced that sooner or later the quiet would break. It never did. And yet that steady absence became the background of my childhood faith: the expectation of a voice, and the persistent lack of one.

In those days, the stillness felt vast, something that had to mean more than it appeared to. I was told that God answered in His own way, in His own time, so I tried to meet Him halfway. I prayed more earnestly, confessed more thoroughly, whispered the same hopes with greater sincerity. Still nothing changed. Only later did I understand that what I took for divine restraint was simply the world behaving as it always had, indifferent to my petitions.

Not that I saw it that way at first. I searched for signs everywhere. The flicker of a lamp, a passing breeze, a perfectly timed song—all of them became potential messages if I strained hard enough to see them that way. For a while, they comforted me. But a pattern emerged: the coincidences didn't line up, and the world didn't respond differently whether I prayed or didn't. What felt like subtle communication one night felt like coincidence the next. Eventually, I had to admit that the "answers" I thought I saw were projections of my own need. I was learning, without realizing it, how easily humans mistake pattern for purpose.

The strange thing is that the absence remained steady even after those interpretations fell apart. It began to feel less like rejection and more like equilibrium, the natural state of things. The universe was not hiding signs; it simply was not offering them. The hum of the refrigerator, the distant whoosh of a car on the road, and the settling of the house were the only nightly constants. At some point, I stopped trying to convince myself they meant something. Their indifference felt almost honest.

What I didn't recognize then was that I was already thinking like someone who needed evidence, not reassurance. I would whisper a prayer one night and wait for something, anything, to change. When nothing did, I tried again the next night, adjusting the wording as if phrasing mattered. The outcome was always the same. The variable was trust; the constant was quiet. Without knowing the term, I was running experiments. And the experiments were telling me something my theology wasn't prepared for.

This wasn't cynicism. I still wanted God to be real. I still wanted the universe to be personal. But the longer that stillness endured, the more I realized that wanting and knowing were not the same thing. If an all-powerful, all-knowing being was present, attentive, and engaged with human life, the evidence should appear somewhere—especially in the small, sincere prayers of a child. Instead, I was left with the same unbroken calm. I didn't yet call that a conclusion, but I felt its weight.

And that weight changed me. When I prayed less, I noticed my thoughts more clearly. If there was no divine audience, then the responsibility for my choices fell back on me. I couldn't blame bad luck on God's plan or credit good fortune to His favor. The absence forced a kind of honesty: my actions mattered because I chose them, not because someone was watching. That realization was unsettling at first. Faith had offered comfort through the idea that someone else held the reins. Without that, I had to learn how to steer.

Meaning didn't disappear when the prayers went unanswered; it shifted. Instead of waiting for the universe to speak, I began to pay attention to the world as it was. Kindness, loyalty, small moments of care; they took on more significance because they weren't commanded or tallied. They were simply choices I could make, and their value didn't depend on divine approval. In that way, the silence remained—but no longer as a void. It became a condition of reality, forcing me to see that the world owed me nothing, and that meaning wasn't given—it was made.

That shift, subtle at first, became the foundation for everything that came later. The stars I once imagined as distant witnesses no longer felt like silent judges; they felt like reminders of a universe that persisted on its own terms. Not designed, not arranged, but enduring. The silence wasn't empty. It was full of movement and coherence, energy transforming and matter rearranging without need for permission. What I once interpreted as divine restraint began to look like the natural order itself.

Even now, I'm not sure faith ever fully leaves us. The longing behind my childhood prayers didn't vanish; it redirected. I found myself searching for meaning in science, in philosophy, in conversations about what it means to be human. The curiosity remained; only the vocabulary changed. The quiet I once feared became a space for questions instead of expectations.

In hindsight, those unanswered prayers marked the beginning of a gradual change. They taught me to live without guarantees, to rely on inquiry rather than tradition, and to accept uncertainty as an ordinary part of life. The silence provided no answers, but it required greater attention to evidence and experience. Disappointment gradually became a practice of careful observation. The world's indifference was not something to be taken personally. It was a reason to learn how to understand reality as it is, rather than as I wished it to be.

PRAYERS THAT WENT NOWHERE

Those prayers were not lofty meditations. They were small, personal petitions: that my parents would remain healthy, that my family would stay safe, that life would remain steady. Sometimes I asked simply for acknowledgment; not a miracle, just some sign that my words were heard. But nothing came.

There was a logic to the way I prayed. If God was real and cared about us, surely He would answer a child who asked in faith. When prayers went unanswered, the explanations always seemed to shift;

maybe I hadn't prayed hard enough, maybe God was testing me, maybe He was saying no. In every case, the quiet was reinterpreted as meaning.

After enough disappointments, I began lowering the bar. I stopped asking for miracles or outcomes and instead begged for a sign, any sign at all. A flicker of light, a sudden breeze, a word in a dream. I watched the shadows on my bedroom wall, waiting for movement. I listened in the stillness for a voice that never came. The calm grew heavier, not because it was hostile, but because it was indifferent.

I tested those expectations in small, childish ways. One night I asked for a sign and promised not to tell anyone if it came. Another time I tried the opposite, telling God out loud that I didn't believe, half expecting a reprimand from the heavens. Both times, the room remained unchanged. The ceiling, the moonlight, the hum of the refrigerator—none were responsive.

Looking back, those unanswered prayers did more to shape my doubt than any argument I would later read. They were experiments, repeated nightly, with the same result: no reply. Faith asked me to treat stillness as presence, but in my own experience, stillness was simply stillness. The more I prayed and heard nothing, the more it felt like I was speaking into an empty room. Those nightly experiments taught me something I didn't yet have the language for: silence doesn't need explaining—only claims about what it means do.

Years later I learned that philosophers had a name for the imbalance I had felt as a child. At the time, I wasn't thinking about arguments or evidence. I was just a kid waiting for something—anything—to happen, and nothing ever did.

Even after I stopped praying, the habit of waiting remained. For a while I kept a quiet mental record—and later an actual journal—writing things down so I would not miss anything, convinced that meaning would reveal itself if I watched closely enough. Whenever something went right, I caught myself wondering if it might be a late reply from heaven, proof that patience had finally paid off. Yet the pattern never appeared. What looked like divine timing one week looked like ordinary cause and effect the next. The silence had not changed; only my need to interpret it had.

I used to envy those who claimed that prayer had transformed their lives. They spoke as though devotion were a transaction: ask sincerely, receive accordingly. But I noticed that their evidence was always retrospective. A recovery was called a miracle, even when medicine explained it. An escape from danger became divine protection, though others in the same peril were not spared. Success confirmed God's favor, and tragedy confirmed His mysterious plan. The story always bent to fit conviction. Even as a child, I sensed how fragile that logic was.

What I didn't yet have words for was how selective the evidence always seemed. We heard the voices of those who survived, the ones whose prayers happened to align with good fortune, but never the silence of those who did not. Their stories ended before they could testify, leaving only the successes to be counted. Faith, I realized, often speaks from the side of the living, mistaking survival for evidence.

One evening I decided to test it in a way that only a child could. I prayed for two impossible things at once, small but contradictory requests, certain that whatever happened would prove something. Nothing did. The outcome was neither blessing nor punishment; it was simply ordinary. The realization came slowly: the world would go on, with or without my permission.

In hindsight, those unanswered prayers marked the start of a gradual change in how I understood the world. They taught me to live without guarantees, to place greater trust in inquiry than in tradition, and to accept uncertainty as a normal feature of human life. The silence did not provide answers, but it shifted my attention toward evidence, experience, and patterns that could be examined. Disappointment slowly turned into a more disciplined way of thinking. The apparent indifference of the world was not an injury to be explained, but a condition to be understood on its own terms rather than through personal expectation.

In later years I would discover that others had wrestled with the same conclusion and had given it a vocabulary far more precise than mine. What I had reached through childhood frustration, they had expressed through reason: conviction carries the burden of its own proof. I did not know it then, but I had already taken the first step toward that understanding.

PRESUMPTION OF ATHEISM

That unease eventually took on a philosophical shape. Philosopher Antony Flew, one of the most influential atheists of the twentieth century, gave this principle its sharpest form in what he called the *presumption of atheism*.[1] Just as a courtroom begins with the defendant presumed

1. Flew, "Presumption of Atheism," 13–23.

innocent until proven guilty, Flew argued that the conversation about God should begin with nonbelief until evidence is presented. Disbelief, he said, is the rational default. The burden of proof rests not with the skeptic to disprove God, but with the believer to demonstrate that faith has grounds beyond assertion.[2] For Flew, faith without evidence was not a virtue; it was a reversal of reason itself.

That comparison to the courtroom struck me as immediately practical. Our judicial system is built on this very principle. No one would expect a defendant to prove they did not commit a crime. The responsibility rests squarely with the prosecution to show, beyond a reasonable doubt, that the charge is true. Without that safeguard, justice would collapse into chaos. We would all be guilty until proven innocent.

The same reasoning applies to religion. If someone affirms that an all-powerful, all-knowing being governs the universe, the responsibility for supporting that affirmation falls entirely on them. It is not the skeptic's task to disprove every possibility. You cannot be asked to prove that something is not there, whether a god, a ghost, or a guardian angel. The absence of proof is not a weakness in skepticism; it is the natural position until verification is provided.

When I first encountered Flew's writing, it felt like a quiet act of permission. For years I had been told that disbelief was the harder stance, the one that needed justification. Here, at last, was a framework that restored balance. It did not make grand claims or offer easy comfort. It simply required that extraordinary statements meet ordinary standards of proof. Flew's logic did not mock belief; it asked that conviction stand on its own two feet.

That realization unsettled me as much as it liberated me. To say that belief carries the burden of evidence also means that doubt carries a burden of honesty. It cannot hide behind anger or disappointment. It must be willing to accept the facts if and when they appear. The presumption of atheism was not an excuse to stop asking questions; it was an invitation to keep asking them carefully.

I began to see how many conversations about faith avoided that discipline. People spoke as though sincerity were evidence, as though longing itself proved what was longed for. But sincerity and truth are not the same thing. The intensity of a feeling tells us nothing about the accuracy

2. Flew, *God and Philosophy*, 48–52.

of its object. To recognize that difference was freeing. It meant I no longer had to treat comfort as confirmation or emotion as evidence.

Flew's argument also helped me understand why doubt is so often misunderstood. Within many faith communities, disbelief is portrayed as pride or rebellion, a refusal to bow before mystery. In reality, it can be an act of fairness. The skeptic is not closing doors but keeping them open until something real walks through. The believer begins with a claim; the doubter begins with a question. Both are searching for truth, but only one insists that it be demonstrated rather than declared.

Over time I realized that Flew's principle extended beyond religion. It applied to politics, science, and ordinary life. Whenever someone made a sweeping claim, I found myself returning to that courtroom image: the claim stands accused until proven true. The rule protects not only reason but humility, reminding us that conviction is easy to claim and hard to earn.

The presumption of atheism did not end my search; it gave it structure. It taught me that unbelief is not a conclusion but a method, a way of beginning from honesty and working forward. In that light, doubt ceased to feel like absence. It became a kind of integrity, a refusal to pretend to know what I did not.

ON BEING THE ODD ONE OUT

When skepticism appears inside a community of faith, it is rarely greeted with curiosity. Doubt is often cast not as a question to consider but as a weakness to correct. In church classrooms, questions about God's silence were usually met with assurances about trust. In sermons, doubt was portrayed as the enemy of devotion, the first step down a dangerous slope. They were questions that should not be asked at all, the kind that marked you as different simply for voicing them.

In the world I grew up in, being a nonbeliever was not a neutral stance. It was treated as a flaw, a mark against your character—not so much by my family, but by the broader world around me. To doubt was to invite suspicion: maybe you were arrogant, maybe you lacked gratitude, maybe you were drifting toward moral collapse. Faith was seen as a sign of goodness; unbelief, of something gone wrong. Even before I could articulate my own questions, I understood that disbelief carried a kind of stigma.

I learned to measure silence differently. At church gatherings, the talk around me revolved easily around prayer and blessing, but I learned how to nod without agreeing, how to join in a hymn without letting the words reach conviction. The skill of blending in became its own quiet form of survival. I began to understand how social belonging can outweigh honesty. A single doubt voiced aloud could cool an entire room.

Being honest had real consequences. My mother's faith was steady and unquestioned, and I had always respected the comfort and strength it gave her. One evening, I told her that I was no longer sure I believed. She became very still and asked, quietly, why I would say that. Her response was not anger but concern. She suggested that I speak with a priest. To her, belief was not something to examine but something to protect. We sat in silence, aware that the conversation had changed something between us. I understood then that disbelief does not need to be dramatic to be unsettling; even a simple expression of doubt can be enough.

This dynamic is not unique to my experience. History shows the same pattern again and again. Augustine of Hippo, the fourth-century bishop whose writings became foundational for Western Christianity,[3] described his own pre-conversion doubts as though they were an illness cured only by faith. In medieval Europe, to question official doctrine risked being branded a heretic, with punishments ranging from public shaming to execution.[4] Even in less extreme times, religious communities have often treated unbelief as a kind of betrayal. To step outside the shared conviction is to unsettle the harmony of the group.

Flew's courtroom analogy revealed how deeply that imbalance runs. The skeptic is placed in the role of defendant, expected to justify refusal, while the believer assumes the role of accuser, presenting claims as though they require no defense. The reversal of responsibility gives the appearance of fairness but preserves authority where it has always been. To challenge that structure is to disrupt not only theology but the social order that protects it.

Yet reason alone cannot erase the human cost. Communities bond through shared devotion, not shared doubt, and the pressure to conform can be immense. In modern surveys, atheists still rank among the least trusted groups in the United States, below nearly every other minority.[5] To admit disbelief is often to risk being seen as less moral, less trustworthy,

3. Augustine, Confessions, bk. VIII.

4. Moore, The Formation of a Persecuting Society, 18–35.

5. Pew Research Center, "Americans' Feelings About Religion," 2019.

less American. The suspicion may not always be voiced, but it lingers like static in the air.

The irony is that doubt often arises from the same place as faith—a concern for what is true, what is good, what is worthy of commitment. The doubter's questions are not acts of rebellion but of conscience. Yet in a setting where answers are sacred, questions themselves can feel dangerous.

There is a solitude that comes with standing apart from belief, a quiet that feels different from the stillness of prayer. It is not cosmic but social, the hush that follows when you withhold an expected amen. I learned that skepticism requires a kind of courage rarely celebrated: the courage to live without applause.

What sustained me was the belief that careful questioning is not cynicism but responsibility. It is a way of taking truth seriously, rather than accepting claims too easily. Asking honest questions reflects respect for reality as it is, not automatic deference to authority. To question is to recognize that truth and error both exist, and that distinguishing between them matters.

If doubt was treated as weakness in the pews, philosophy and science reframed it as strength. To ask for evidence was not to diminish belief but to elevate honesty. I began to see that skepticism, at its best, was a way of keeping conviction accountable to the same standards we apply everywhere else.

SAGAN'S MAXIM: EXTRAORDINARY CLAIMS

Among those who gave voice to that fairness was Carl Sagan, the American astronomer and science communicator whose book and television series *Cosmos* reached millions.[6] He put the principle in the plainest terms: extraordinary claims require extraordinary evidence.[7] That simple sentence carried the clarity of sunlight. It was not hostile to faith, only precise about the rules of inquiry.

When I first heard the phrase, it struck me with the force of recognition. I had spent years wondering why some ideas were accepted without question while others were expected to justify themselves. Sagan's maxim gave that imbalance a name. It was not arrogance to ask for proof; it was

6. Sagan, *Cosmos*, 1–5.

7. Sagan, *The Demon-Haunted World*, 73.

the foundation of understanding. To expect more support for larger assertions was not unfair—it was consistency.

We already practice this principle in nearly every area of life. If a neighbor says they saw a cat in the yard, we do not ask for proof. If they claim it was a mountain lion, we want a picture. But if they insist they saw a pink unicorn trotting down the street, we demand something more substantial than a story. The greater the claim, the higher the bar. We adjust our skepticism without needing to be told. Religion, however, often asks for exemption from that logic.

When I began reading Sagan's work in depth, what stood out was not only his reasoning but his tone. He wrote with a scientist's precision but also with a poet's sense of wonder. His call for proof was never a dismissal of mystery. It was a way of honoring it. He seemed to say that to truly appreciate the universe, we must be willing to separate what we know from what we only wish to be true.

That insight reshaped the way I saw beauty itself. The same sunset that had once been described to me as proof of divine artistry became no less beautiful when explained through physics and light. Understanding did not drain the wonder; it refined it. To know that color scatters through air molecules or that a star's glow bends across the horizon does not make the scene smaller. It makes it more intricate, more astonishing for being real.

The first time I watched *Cosmos*, I was caught off guard by how reverent it felt. Sagan spoke about the birth of galaxies and the chemistry of life with the same awe others reserve for scripture. Yet his reverence was grounded in observation, not authority. He invited questions instead of forbidding them. That invitation became a kind of permission: to be moved by existence without needing to worship it.

Religion, by contrast, often sidesteps that demand for proportion. I recall reading about a piece of toast that seemed to bear the face of Mary, celebrated as a sign of divine presence. Even as a child I wondered whether a creator of galaxies would choose to reveal Himself through breakfast. The claim was extraordinary, yet the evidence was crumbs. The imbalance was obvious. For unicorns we demand proof; for visions in food we suspend it.

The kinds of evidence typically offered for God's existence rarely rise above this level. Personal feelings, inherited traditions, or verses from ancient texts are treated as though they could support the most sweeping assertion imaginable: that an all-powerful and all-knowing being created the universe and watches over every human life. Against such a claim, sincerity cannot serve as validation.

Sagan's evidentiary principle does not reject the possibility of God. It simply insists that the scale of a claim be matched by the scale of the support. If someone asserts something infinite, the proof must reach beyond the ordinary. Otherwise, conviction becomes a matter of preference rather than proportion.

What affected me most was that Sagan did not argue as someone trying to defeat belief, but as someone urging intellectual humility. His insistence on evidence was not meant to diminish wonder, but to prevent it from becoming careless or misleading. He modeled a balance between curiosity and restraint, showing that skepticism does not exclude a sense of awe. I began to see that treating existence seriously requires not uncritical acceptance, but careful and disciplined attention.

That spirit became my compass. It guided how I approached every claim afterward, sacred or secular. If an idea could not survive the request for evidence, it did not deserve the name of truth. And if the truth was genuinely extraordinary, it could bear that weight. In time I came across a thought experiment that captured that principle perfectly.

RUSSELL'S TEAPOT

Bertrand Russell, the Nobel Prize–winning philosopher and logician known for his defense of reason, asked us to imagine a small china teapot orbiting the sun somewhere between Earth and Mars.[8] The teapot is too small for any telescope to detect, so its existence can never be confirmed or denied. If someone insisted that the teapot was really there, how should we respond?

Russell's answer was simple. The burden of proof rests entirely with the person making the claim. No one else is obliged to disprove the existence of an undetectable teapot. If it cannot be tested, measured, or shown, it cannot demand belief. The image is striking because it is absurd. Its very absurdity reveals the logic.

When I first encountered this idea, I smiled at its playfulness, but it stayed with me for reasons that went beyond humor. As a child I had prayed into silence, waiting for a reply that never came. Russell's teapot gave that quiet a shape. It illustrated, in miniature, what I had already

8. Russell, "Is There a God?," 547–48.

learned by experience: that claims without support are not equal to claims with it. The teapot may exist, but if no one can demonstrate it, the only honest answer is that we do not know.

The thought experiment may seem trivial, yet it carries enormous weight. It reminds us how language can smuggle certainty into places where knowledge has not earned it. Once a claim is made, the pressure shifts unfairly to those who question it. The teapot becomes a symbol for every untestable conviction; every idea protected from scrutiny by its own vagueness.

I began to see this pattern almost everywhere. Someone insists that a prophecy came true, but when pressed for details, they claim its fulfillment is invisible to unbelievers. Another person says that fate has a plan for every soul, and when asked for evidence, replies that the plan is hidden for our own good. Each time, the same move occurs: the burden slides from the speaker to the skeptic. The claim becomes safer precisely because it cannot be examined.

Russell's analogy dismantles that protection. It insists that belief earns its standing through demonstration, not exemption. Just as we would not believe in the teapot without evidence, we should not accept supernatural claims that exist only in assertion. The purpose is not ridicule but clarity. Without this standard, we lose the ability to distinguish between what is plausible and what is merely comforting.

The relevance of his point extends far beyond theology. The same logic applies to conspiracy theories, pseudoscience, and superstition. Someone insists that a secret group controls world events, or that unseen forces shape our destinies. When asked for proof, they reply that the absence of evidence is itself proof of how well the secret is kept. The skeptic is told to disprove a claim designed to be unfalsifiable. The teapot principle exposes the flaw. It is not the task of the doubter to refute every fantasy; it is the responsibility of the claimant to provide reason to believe.

What struck me most about Russell's image was its fairness. It did not sneer or condemn. It simply asked that statements about reality be treated with the same care we give any other assertion of fact. To live by that rule is to accept humility as the cost of knowledge. It means admitting when we do not know, and refusing to dress uncertainty in the language of conviction.

For me, the teapot did not disprove God, but it clarified what belief demands. It showed how easily tradition can shift the weight of proof, how often we begin with an assumption and then ask the world to justify our comfort. The teapot returned the responsibility to where it belongs. If someone claims to know the mind of the universe, they must show why that claim deserves trust.

I often think about how radical that simple fairness still is. It cuts through centuries of inherited authority and reduces the grandest metaphysical declarations to a single test: what can be shown? Everything else remains possibility, speculation, or poetry. None of that is shameful, but none of it is knowledge. What survives the collapse of evidence is not argument but faith.

THE LIMITS OF FAITH

The best way to define faith is as the commitment of one's consciousness to beliefs for which there is no sensory evidence or rational proof. It is the acceptance of a claim despite insufficient or even contradictory evidence. At some point in almost every debate between atheist and theist, faith will enter the conversation. It becomes the final refuge, invoked when all other arguments have failed. Yet this is no argument at all. By its very invocation, faith concedes that religious claims cannot stand on their own merits.

To admit that something is non-intellectual is to remove it from the realm of serious inquiry. In daily life we act on assumptions we cannot absolutely prove, but we do so because they are probable, not because we sanctify them as truth. If someone steps out of a ten-story window, they could claim faith that they will walk on air—but gravity does not negotiate with conviction. We rely on evidence, not hope, to keep us alive. Faith decides nothing here. And yet we do have very good reasons for not stepping out of that window.

Still, faith rarely ends with logic; it reaches for something to feel, and that is where miracles begin.

ALLURE OF MIRACLES

By this point, I had begun to notice the same pattern repeating itself in different forms. When I was young, miracle stories held a special fascination. They were moments when faith seemed to spill into ordinary life, proof that God was still active in the world. I heard about statues that wept, about saints who healed the sick, about apparitions of Mary appearing to the faithful. These tales were told not with doubt but with reverence, as if the very act of repeating them confirmed their truth.

To believe in such wonders was to belong. They gave religion its color and urgency. A faith without marvels would have felt thin, almost lifeless. Miracles promised that the stories in Scripture were not locked in the past but could reappear at any moment. To question them was to risk more than disbelief; it was to risk being seen as irreverent, as someone unwilling to recognize divine power.

For a long time I accepted them as others did. I was told about a woman in a nearby town whose cancer had vanished after a prayer circle gathered around her hospital bed. The account passed from family to family until it became legend. No one could name the doctors or verify the diagnosis, but that was part of its allure. The less it could be traced, the more sacred it seemed. Evidence would have diminished it. The mystery was the message.

As I grew older, I noticed how these stories multiplied in times of fear. During illness, disaster, or uncertainty, people needed wonders more than ever. They offered reassurance that the universe was still under supervision, that someone was watching, that pain had purpose. Every culture, every generation, has produced its own version of this comfort. The details change, but the longing remains the same: the wish that the laws of nature might bend, just once, to show that we are seen.

History is filled with examples. In the Middle Ages, shrines across Europe drew pilgrims with claims of relics that cured blindness or raised the dead. Entire towns prospered on the strength of these tales. The miraculous served to renew what was already assumed, not to prove what was in doubt. Its purpose was never to persuade skeptics but to reassure believers.

The Scottish philosopher David Hume, writing in the eighteenth century, pointed out the weakness in this pattern.[9] Human testimony, he argued, is far more likely to be mistaken—through error, exaggeration, or deceit—than for the laws of nature to have been suspended. No account of a marvel could ever outweigh the ordinary reliability of experience. What Hume observed with logic, I had begun to see in practice.

Many of the most famous wonders do not survive scrutiny. Statues that appeared to weep were found to be leaking condensation or oil from

9. Hume, *An Enquiry Concerning Human Understanding*, 114–16.

hidden cavities. Relics that drew pilgrims by the thousands turned out to be animal bones. Reports of sudden healings unraveled when medical records were examined. Even biblical events, once accepted as literal history, have been traced to natural phenomena magnified by centuries of retelling.

Other cases show how the desire for meaning can overtake perception itself. In 1917, tens of thousands gathered in Fatima, Portugal, claiming to see the sun dance in the sky.[10] To believers it was a sign from heaven; to skeptics, a collective illusion shaped by expectation and light. At Lourdes in France, millions still line up for healing waters, though of the thousands of reports, only a handful have ever been recognized as unexplained.[11] In modern times, televangelists have staged dramatic healings for broadcast audiences, later exposed for using hidden microphones and planted actors. Each generation produces its miracles, and each generation produces its debunkings.

Yet the stories endure. They persist not because they are verified but because they satisfy an emotional need that evidence cannot touch. The miraculous offers reassurance that life is not random, that suffering is not wasted, that we are not alone.

People sometimes argue that our existence is a miracle, claiming that the odds of life arising are so small that it must have been intended. But improbability alone is not evidence of design. Imagine a golfer hitting a ball across a large field. After a long flight, it lands on a few particular blades of grass. Looked at afterward, that spot can seem extraordinary simply because it is the one the ball reached. But was it a miracle that the ball hit those blades of grass and not others? No—the ball had to land somewhere. Our existence works the same way. We notice the outcome because we are standing inside it, not because it was chosen.

We rarely notice how selective our idea of a miracle can be. When one patient recovers unexpectedly while others in the same ward do not, the recovery is often described as a miracle by the patient's family. But the families of those who do not survive would not see it that way. Their experience is usually absent from the story. The few who recover are remembered as evidence of intervention, while the many who die are quietly excluded from the account.

10. Nickell, *Looking for a Miracle*, 179–86.

11. Barrett, *Healers and the Healing Process*, 92–105.

To abandon miracles is to confront a universe that may not intervene, no matter how much we plead.

I began to see that the craving for miracles is really the craving for significance. To live without them is to accept that the cosmos may be vast and indifferent, and that our worth must arise from one another rather than from intervention. But there is dignity in that acceptance. The absence of divine interruption does not make the world smaller; it makes human compassion larger, because it must come from us.

In that realization, the loss of the supernatural became its own kind of grace. Wonder did not die when the miraculous faded. It simply found a new home. It now lived in discovery, in empathy, in the quiet persistence of people helping one another without expecting celestial approval. The extraordinary, I learned, was still with us—it just no longer needed to break the laws of nature to be real.

TRADITION AND POPULARITY AREN'T EVIDENCE

Another argument I often heard growing up, including from my mother, was an appeal to tradition or sheer numbers. The reasoning was straightforward: if so many people believe in God, and if those beliefs have been passed down for generations, then there must be something to them. At first, this seemed convincing. How could so many people be wrong? History, however, offers many examples showing that widespread belief and long tradition are not reliable measures of truth.

For centuries, nearly everyone believed the sun revolved around the earth. Doctors prescribed bloodletting and mercury as cures for disease. Millions once believed that witches were real and should be hunted; between the fifteenth and eighteenth centuries, tens of thousands were executed and hundreds of thousands accused.[12] People thought illness came from "bad air" instead of germs, that slavery was part of the natural order, that the earth was only a few thousand years old. Each of these convictions was shared by entire civilizations—widely held, fiercely defended, and completely wrong. Popularity and longevity made them feel secure, but neither made them true.

Part of the power of tradition lies in its invisibility. It surrounds us like air, shaping thought long before we can name it. What has always been believed feels natural simply because it is familiar. The mind

12. Levack, *The Witch-Hunt in Early Modern Europe*, 21–30.

confuses repetition with truth. When the same creed is recited every Sunday, or the same rituals are practiced generation after generation, belief begins to feel inevitable. Few stop to ask whether its foundations have ever been tested.

As a child, I never thought of religion as a choice. It was the background of life, as ordinary as the calendar. The songs, the prayers, the rhythm of holidays—all of it seemed to confirm itself by sheer repetition. I did not encounter faith as a claim but as a climate. Only later, when I began to notice that others lived under different skies, did I realize that my certainty was a product of geography as much as conviction. At the time, none of this felt like philosophy; it felt like learning, slowly and awkwardly, how to stand apart.

The psychologist Solomon Asch demonstrated how powerful that pull can be. In the 1950s, he showed volunteers a set of lines on a card and asked them to identify which matched in length. When participants were alone, their answers were almost always correct. But when surrounded by a group who deliberately gave the wrong answer, many conformed, even when the truth was obvious to their own eyes. The experiment revealed how easily social pressure can override perception. If people can be swayed on something as simple as line length, how much stronger is the pull of belief when it is tied to eternity, morality, and family identity?[13]

I often think of that experiment when I recall church gatherings from my childhood. Everyone stood, knelt, and prayed together. The people around me spoke with confidence, and I joined in because not doing so would have felt unacceptable. Being part of the group carried strong pressure. Even when I doubted what was being said, I went along with it. I later understood that conformity is not always a sign of belief; it is often a response to social pressure and a desire to belong.

Over time, the whole routine began to feel automatic. Everyone seemed to know exactly when to stand, kneel, and respond to the priest without thinking. The same prayers were repeated word for word each week, and the hymns rolled out on cue, voices rising and falling in unison. It was impressive in its precision, but it also felt mechanical—like a robotic performance that had forgotten its reason for being. During one service, it felt as though everyone, myself included, was moving on instinct, following along because that was what you were supposed to do. I started to wonder if anyone else ever felt the same disquiet—if, behind

13. Asch, "Opinions and Social Pressure," 31–35.

the bowed heads and murmured words, there were others thinking the same forbidden thought: what if none of this was being heard? The idea both frightened and comforted me. If I wasn't alone in doubting, maybe the silence wasn't just mine to bear. It reminded me of watching a line of lemmings, each one following the next without ever asking where we were going or why we were going there.

Tradition, in that sense, does not only preserve belief—it manufactures confidence. What has been repeated long enough comes to seem self-evident. The familiar rhythm of a creed can sound like proof simply because it has been heard since childhood. I began to understand that endurance is not the same as truth.

When I recognized this, the weight of consensus lost its hold on me. I no longer mistook inheritance for evidence. If a claim cannot stand on reason, no amount of repetition can strengthen it. A thousand voices echoing the same idea do not make it right; they only make it louder.

This realization was both relieving and unsettling. Once numerical authority was removed, belief could no longer rely on the reassurance of community support. It had to be evaluated on its own grounds. This change altered how I understood conviction. If the validity of an idea depends on how many people accept it, then belief becomes a matter of popularity rather than accuracy. Facts are not determined by majority agreement.

FAITH BY GEOGRAPHY

I grew up assuming that my prayers and rituals were simply the way the world worked. It never occurred to me that the same conviction could exist in completely different forms elsewhere. Only later did I understand that if I had been born in another place, my beliefs would almost certainly have been different.

That realization carried an uncomfortable symmetry. Every believer rejects thousands of other gods without hesitation, convinced their god is the real one, the one they happened to inherit. In that sense, we are all atheists to most of the world's deities; we simply draw the line one god later.[14] I began to see that what separated belief from disbelief was often geography, not revelation. Every faith seemed to mirror the culture that sustained it, each offering certainty shaped by its own sky.

14. Dawkins, *The God Delusion*, 54.

When and where we are born largely decides the religion we inherit, and by extension, the god we are told to worship. A child raised in Saudi Arabia is overwhelmingly likely to be Muslim; in rural Mexico, Catholic; in India, Hindu.[15] What feels like eternal truth in one culture may be entirely absent from another.

It was hard not to notice the pattern. When people explained why they did not believe in other gods—Zeus, Odin, Vishnu—their reasons matched my own growing doubts about the one I had inherited. The same absence of evidence, the same dependence on tradition, the same human need to find meaning in uncertainty. I realized I was simply following their logic to its conclusion.

This realization was both humbling and unsettling. As I learned more about other faiths, it became harder to view my own as uniquely authoritative. I read about Hindu families beginning their mornings with offerings to Ganesha, Buddhist monks rising before dawn to meditate, and Muslim children memorizing verses of the Qur'an in much the same way I had memorized Bible stories. In each case, children were taught their beliefs with confidence and certainty. It became clear that religious belief is often inherited through upbringing and culture rather than discovered independently.

That thought was not meant to diminish devotion but to place it in perspective. If conviction depends on birthplace, then certainty must be handled with care. The map of belief looks less like divine design and more like an atlas of human adaptation, shaped by landscape, climate, and need. The gods of the desert promise water and shade. The gods of the sea promise safe passage. The gods of the harvest promise abundance. Each reflects the fears and hopes of its people more than the dictates of the cosmos.

When I studied ancient civilizations, I saw this pattern everywhere. A child born in Athens would have worshiped Zeus and Athena. In Mesopotamia, the names were Marduk and Ishtar. In Viking Scandinavia, they were Odin and Thor. In Egypt, Osiris and Ra. Each of these deities commanded loyalty, sacrifice, and reverence. Each felt timeless in its day. Yet all eventually passed into myth, their temples left in ruins or preserved only as artifacts in museums. The ruins were not failures of faith but reminders of how belief evolves with circumstance.

15. Pew Research Center, *The Global Religious Landscape*, 2012.

I remember standing in a museum once, looking at a glass case that held fragments of an Assyrian tablet. The carvings told of prayers offered to a god meant to guard the city from famine. The words were ancient, but the plea was familiar: keep us safe, protect our children, make sense of our suffering. I realized then that every age asks the same questions and gives them different names. The vocabulary changes, but the yearning remains.

Inherited belief is powerful largely because it is rarely recognized as inherited. People raised within a particular faith often experience it as the normal way the world works, not as one tradition among many. Leaving that framework can be unsettling, because ideas once taken as universal begin to appear tied to a specific culture and history. Although this shift can be disorienting, it also makes it possible to see belief more clearly and critically.

It was in that clarity that I finally saw my own position, not as rebellion but as consistency. Every generation inherits a set of gods and calls them timeless. I had simply stopped making the exception.

THE ASYMMETRY OF BELIEF

When belief settles into the fabric of daily life, it rarely feels like a claim at all. It is taught in childhood, repeated in rituals, reinforced by authority, and soon treated as common sense. From there, the tables turn: the believer no longer feels the need to defend conviction, but the skeptic is asked to explain refusal.

I saw this pattern everywhere growing up. In church, it was taken for granted that God was real. In catechism, lessons began not with whether God existed but with what He expected of us. At home, devotion was assumed in the same way the sky is assumed to be blue. To ask questions was to push against the weight of an entire community.

Once belief becomes normalized, it hides inside language, habit, and social expectation. When someone says, "Thank God," or "I'll pray for you," the words sound like kindness, not theology. The assumption of a divine listener passes unnoticed. Only when that expectation is challenged does the imbalance appear. The believer speaks from tradition; the doubter speaks from deviation.

I began to recognize how powerful that structure is. The burden of explanation always falls on the minority view. The atheist must account for disbelief, while the believer rests comfortably in convention. Even the vocabulary exposes the bias. We say someone "loses their faith," as though faith were the natural state and doubt a deficiency. No one speaks of "losing their skepticism." The very grammar of religion favors belief.

This imbalance extends well beyond theology. In science, politics, and culture, dominant views are often treated as normal, while those who question them are expected to explain themselves. This pattern shields institutions from scrutiny and reinforces group cohesion. When agreement is widespread, individual positions rarely need to be defended. Shared certainty becomes reassuring, and questioning it is often treated as socially inappropriate.

When I was a child, I learned how subtle that pressure could be. In Sunday school, a teacher once asked the class to describe a moment when they felt God's presence. When it was my turn, I said I never had. I didn't mean it as defiance; it was simply the truth. The room went quiet, and the teacher's smile tightened. After class, she told me, "Keep searching. God will speak when you are ready to listen." It was meant as encouragement, but it carried a message I understood too well. The problem was not that God was silent; it was that I had not yet become worthy of hearing. The assumption remained untouched. In that moment, the onus shifted from God to me; His silence wasn't the issue, my supposed failure was.

That experience stayed with me. It showed how easily belief can reverse responsibility. When answers do not appear, the fault is placed on the seeker, not the system. The structure of faith protects itself by redefining doubt as failure. To question becomes a flaw of character rather than an act of conscience.

Bertrand Russell and others warned of this dynamic long before I could name it.[16] Once conviction takes root, repetition is mistaken for proof. Institutions defend it, families pass it down, and soon the skeptic is the one on trial. Instead of asking believers to provide reasons, the question is turned around: why do you not believe? The principle of proof is inverted, as though doubt were an accusation and belief its defense.

But logic does not change just because the numbers do. The responsibility to justify extraordinary claims does not vanish because a doctrine has aged well. It does not shift because questioning feels uncomfortable. Whoever makes the grand assertion still carries the duty of support.

16. Russell, "Is There a God?," 547–48.

This imbalance explains why doubt so often feels heavier than faith. Belief is buoyed by habit, culture, and company. Skepticism stands alone. Yet if reason is to mean anything, the weight must fall where it belongs: not on the one who asks the question, but on the one who declares the answer.

Over time, I came to see that what many call faith is often a wager rather than a conclusion—an instinctive bet placed not on evidence but on hope. People believe not because proof compels them, but because belief itself feels safer, more comforting, and more meaningful than the alternative. Even when silence remains, the wager is clear: better to risk believing in something that might not exist than to face the thought that nothing does.

That shift in motive fascinated me. It was no longer about proof but about stakes. What does one stand to gain or lose by believing—or by refusing to? The question had moved from evidence to risk, from logic to survival. It was there, at the point where evidence gave way to risk, that Blaise Pascal entered the story.

2

Faith as a Gamble

"Pascal's Wager could only ever convince a hypocrite."

Richard Dawkins

THE FIRST BET

Long before I knew it had a name, I had already heard the argument now called Pascal's Wager.[1] It goes like this: if God exists and you believe, you gain everything; if He doesn't, you lose nothing. But if you refuse to believe and turn out to be wrong, the loss is infinite. By that math, belief seems like the safer bet.

I first encountered that logic as a teenager, though stripped of philosophy and probability. I had been hearing some version of it for as long as I could remember, woven into conversations at church, school, and home. Eventually it reached me as a warning: *What if you're wrong? What if there really is a hell?* The message was clear—better to believe and be safe than to doubt and risk eternal punishment.

At that age, the argument carried more weight than it deserved. Doubt was already difficult enough, and the threat of being eternally mistaken made questioning feel dangerous. The wager reached me not through a sermon or a philosophy book but in a quiet conversation with my mother. She asked it gently, almost tenderly, as if concern could

1. Pascal, *Pensées*, 233–34.

substitute for proof. "You don't want to take that chance," she said. Her voice wasn't stern; it was protective, filled with the same worry behind countless other warnings: don't run into the street, don't talk to strangers, don't risk what you can't replace. She meant it as love, and I understood it that way. Still, something in me resisted. The appeal wasn't to evidence but to vulnerability.

Later, sitting alone in my room, I tried to reason it through. If belief could keep me safe, then disbelief was reckless. The logic looked neat, almost elegant. But it felt hollow. Faith, as I had been taught, was supposed to be trust, not calculation. Yet this version of faith sounded less like trust than like a contingency plan—a way of bracing against cosmic disaster rather than committing to anything at all.

Only years later did I learn the wager came from Blaise Pascal, a seventeenth-century mathematician and philosopher. Pascal lived in a world shaped by religious war, disease, and early death, where belief carried real consequences and salvation felt desperately uncertain. Against that backdrop, his argument made sense. If the world was brutal and the stakes eternal, why not believe?

When I learned that history, the distance between his world and mine became clear. I had grown up riding bikes and playing in neighborhood streets, attending public schools—not surrounded by monasteries and relics. Yet the argument had crossed centuries with little change. The language was different, but the underlying fear remained. What once was delivered from pulpits now appeared in quieter, more personal forms, presented as reasoning but driven by the same unease.

The question *What if you're wrong?* lingered long after that conversation. It followed me into the dark when I tried to pray and could not. It turned belief into a kind of gambling, with eternity treated not as meaning but as leverage. Lying awake, I tried to reason it through like a calculation: if heaven meant infinite happiness and hell infinite pain, even a small chance of either seemed to outweigh everything else. The arithmetic looked clear. The feeling did not. What kind of belief could grow out of that kind of calculation?

For a while, I tried to make it work. I prayed more, acted as though conviction might follow. I whispered apologies into a silence that never answered. The problem wasn't that I wanted to reject faith. It was that I couldn't pretend it felt real simply because the odds seemed to demand it. I wanted conviction, not coverage. The wager offered the latter and called it wisdom.

Looking back, I can see why the idea endures. It gives uncertainty a simple shape and converts fear into arithmetic. It promises that the safest path is also the smartest one. But safety is not the same as truth. I didn't have the words for that realization then—only the unease that comes when something sounds clever but feels wrong. Belief born of anxiety cannot sustain itself for long.

When I eventually read Pascal's *Pensées*, where the wager first appeared, the tone felt familiar. Pascal urged those who wanted to believe but could not to begin by acting as if they already did—to attend Mass, take holy water, live as though belief were true until conviction followed.[2] I recognized the same impulse I had heard years earlier: belief as performance, uncertainty disguised as obedience.

That was my first real encounter with Pascal's Wager. What struck me was not its brilliance but its bluntness. It told me to believe not because it was true, but because the alternative was terrifying. Even then, I wondered whether a God worth worshiping would be fooled by faith adopted out of fear. The argument unsettled me because it confused fear with faith, calculation with conviction. It didn't invite a search for truth; it urged surrender to safety. And for a long time, its shadow stayed with me, quietly shaping how doubt itself felt dangerous.

WHY IT SOUNDED PERSUASIVE

Pascal's Wager endures because it feels like common sense. Faced with uncertainty, people tend to choose the safer path. When the stakes are high, comfort often disguises itself as logic. At its core, the wager appeals to self-preservation, one of the most powerful instincts we have.

Behavioral science later gave names to what Pascal intuited. Daniel Kahneman and Amos Tversky, whose research reshaped our understanding of human judgment and decision-making, showed that people are not primarily rational optimizers but deeply sensitive to perceived risk. Their work revealed that losses loom larger than gains, and that this imbalance quietly governs everyday behavior.[3] We buy insurance for trips we never take, pay for extended warranties we never use, and check weather forecasts repeatedly before routine trips. We arrive at airports hours early and

2. Pascal, *Pensées*, 418–19.

3. Kahneman and Tversky, "Prospect Theory: An Analysis of Decision under Risk," 263–91.

keep backup plans we rarely need. These choices are not mathematically rational, but they reduce anxiety and create a sense of control.

Pascal's Wager magnifies that instinct. If people are willing to pay to protect their possessions, how much more will they yield to protect their souls. The argument fits neatly into the mental habits that help us survive. It feels reasonable not because it is sound, but because it aligns with how fear already works.

The same pattern appears well beyond religion. Superstitions operate on similar logic. Knock on wood. Avoid tempting fate. Politics often relies on it as well, appealing to worst case scenarios rather than evidence. Warnings about crime, disease, or moral collapse are framed as bets. Act now, or regret it later. When uncertainty increases, fear becomes persuasive.

Religion amplifies this effect by raising the stakes to infinity. The question *What if you are wrong* becomes a kind of psychological gravity, pulling belief toward safety. Once that fear takes hold, even weak arguments feel immovable. It is not logic that persuades, but the promise of relief.

Pascal's insight was to disguise that promise in mathematics, turning belief into a calculation and giving anxiety the appearance of reason. Even the smallest chance of infinite reward outweighs any finite cost. On paper, the equation looks decisive.

But equations hide assumptions. Behind Pascal's numbers lies an emotional bargain. Fear presents itself as prudence. Infinity is treated not as a concept but as a threat. Once anxiety enters the equation, proportion disappears. The math looks clean, but what it measures is desperation.

The argument also survives because it sounds modern, even scientific. It presents itself as a bridge between faith and rationality. As a teenager, I was drawn to that surface logic. It felt disciplined and intellectual, a defense of belief that did not rely on scripture or miracle stories. Yet beneath the polish I could still feel the same pulse of fear I had heard so often before. The wager did not build faith. It taught hesitation to pose as wisdom.

Part of its power lies in how easily it slips into ordinary language. Versions appear in everyday conversation. *It cannot hurt to believe. You might as well pray. Why take the risk.* These phrases sound harmless, but they carry a quiet instruction. Fear is safer than doubt. Once accepted, belief shifts from a search for truth to an effort to avoid regret.

Even people who reject religion often reason the same way. The precautionary principle in public policy reflects a similar instinct. Act to prevent the worst possible outcome even without full proof. That logic has practical value, but when applied to belief it distorts the idea of truth. The goal becomes not to know, but to avoid being wrong.

I saw this reasoning at work in my own family. My mother's warning came from love, but beneath it was an inherited caution passed down over generations. Belief was treated as the safer choice, not because it was proven, but because disbelief carried unthinkable consequences. To question felt like stepping outside a fence everyone else trusted to keep them safe. I did not yet have the words for it, but I could feel the discomfort of watching comfort replace conviction.

What gives Pascal's argument its staying power is that it appears humble. It asks for so little. *Just believe, in case.* But the humility is false. The wager assumes the universe can be managed through risk assessment, that God can be satisfied by statistical obedience. It turns belief into a transaction, as though eternity could be negotiated. Caution hides an arrogance of its own.

And for many, it works. The wager quiets fear, at least temporarily. It offers relief and teaches people to mistake emotional safety for spiritual truth. Its simplicity is exactly what makes it effective.

Eventually, I began to see that its power came not from reason but from fear. It offered a way to stop asking questions without admitting that the search had ended. Once I recognized that, the argument lost much of its hold. What had sounded like logic revealed itself as surrender wearing the mask of prudence.

CALLING PASCAL'S BLUFF

The more I examined Pascal's Wager, the more its simplicity collapsed. What first looked like a clean ledger of risks and rewards began to fray as soon as I tested its assumptions. The argument promised clarity, but it could not withstand even basic scrutiny.

The first problem was obvious. Which God was I supposed to bet on. Pascal assumed his own, but history offers countless others, each claiming exclusive truth. Every religion promises salvation and warns of consequences for disbelief. If belief is a wager, then the table is crowded. Choosing among competing infinities is not reasoned faith.[4] It is guessing with eternal consequences.

4. Mackie, *The Miracle of Theism*, 202–5.

One night, I lay awake picturing a hallway lined with doors, each marked by a different symbol. I was told that choosing the wrong one would close all the others forever. Nothing about that felt rational. It felt like coercion dressed as choice.

Some critics have pushed the logic further. If the goal is truly to minimize risk, then the rational move would be to choose the belief system with the harshest punishment for unbelief. If one tradition threatens torment, another endless rebirth, and another annihilation, then fear itself becomes the deciding factor. By that logic, cruelty is rewarded and terror becomes sacred. A God worth believing in would not be discovered through a contest of threats.

The second flaw lies in the nature of belief itself. The wager assumes belief can be switched on at will, as though sincerity were a lever that could be pulled when convenient. But belief does not work that way. You can imitate belief. You can perform its rituals and repeat its language. But genuine conviction resists self-interest.

There was another inconsistency I could not ignore, not in the logic of the wager itself, but in how belief appeared in the lives of those who said they cared about me. If the consequences were truly as severe as I had been told, their behavior should have reflected that belief. Eternal torment is not a minor risk. If someone genuinely believes that a person they love is headed for infinite suffering, concern would not be occasional or restrained. It would be urgent and persistent.

Yet that urgency was largely absent. Warnings were offered briefly and then allowed to fade. Conversations shifted away from the subject. Invitations to reconsider were made once or twice and then quietly abandoned. If my soul was truly in danger, that restraint was difficult to reconcile with genuine concern. Love, if paired with belief in hell, should have demanded far more insistence.

The pattern was revealing. Many people spoke as if the doctrine were true, but their behavior did not reflect the seriousness of its stated consequences. Although the stakes were described as infinite, they were treated as matters of social discretion. Ideas presented as urgent in sermons were often avoided or minimized in personal conversations. This difference was informative. It suggested that belief frequently persisted as language and routine, while certainty diminished into assumption or hope.

This did not appear to be hypocrisy, but avoidance. Fully accepting the doctrine would require treating its consequences as urgent, while openly questioning it would risk social tension. The more manageable response was to affirm belief in principle while behaving as though the consequences were remote. In this way, faith remained part of personal and social identity even as its claims were no longer treated as immediate or decisive.

I learned this firsthand when I tried to force it. After my conversation with my mother, I treated belief like an experiment. I prayed longer, read more scripture, attended every service. I waited for assurance to arrive on schedule. It never did. There was no peace, no sign of approval, only the same silence that had followed every honest question. Pretending belief just in case did not bring me closer to faith. It hollowed it out. I was not fooling God or myself. I was rehearsing a feeling I did not have.

Philosophers have long recognized this tension. J. L. Mackie, known for his systematic critique of theism, argued that belief cannot be justified by calculation or pragmatic payoff alone. William James, writing with more sympathy, approached belief as a lived commitment rather than a wager. In *The Will to Believe*, he allowed that faith can be a legitimate choice when evidence is incomplete—but only when the decision is momentous, unavoidable, and freely made, grounded in sincerity rather than fear or coercion.[5] Both understood what Pascal's wager ignores. Fear cannot produce authentic belief.

A third problem appears in the kind of God the wager implies. Even if one accepted its logic, what sort of deity would it reveal. Would a just and merciful being reward those who feigned belief to avoid punishment while condemning those who searched honestly but remained unconvinced. A God who valued obedience over integrity would be indistinguishable from a tyrant. Fear might secure compliance, but it would never inspire reverence.

I found myself returning to that question often. Would a God worthy of worship really prefer pretense to honesty. Would He rather hear prayers spoken out of fear than silence chosen out of truth. Once I allowed myself to ask it plainly, the answer felt unavoidable.

The wager also carries a deeper moral cost. If belief is motivated by self-preservation, morality itself becomes transactional. Acts of kindness are performed to earn reward or avoid punishment. They become strategies rather than choices. Genuine goodness cannot grow under threat. Albert Einstein, who rejected religious authority while defending moral

5. James, "The Will to Believe," 459–60.

responsibility grounded in reason, warned that morality based on fear of punishment or hope of reward strips ethical action of its dignity.[6]

Over time, the comfort the wager promised began to collapse. At first it seemed to offer safety. Believe and you are secure. But when I tried to adopt that posture, the safety proved brittle. Every prayer offered just in case widened the distance rather than closing it. The more I tried to believe for protection, the more trapped I felt inside a performance.

The pattern revealed itself slowly in others. In religious settings, faith was often spoken of as a guarantee, a shield against doubt. When questions arose, the response was predictable. Better not risk it. Beneath the calm language I sensed quiet fear. People were not convinced. They were afraid of what might happen if they stopped pretending.

Once I saw that clearly, the wager no longer looked like faith's defender. It looked like its enemy. It encouraged submission instead of sincerity and replaced wonder with calculation. To believe out of fear is not devotion. It is compliance.

Pascal's Wager fails for the same reason all fear-based reasoning fails. It confuses safety with truth. It promises protection at the cost of honesty. That bargain may comfort the anxious, but it cannot satisfy the seeker. What had once seemed like a bridge between faith and reason now looked like a warning about how easily fear can masquerade as wisdom.

THE REAL COST OF PLAYING SAFE

At first, Pascal's Wager looks like a bargain. You surrender a small measure of faith and obedience and, in return, insure yourself against eternal loss. The math appears simple. Infinite gain for finite cost. What could be more reasonable.

But I began to see that this bargain carries a hidden price. To believe only as a precaution is to hollow out belief itself. Faith becomes calculation rather than conviction.

I saw this tension in my own life and in the religious culture around me. Belief was often spoken of as protection against disaster. Sermons leaned on the language of risk. Better to be safe than sorry. Revival services turned this logic into spectacle. A preacher once warned that failing to come forward might be the last mistake you would ever make.

6. Einstein, "Religion and Science," 39–40.

The air was thick with anxiety, and every invitation carried the same message. Act now, before it is too late.

For those who responded, the relief was real but short lived. Many returned again and again, as though faith required constant renewal. The fear never disappeared. It only changed shape. What they were seeking was not communion with God but escape from punishment. That kind of belief can sustain ritual, but it cannot produce peace.

What became clear instead was that when faith is chosen for safety, sincerity is the first casualty. What begins as reassurance becomes performance. I felt it myself, the gap between the words I spoke and the doubt I carried. To pray while wondering whether anyone is listening is one thing. To pray only to quiet fear is another. One keeps searching for truth. The other stops as soon as it feels secure.

This pattern shapes entire communities. When belief is sustained by fear, questions become dangerous. Inquiry is treated not as curiosity but as disobedience. To ask for evidence is to threaten the shared illusion of safety. I saw it repeatedly. Someone raised a difficult question, and instead of discussion came gentle warnings. The goal was not understanding but preservation.

That fear is often passed on with good intentions. Parents hand it to children not out of cruelty but out of care. They believe they are protecting them. What they pass along, however, is anxiety dressed as faith. The message is subtle but clear. It is safer to believe than to think too much. Over time, conformity replaces conviction.

Philosophers have long warned about this trade. Søren Kierkegaard argued that faith has meaning only when it confronts uncertainty honestly; belief without risk, he insisted, is not faith at all.[7] Jean-Paul Sartre, writing from a secular existential perspective, described the same failure as *bad faith*—the act of surrendering freedom by disguising fear as necessity.[8] Both recognized that belief adopted to avoid punishment empties life of authenticity.

Immanuel Kant, who grounded morality in reason rather than reward, made the ethical cost even clearer. He argued that actions have moral worth only when they are chosen from duty, not performed to gain favor or avoid punishment.[9] A goodness that must be coerced is not goodness at all.

7. Kierkegaard, *Fear and Trembling*, 46–49.
8. Sartre, *Being and Nothingness*, 86–90.
9. Kant, *Groundwork of the Metaphysics of Morals*, 13–15.

Modern psychology explains what happens next. When people adopt beliefs they do not genuinely hold, they experience cognitive dissonance, the tension of living against their own understanding.[10] To relieve it, the mind suppresses questions, rationalizes inconsistencies, and reframes doubt as temptation. What begins as a compromise hardens into habit.

Only later did that cycle show itself in my own life. For a time, I tried to make my mind follow what fear had already chosen. I went through the motions of belief, hoping the feeling would return. It never did. Belief adopted as a precaution did not deepen faith. It thinned it, leaving only the outer form intact. You can perform belief for others, but not for yourself.

The cost does not stop with the individual. A community built on fear quietly polices sincerity. Members display confidence even when it has faded. I saw people reciting creeds they no longer trusted, afraid that honesty would make them outsiders. Each assumed the others were certain, and so the performance continued. Silence became a form of safety.

The moral consequences are just as real. When belief is practiced only to avoid punishment, morality becomes transactional. Kindness turns into strategy. Help others now, earn reward later. A deed loses meaning when it is done under threat. A system that requires fear to produce goodness reveals its own emptiness.

Even the image of God changes under this logic. In the world of Pascal's Wager, God becomes less a source of meaning than a cosmic accountant, tallying belief and disbelief. It is a portrait of divinity shaped by suspicion rather than trust. I could not see how a God worth worshiping would value obedience over honesty. A faith that demands the silence of the mind asks too much.

The irony is that Pascal's argument tries to defend faith by turning it into fear. It reduces belief to strategy and caution to devotion. In doing so, it drains both faith and doubt of dignity. Faith becomes compliance. Doubt becomes forbidden thought.

What the wager offered as comfort ultimately felt like captivity. It promised shelter at the cost of honesty and reassurance at the expense of growth. The price was too high. What I feared most was not punishment, but the slow erosion of integrity.

10. Festinger, *A Theory of Cognitive Dissonance*, 2–18.

Letting go of that bargain did not bring certainty, but it brought clarity. When I stopped treating belief as insurance and began treating truth as pursuit, the fear began to loosen its grip. Safety had demanded too much. I was no longer willing to pay.

BEYOND THE WAGER

For a long time, Pascal's Wager lingered even after belief itself had faded. It no longer felt like an argument so much as a reflex. It surfaced in hospital rooms, on sleepless nights, in moments when uncertainty pressed close. The question returned without logic or explanation. *What if you are wrong.* It carried no evidence, only weight. Pascal's genius was not philosophical but psychological. He turned fear into arithmetic, and arithmetic into obligation.

For years, I mistook that reflex for humility. I told myself I was being careful, that keeping one foot inside belief was a form of balance. Only later did I recognize the truth. I was not being cautious. I was being afraid. The wager had trained me to see courage as recklessness and honesty as danger.

Once I saw that, its hold weakened. The question that finally broke it was simple. What kind of God would this logic reveal. Would a being worthy of reverence truly prefer pretense to sincerity. Would He reward belief adopted out of fear while condemning those who followed evidence as far as they could see it. A deity who prizes obedience over honesty would demand submission, not understanding. I could not find reverence in that image.

Letting go of the wager did not bring certainty. It brought clarity. I no longer needed belief as insurance against fear. If I was wrong, I wanted to be wrong honestly. I wanted error born of integrity, not safety purchased through silence or sustained by fear. The courage to question mattered more than the promise of protection.

When fear stopped posing as wisdom, the space to think widened. Doubt no longer felt like rebellion. It felt like fidelity to reality. There was a quiet dignity in uncertainty once it was no longer framed as danger. The wager had tried to frighten me into belief. Instead, it forced me to decide what belief should mean at all.

That decision did not end my questions. It sharpened them. If faith could no longer rest on fear, then its claims would have to stand on reason. And if belief insists on a creator, then one question cannot be avoided.

Who created God?

3

Who Created the Creator?

"If everything must have a cause, then God must have a cause."

BERTRAND RUSSELL

THE UNASKED QUESTION

Long before philosophy tried to formalize the origin of causes, people explained the world through stories that gave natural events intention. Storms acted with purpose, winds carried messages, and the sea behaved like a willful being. These explanations did not arise from ignorance so much as perception. The world appeared alive. Lightning did not simply strike. It seemed to choose.

To explain an event was to imagine an agent behind it. That instinct shaped the earliest gods and later hardened into philosophical systems. When something moved, something must have moved it. When something happened, someone must have intended it.

This tendency did not belong to any single culture or tradition. Long before Christianity, human societies across the world explained origins and natural events through intentional agents. Creation stories, divine ancestors, and purposeful forces appear independently in ancient civilizations separated by geography and time. These similarities do not require borrowing or imitation. They reflect shared features of human cognition, especially the expectation that significant events must be caused by someone rather than something. Familiar structures recur because the minds producing them recur. What feels revealed often feels that way because it fits expectations already in place.

This same intuition guided early philosophy. Aristotle, the fourth-century BCE thinker who laid much of the groundwork for Western logic, argued that motion requires a cause. Every movement must be set in motion by something else. To avoid an infinite chain that never begins, he proposed an "unmoved mover," a final source that initiates all motion without itself needing to move.[1] The idea was meant to solve a problem, not create one. If every effect required a cause, then explanation needed a stopping point.

Thomas Aquinas, a thirteenth-century Christian theologian and philosopher, sought to reconcile Aristotle's philosophy with Christian doctrine. Drawing on Aristotle's causal reasoning, he identified God with the unmoved mover—the first cause invoked to explain motion and order in the world.[2] In Aquinas's work, what began as a philosophical account of causation was extended into a theological framework for understanding meaning and purpose.

What both Aristotle and Aquinas assumed, without fully defending, was that the chain of causes must end somewhere. An infinite regress felt intolerable, so a final answer was declared. The decision was driven less by evidence than by a desire to bring explanation to an end. The explanation did not emerge from observation. It emerged from discomfort with uncertainty.

I grew up with a simplified version of the same idea. I was told that everything must come from something, and that God stood at the beginning of all things. For a time, that explanation felt sufficient. I imagined causes leading backward like a line of ancestors: parents, grandparents, distant forebears, and finally the Creator. The picture felt orderly. It felt complete.

But one question always lingered just behind it. If everything needs a cause, where did God come from?

The answer I was given was always the same. God had always existed. The statement closed the discussion, but it did not resolve the question. Even as a child, I sensed the difference between an explanation and a declaration meant to end curiosity. Saying that something has no beginning does not explain it. It exempts it.

1. Aristotle, *Metaphysics*, bk. XII.
2. Aquinas, *Summa Theologiae*, I.2.3.

Years later, that early discomfort returned with sharper focus. If God could exist without a cause, then the rule itself was not universal. And if the rule was not universal, there was no reason to apply it to the universe alone. The logic no longer felt consistent. The same principle that demanded an explanation for everything else suddenly stopped at the point where explanation mattered most.

This was not rebellion disguised as inquiry. It was an attempt to apply the same standard evenly. If existence requires a cause, then God must have one. If God does not require a cause, then existence itself may not either. The argument for a creator rested on an exception that could not be justified without undermining the rule it depended on.

That realization did not arrive with certainty or relief. It arrived as a recognition that the explanation I had inherited depended on a preference rather than a principle. The question I had been taught not to ask was not dangerous. It was necessary. Once raised, it did not demand an answer. It revealed an assumption.

And once that assumption was visible, it could no longer support the weight placed upon it.

WHEN THE CIRCLE BREAKS

There came a point when the question stopped feeling theoretical and began to feel personal.

It did not arrive as a victory. It arrived as disorientation. I had grown up with a stable chain of explanations: God created the world, the world carried meaning, and my life fit within that order. When the chain no longer held, the sense of structure it provided weakened as well.

The shift did not come during a crisis. It emerged gradually, as unanswered questions accumulated. I began looking for thinkers who had confronted the same doubts without retreating into reassurance. That search led me to Bertrand Russell's *Why I Am Not a Christian*.[3] I did not read it to abandon belief. I read it to understand the discomfort that had followed me since childhood.

Russell's writing was strikingly restrained. He did not argue with anger or mockery. He relied on consistency. His objection to the First Cause argument was simple. If everything requires a cause, then God must

3. Russell, "Why I Am Not a Christian," 6–7.

require one too. If God does not require a cause, then the universe does not either. The rule cannot be applied selectively without collapsing.[4]

What mattered to me was not the conclusion but the method. Russell refused to grant an exception where none could be justified. He treated God and the universe by the same standard. That refusal alone dissolved much of the argument's force. The appeal of the First Cause had never been evidence. It had been exemption.

What unsettled me was not simply the possibility that the argument was flawed, but that belief itself might be unnecessary. If the universe did not require a creator to exist, then faith was no longer the foundation beneath meaning. It became something added afterward. That realization did not feel liberating. It felt like standing on ground that had quietly shifted.

Russell did not invent this line of reasoning. He inherited it from David Hume, who questioned whether causation itself is as solid as people assume. Hume observed that we never directly perceive causes.[5] We see one event followed by another and infer a connection. The hammer strikes and the glass breaks. The necessity linking the two is supplied by the mind, not by observation.

This insight changes the problem entirely. If causation is a habit of thought rather than a law written into reality, then the demand for a first cause loses its urgency. The chain of causes is a way the mind organizes experience. It is not proof that the universe requires an originating agent.

Hume illustrated this with ordinary examples. We expect fire to produce heat because it always has, not because logic demands it must. The future resembles the past because we assume it will. That assumption works well enough for survival, but it does not justify metaphysical conclusions. Building a theory of God on that foundation stretches habit into certainty.

Together, Hume and Russell exposed the same flaw from different angles. Russell showed that the First Cause argument contradicts itself. Hume showed that the rule it relies on may not be absolute in the first place. The circle does not close because the reasoning was never as firm as it appeared.

When I tried to preserve belief by defining God as existing outside time and causation, the problem did not disappear; it changed form.

4. Russell, "Why I Am Not a Christian," 7–8.

5. Hume, *An Enquiry Concerning Human Understanding*, 26–29.

Exempting God from ordinary rules of explanation also placed that idea beyond meaningful explanation. A cause that cannot be examined, tested, or compared does not add clarity. It serves as a label rather than an explanatory account.

There was an irony in this realization. The instinct that had once made belief feel logical, the desire to trace everything back to an origin, was now revealing its limits. I had mistaken a mental habit for a feature of reality. The need for a starting point was not imposed by the universe. It was imposed by the mind.

The circle broke without a dramatic conclusion. What remained was not despair but exposure. The world no longer pointed beyond itself for justification. It stood on its own, vast and indifferent. Meaning was no longer delivered from outside. It had to be constructed from within experience itself.

That moment did not answer every question. It made one thing clear. The argument that once promised certainty depended on assumptions that could not support it. Once those assumptions were visible, they could no longer do their work unnoticed. The circle did not close. It dissolved.

COMFORT OF COMPLETION

Human beings are uncomfortable with unfinished explanations. We complete half-heard melodies, finish other people's sentences, and connect scattered stars into familiar shapes. The same impulse drives many theological answers. Invoking God brings inquiry to an immediate stop. The chain of causes ends not because it has been traced, but because it has been named.

Psychology describes this impulse as the need for cognitive closure.[6] Faced with uncertainty, most people prefer a definite answer, even an incorrect one, to remaining in doubt. The mind treats ambiguity as a problem that must be resolved. An unresolved question feels like tension, and tension seeks release.

This tendency is closely tied to another well-documented habit: the attribution of intention. When something unexpected happens, people instinctively look for an agent behind it. A sudden noise in the dark becomes a threat. A fortunate coincidence feels like a sign. These reactions

6. Kruglanski, *Motivated Social Cognition*, 333–44.

evolved as survival mechanisms. Assuming intention was safer than assuming randomness. Over time, that same instinct was carried into explanations of the natural world.

Cognitive scientist Justin Barrett describes this tendency as a hyperactive agency detector.[7] When events violate expectation, the mind searches for a hidden actor. A storm feels purposeful. A disaster feels meaningful. A stroke of luck feels earned. The same pattern that once helped people avoid predators also helped them populate the world with gods.

That satisfaction, however, is psychological rather than logical. The cosmological argument begins by insisting that everything requires a cause. As the reasoning tightens, it quietly introduces an exception. God is exempt. The rule applies universally until it no longer can.

This is the moment where explanation gives way to preference. The exception appears minor until it is examined closely. If everything requires a cause, then God must as well. If God does not, then causation is not a universal rule. The argument does not resolve the problem of origins. It avoids it. Russell stated the problem with the same directness.

Bertrand Russell captured this problem in a single sentence.[8] If everything must have a cause, then God must have a cause. His point was not theological. It was logical. The reasoning used to prove a creator collapses under its own rule. Either causation applies universally or it does not. It cannot be both.

This realization often comes gradually. It is not the result of winning an argument, but of recognizing how a line of reasoning functions. The desire for a final answer remains. Confidence in the explanation that once supported it begins to weaken. What previously seemed like an explanation is revealed instead as a way of relieving discomfort rather than addressing uncertainty.

The appeal of closure is strong. It helps explain why the idea of a first cause persists even when its logic is questioned. Bringing a question to an end can feel like understanding it. However, the relief that follows is psychological rather than evidential. The argument is persuasive not because it explains the universe, but because it reduces the need to continue asking questions.

7. Barrett, *Why Would Anyone Believe in God?*, 31–52.

8. Russell, "Why I Am Not a Christian," 6–7.

FRAGILITY OF CERTAINTY

When the idea of a first cause gives way, the mind does not immediately follow. Logic can dismantle an argument in a moment, but emotional certainty erodes more slowly. People are not designed to rest easily in uncertainty. Even after belief weakens, the desire for an anchor remains. This tension is often where faith persists long after its foundations have begun to crack.

This fragility is not a defect of reason. It is a feature of consciousness. Human thinking depends on patterns. We rely on continuity to navigate the world, and when continuity breaks, the mind works to restore it. Asking a question carries an unspoken promise that an answer exists. When no answer appears, discomfort follows.

Living without a first cause requires accepting that some explanations remain unfinished. It can feel like stepping into deep water without seeing the bottom. Theologians often describe faith as courage, but there is another form of courage involved here. It is the willingness to resist premature resolution and to remain with a question that does not close.

Mythology offers clear examples of this impulse. Origin stories do more than explain how the world began. They assign intention, moral order, and meaning. Even tragedy follows a structure. Suffering is framed as consequence or test. When that structure dissolves, events no longer point beyond themselves. Loss is not redeemed by explanation. The discomfort that follows is not philosophical. It is emotional.

The same desire for resolution appears outside religion. A mystery novel that ends without revealing the culprit frustrates readers. An unresolved melody leaves listeners uneasy. A sentence cut short feels incomplete. These reactions are not failures of intelligence. They reflect how deeply the mind associates completion with understanding.

Science itself reflects this tension. Researchers seek unified theories and elegant explanations. They pursue coherence because it has proven useful, not because the universe guarantees it. When a theory explains much but not all, the remaining gap becomes a source of irritation. The search continues, driven as much by discomfort as by curiosity.

The universe, however, does not share that preference. It continues without regard for closure. Each explanation opens further questions. Every boundary reveals another horizon. The lack of finality is not an error. It is a characteristic of existence itself.

Understanding this helps explain why belief remains compelling even as its arguments weaken. Certainty provides rest. It allows the search to stop. The believer feels secure in having arrived. The skeptic continues moving, aware that arrival may not be possible. Both respond to the same psychological need, but only one acknowledges its limits.

There are moments when I miss the simplicity of childhood belief. A universe with a beginning and an author offered emotional symmetry. Heaven above and purpose below made the world feel complete. But comfort does not determine truth. Once the structure behind belief becomes visible, it cannot be unseen.

Moving away from certainty does not require despair, but adjustment. It involves learning to function without final answers. Meaning develops through continued engagement rather than inherited conclusions. Coherence is found in ongoing inquiry rather than in fixed endpoints.

Certainty weakens not because understanding collapses, but because it expands. When explanations reach their limits, they clarify the difference between knowledge and emotional reassurance. Lacking definitive closure does not make reality less significant. It encourages a more direct and honest engagement with it.

THE CHAIN WITHOUT END

Even after the idea of a first cause begins to loosen, the mind still reaches for beginnings. The habit runs deep. We are accustomed to tracing events backward until we arrive at a starting point. When that point does not appear, unease follows. The absence of an origin can feel like standing on a staircase that never touches the ground.

This discomfort reveals how strongly human reasoning gravitates toward linear narratives. We expect explanations to do the same. Yet not all structures follow that pattern. Some sequences do not originate from a first link. They simply extend.

An infinite chain is difficult to imagine, but difficulty is not impossibility. Consider the number line. There is no first number. Any point selected can always be preceded by another. The absence of a beginning does not make the system incoherent. It simply resists the kind of closure the mind prefers. Searching for a first cause in an infinite sequence may be like searching for the first number. The problem lies in the question itself.

For those raised within a religious framework, this idea can feel like loss. A beginning offers security. It suggests intention and direction. Without it, existence can feel exposed. Yet once the initial discomfort passes, something else appears. The absence of a starting point does not strip the universe of meaning. It removes a demand that meaning arrive fully formed.

Bertrand Russell later expressed this conclusion with characteristic economy when he wrote that the universe is just there.[9] The statement sounds dismissive, but it carries a quiet humility. It acknowledges the limits of explanation without pretending to resolve them. The universe exists, and that fact does not require embellishment to be extraordinary.

In science, this perspective appears repeatedly. Each discovery opens further questions. Matter becomes energy. Energy becomes fields. Fields dissolve into probabilities. Cosmology traces the universe back to dense early states, but even there, the question of what preceded them remains unanswered. The chain stretches beyond the point where current tools can reach.

Accepting a chain without a beginning does not mean abandoning inquiry. It means recognizing that explanation may not terminate in the way stories do. Understanding advances without closure. The universe does not owe us a starting point. It offers patterns, regularities, and surprises. That may be enough.

The endless chain challenges the desire for certainty, but it also invites intellectual honesty. It asks whether the demand for a first cause is a feature of reality or a reflection of the mind's preference for completion. Once that distinction becomes clear, the absence of an origin no longer feels like a failure. It feels like a boundary that marks where explanation gives way to wonder.

FINE-TUNED ILLUSION

As philosophical arguments for a first cause weakened, scientific language began to fill the same explanatory role. Instead of invoking metaphysics, some pointed to physics. The universe, they argued, appears finely tuned for life. The precision of its laws seems too exact to be accidental. Where God once explained order, equations now appeared to whisper intention.

9. Russell, "Why I Am Not a Christian," 16.

The fine-tuning argument often centers on physical constants, especially the cosmological constant, which governs the rate of the universe's expansion.[10] Its value is extraordinarily small and specific. If it were slightly larger, matter would disperse too quickly for stars or galaxies to form. If it were slightly smaller, gravitational attraction would dominate and the universe would collapse before complex structures could develop. Based on this narrow range, some conclude that the value was deliberately set, by God.

At first glance, the argument feels compelling. Precision suggests purpose. But the impression of design may arise from perspective rather than structure. We observe a universe capable of supporting life because only such a universe can be observed by living beings.[11] This is not evidence of intention. It is a selection effect.

Fine-tuning explains why life is possible under certain conditions; it does not explain why the universe exists at all. At most, it describes the narrow range within which observers can appear. It does not reduce mystery. It relocates it. Whether the universe was designed, necessary, or simply given, the question of existence remains unchanged. Precision answers how life fits the universe, not why the universe is here.

A familiar analogy helps clarify the point. Imagine a puddle of water that exactly fits the shape of a hole in the ground.[12] The fit may look remarkable, but the water did not shape the hole. The hole shaped the water. Life conforms to the universe in the same way. We are suited to the conditions that exist because only those conditions allow observers to appear.

Modern cosmology offers additional explanations. Some theories propose a vast number of universes, each with different physical constants.[13] Most would be sterile. A small fraction would permit complexity. If such a multiverse exists, our universe would not require design to explain its properties. It would simply be one of the rare configurations in which observers can emerge.

Even without invoking multiple universes, fine-tuning does not require intention. The constants we observe may arise from deeper physical laws not yet understood. What looks precise at one level may

10. Weinberg, *Dreams of a Final Theory*, 221–26.

11. Carter, "Large Number Coincidences and the Anthropic Principle," 291–98.

12. Adams, *The Salmon of Doubt*, 131–33.

13. Tegmark, *Our Mathematical Universe*, 105–32.

be inevitable at another. The appearance of improbability often reflects limited knowledge rather than design.

Fine-tuning arguments also confuse outcome with cause. The fact that a universe supports life does not mean it was created for life. Snowflakes form intricate patterns without a designer. Crystals assemble according to physical constraints. Complexity can arise naturally when conditions allow it. Precision does not imply purpose.

What fine-tuning reveals most clearly is a human tendency to interpret surprise as intention. When conditions align in unexpected ways, the mind looks for agency. This instinct predates science. It once helped people survive by assuming intention where none existed. In cosmology, it can mislead in the same way.

The universe appears ordered in part because only an ordered universe can be observed. This does not lessen its significance, but it changes how that significance is understood. A sense of awe does not depend on the existence of a planner; it can arise from recognizing that simple physical laws produce complex outcomes. The fine-tuning argument remains appealing because it serves the same psychological function as the first-cause argument: it provides a sense of closure in the face of uncertainty.

A UNIVERSE WITHOUT A MAKER

When the argument for a first cause weakens, many people attempt to replace it with scientific language. The vocabulary changes, but the underlying desire remains. Instead of asking what God initiated, the question becomes what set matter and energy in motion. Physics inherits a search that once belonged to theology. Yet modern cosmology increasingly suggests that the universe does not require an external agent to exist.

Biology offers a particularly clear window into this shift. If life were the product of deliberate design, we would expect evidence of careful planning. Instead, living organisms display the marks of adaptation, compromise, and historical constraint. The human body is not a finished blueprint. It is a record of what worked well enough to persist.

The human eye provides a familiar example. In humans, the retina is arranged backward. Light passes through layers of nerve fibers before reaching the photoreceptors. This arrangement creates a blind spot where the optic nerve exits the eye. Octopuses and squids, which evolved their eyes independently, do not share this flaw.[14] Their retinas face the correct direction and have no blind spot. If intentional design were the goal, there is no reason to favor the inferior arrangement.

The same pattern appears throughout the body. The recurrent laryngeal nerve takes a long detour from the brain to the larynx, looping down into the chest before returning upward. In giraffes, this route stretches to extraordinary lengths. The path makes sense only when viewed as an evolutionary remnant, not as a product of foresight.[15] The human spine, adapted from a structure built for four-legged movement, struggles under upright posture. Chronic back pain reflects evolutionary inheritance, not divine testing.

Other examples follow the same logic. Humans still possess prominent canine teeth, originally shaped for tearing flesh from bone rather than for the modern diets they now serve. Wisdom teeth crowd the jaw because our ancestors had larger mouths and tougher diets. The prostate continues to grow throughout a man's life and can obstruct the urethra. The appendix serves little purpose beyond occasionally becoming life threatening. These features do not point to intelligent planning. They point to a process that modifies existing structures rather than designing them from scratch.

Evolution explains this pattern without invoking intention. Small mutations arise and are passed down to offspring. Some persist because they improve survival or reproduction. Over time, these changes accumulate into complexity. The process is gradual and unguided. It produces workable outcomes, not optimal ones.[16] What looks intricate is the result of countless small steps, not a single creative act.

This process is not theoretical. It can be observed directly. In several underground lakes in Nevada, populations of fish live in complete darkness. Over generations, these fish have lost functional eyes. Some retain eye sockets; others show partial eye development that never matures. Eyes require energy to build and maintain, and in an environment with no light, mutations that reduce or eliminate vision are not harmful. They persist because nothing selects against them. What disappears is not designed away; it fades because it is no longer useful.

Where the cave fish illustrate loss through disuse, the peppered moths of industrial Europe show adaptation through environmental

14. Dawkins, *The Blind Watchmaker*, 93–101.

15. Coyne, *Why Evolution Is True*, 79–82.

16. Dennett, *Darwin's Dangerous Idea*, 74–79.

pressure. Before widespread pollution, lighter-colored moths blended more effectively with lichen-covered trees and were less likely to be eaten by predators. As coal soot darkened the trees, darker moths gained a survival advantage. Within a few decades, the population shifted noticeably. When pollution later declined, the trend reversed. No planning was involved. The environment changed, and the population changed with it.

These cases illustrate what evolution actually produces: adaptation shaped by circumstance, not foresight. Traits persist because they work well enough in a given context, not because they were intended. Complexity accumulates through selection acting on variation, not through design aiming at an outcome.

What biology shows at the level of life, cosmology suggests at the level of the universe itself. The Big Bang describes expansion, not creation within space.[17] Space and time themselves are part of the system that emerged from an early dense state. Asking what happened before that event may not be meaningful, because time is part of what began. Without time, causation loses its usual meaning.

Some physicists have proposed models in which the universe is finite yet without a boundary. Stephen Hawking described this possibility by comparing it to the surface of the Earth. The planet has edges, but no edge functions as a beginning. Asking what lies before the universe may be like asking what lies north of the North Pole.[18] The question assumes a framework that does not apply.

Other models suggest that universes can arise from quantum fluctuations within a broader physical context.[19] In such accounts, existence does not require an external cause. The laws of physics supply the conditions under which emergence can occur. Mystery remains, but intention is no longer necessary.

What struck me while reading modern physics after philosophy was how similar their conclusions felt. Hume questioned causation itself. Russell rejected special exemptions. Physicists question whether beginnings require causes at all. Each approach points toward a universe that stands on its own.

At first, this view can feel impersonal. A universe without a maker does not center human concerns. But that indifference carries its own dignity. Stars form and die because conditions allow it. Atoms combine

17. Hawking, *A Brief History of Time*, 116–21.

18. Hawking, *A Brief History of Time*, 134–36.

19. Krauss, *A Universe from Nothing*, 146–52.

because their properties make it possible. Complexity arises without supervision. The universe does not need to intend in order to create.

Standing beneath a night sky makes this tangible. Stars are not symbols. They are furnaces in which hydrogen fuses into helium, releasing energy that travels across vast distances. When massive stars collapse and go supernova, they forge heavier elements—carbon, oxygen, iron—that later form planets and living organisms. We are not creations placed into the universe; we are products of it. In the simplest terms, we are made from the remnants of stars.

Science does not drain the world of wonder. It relocates it. Understanding becomes participation. The universe does not need a maker to be remarkable. It needs only the conditions that allow matter, energy, and consciousness to arise and observers capable of recognizing what has occurred.

THE PARADOX OF DIVINE COMPLEXITY

Defenders of divine creation often argue that the universe is too complex to exist without intention. Life, consciousness, and order are presented as evidence of design. Yet this claim introduces a deeper difficulty. If complexity requires explanation, then a creator more complex than the universe would require explanation as well. Invoking God does not remove mystery. It magnifies it.[20]

This is the central irony of creationist reasoning. Natural complexity is treated as unacceptable without guidance, then resolved by proposing a being of far greater complexity. A divine mind with unlimited knowledge, power, and intention is vastly more difficult to account for than the physical processes it is meant to explain. The solution demands more than the problem it claims to solve.

The issue can be clarified with a simple comparison. If a watch requires a watchmaker because of its intricate parts, then a watchmaker capable of designing countless watches would require an explanation even more urgently. Replacing one unexplained complexity with a larger one does not simplify understanding. It postpones it.

Philosophers recognized this problem long before modern science. William of Ockham, a fourteenth-century English philosopher and theologian, argued that explanations should not multiply assumptions

20. Dawkins, *The God Delusion*, 143–47.

beyond necessity. His principle, later called *Occam's Razor*, is not a law but a discipline of restraint.[21] When applied to questions of origins, it favors explanations grounded in observable processes rather than entities defined beyond examination.

Theological explanations often move in the opposite direction. They introduce the most elaborate being imaginable, defined by perfect knowledge, unlimited power, and eternal existence. These qualities are asserted precisely because they cannot be tested. The result is not clarity but insulation. The creator is placed beyond question, and inquiry ends.

Appeals to transcendence are often offered in defense. God, believers say, is not subject to the rules that govern the universe. Causation, time, and complexity do not apply. But removing God from the rules of explanation removes him from explanation itself. A cause that cannot be described or evaluated does not explain anything. It functions as a placeholder where understanding stops.

There is also a hidden contradiction in the idea of a timeless creator who acts. Thought involves sequence. Choice implies change. Decision requires time. A being that exists entirely outside time cannot think, decide, or create in any meaningful sense.[22] To preserve divine agency, theology quietly reintroduces the very concepts it claims do not apply.

Natural explanations avoid this problem. Evolution, physics, and cosmology describe processes that generate complexity from simpler states. These processes do not eliminate mystery, but they do not add new layers of untestable assumptions. They show how structure can emerge without foresight or intention.

The emergence of consciousness illustrates this clearly. Every mind we know arises from physical systems shaped by natural processes. Thought grows from matter arranged in particular ways. A supernatural designer is not required to explain how awareness appears. Complexity can arise through accumulation rather than command.

Belief persists in part because imagining a divine mind feels familiar. A god who thinks and chooses resembles human cognition on a larger scale, which can provide comfort and a sense of personal connection. Letting go of that model can be unsettling, but understanding thought as a natural phenomenon is consistent with available evidence.

21. Ockham, *Summa Logicae*, I.12.

22. Russell, "The Problems of Philosophy," 108–10.

This creates a continuing problem for belief. The proposed explanation is more complex than the phenomenon it aims to explain. Adding a designer does not simplify questions about the origin of the universe; it expands them and places the explanation outside investigation. The amount of uncertainty is not reduced, only relocated.

Recognizing this does not lessen the significance of human thought. If consciousness arises from natural processes, then the universe includes the capacity for self-reflection. Meaning is something that develops through these processes rather than something externally imposed. Questions about existence remain, but they concern the world that can be examined, not an entity defined beyond it.

DOUBLE STANDARD OF ETERNITY

When pressed on the problem of origins, believers often invoke divine eternity—not as an explanation, but as a stopping rule. The claim is meant to halt the regress. An eternal deity needs no cause. The chain ends. Yet this move introduces a double standard. If an uncaused existence is possible, then the same allowance can be made for the universe itself.

Both claims stop the chain at a chosen point. The difference is not logical but preferential. One points to something we can observe and study. The other points to a being defined beyond observation. Calling God eternal performs the same function as calling the universe eternal. It ends the question by definition rather than by explanation.

Ancient thinkers recognized this possibility long before modern science. Philosophers such as Lucretius considered the universe to be eternal, governed by natural processes rather than divine will.[23] Aristotle himself entertained the idea of an everlasting cosmos.[24] These views were based on reasoning, not revelation. They accepted infinity as a feature of reality rather than a flaw to be corrected.

Modern cosmology echoes this restraint. Some theories describe oscillating or self-renewing universes. Others suggest that what we call the beginning marks the limit of what physics can currently describe. In these models, asking what happened before the universe began may not be meaningful, because time itself is part of the system that emerged.[25]

23. Lucretius, *On the Nature of Things*, bk. I.

24. Aristotle, *On the Heavens*, bk. I.

25. Hawking, *A Brief History of Time*, 134–36.

Causation depends on sequence. A cause must precede its effect. If time began with the universe, then creation cannot be a temporal event. Saying that God caused the universe assumes a before in a context where before may not exist. The language of cause breaks down when applied outside time.

Both positions reach the same boundary. Either something exists without a cause, or the concept of cause does not apply at the deepest level. The difference lies in how each response treats that boundary. One admits the limits of explanation. The other claims certainty without access to verification.

Preferring divine eternity over cosmic eternity does not resolve the mystery of existence. It replaces an unanswered question with a declaration that cannot be tested. The universe remains here regardless of which story is told. Our task is to understand it as far as observation and reasoning allow. Beyond that point lies speculation, not knowledge.

Recognizing the double standard does not eliminate wonder. It clarifies responsibility. If explanation reaches a limit, honesty requires acknowledging it rather than filling the gap with assertion. Mystery does not disappear when it is left unresolved. It becomes part of the landscape of inquiry.

PERSONAL RECKONING

The first time I allowed myself to consider a universe without a creator, the reaction was not relief. It felt like loss. Even after years of questioning religious claims, part of me still expected a central figure behind everything. That expectation does not disappear simply because belief weakens. It lingers as habit, shaped by years of prayer, instruction, and emotional attachment.

For a long time, I lived between understanding and desire. Philosophical arguments had loosened the foundations of belief, but they did not immediately fill the space belief had occupied. Faith had once supplied a framework for interpreting events. Pain could be a test. Joy could be a blessing. Coincidence could be a sign. Within that structure, nothing felt arbitrary. When the structure dissolved, the world initially felt flatter, as though meaning itself had thinned.

It took time to recognize that this sense of loss came from contrast rather than absence. The world had not changed. My expectations had.

Without a divine narrative to supply intention, I began to notice details that had previously been overshadowed by interpretation. Ordinary moments gained weight. Nature no longer pointed beyond itself. It stood on its own, complex and sufficient.

There is a particular clarity that comes with recognizing that the universe does not revolve around human concerns. Stars form and die without regard for meaning. Planets follow their paths because gravity dictates it. From this indifference arise the conditions that make life possible. The absence of intention does not make existence empty. It makes it honest.

I once believed that a godless universe would feel bleak. Instead, responsibility increased. Without a higher authority to assign purpose, meaning became something that had to be chosen. Morality shifted from obedience to consequence. Caring for others was no longer a matter of divine instruction but of shared vulnerability. What we do matters precisely because nothing outside us guarantees that it will.

Awe did not disappear, but took a different form. A sense of wonder no longer depended on belief in an unseen creator. It arose from understanding and explanation. Learning more about the universe increased rather than diminished its significance, and reduced the impulse to describe it in human terms.

The question that once troubled me most, who created God, eventually stopped feeling confrontational. It became descriptive. It stripped away assumptions that had shaped my thinking since childhood. In the space that followed, I found that the reverence I had once associated with faith did not require an object. It arose from attention, from recognizing the improbability of consciousness itself.

To be human may mean learning to create meaning rather than receive it. Instead of inheriting purpose, we participate in it. We shape value through action, understanding, and care. We are not here because a plan required us. We are here because the conditions allowed awareness to emerge.

Once the idea of a creator lost its explanatory force, understanding itself began to feel creative. To learn, to question, and to act deliberately became meaningful in ways doctrine never supplied. The universe did not become smaller without God. It became more immediate.

The silence I once mistook for absence began to feel like space. Not a void demanding explanation, but an openness that allowed inquiry to continue. What replaced certainty was not despair, but honesty. And in that honesty, I found a deeper connection to the world as it is.

Before belief fell away, silence felt threatening. Afterward, it felt truthful. And truth, even when incomplete, proved strong enough to stand on its own.

4

Mystery as an Excuse

"Whereof one cannot speak, thereof one must be silent."

LUDWIG WITTGENSTEIN

THE BOUNDARIES OF REVELATION

I recall the first time I was told that God speaks to us. The idea was comforting because it implied the universe was not silent and that a guiding presence might be waiting to be heard. Yet even then something about it felt uncertain. If God communicated with people, why could I never hear anything? I listened during prayer, during church services, and in the quiet moments before sleep, but nothing ever answered. I assumed the problem must be with me rather than the claim itself. Only later did I notice how many people claimed to speak on behalf of the same silence I had been trying to understand.

Every faith begins by asserting that truth has spoken and that its followers have heard correctly. The divine message is presented as a bridge between confusion and certainty, a voice cutting through doubt. Yet the world is filled with competing versions of that voice. The Hindu listens for the eternal syllable *Om*. The Muslim accepts the words delivered by the angel Gabriel. The Christian sees the Word made flesh. The Buddhist finds insight in stillness rather than speech. Each tradition claims privileged access to the infinite, yet their messages rarely align.[1] At that point, the problem felt less like disagreement and more like a question about how certainty itself takes shape.

I sat in the pew once while a priest described other religions as misguided paths, their followers portrayed as souls in need of rescue. I could not shake the image of those same followers praying in their own temples, equally convinced that *we* were the ones who needed saving. I imagined competing prayers rising into the same sky, each claiming to be the only true voice. That thought unsettled me. It showed me that sincerity could not be the measure of truth, because sincerity existed everywhere. If devotion appeared in every tradition, then devotion alone could not decide which one was correct. I did not take this as an answer, only as the beginning of a longer uncertainty.

If a voice from heaven truly spoke, clarity would be the expected result. Instead, what appears is translation: competing versions, interpretations, and arguments over meaning. Each group claims authority while denying it to the others. The problem may not be confusion at the source, but the demand placed on language to carry certainty it cannot sustain. What we call revelation may fail not because God contradicts Himself, but because human interpretation cannot support the role assigned to it. The question is no longer who is mistaken, but whether the expectations placed on revelation were ever realistic.

Sacred texts illustrate this problem vividly. The Ten Commandments differ from the teachings of the Upanishads. The Qur'an diverges from the Gospels. The Torah conflicts with the Tao. Even within a single tradition, voices differ, commands shift, and the tone of the divine moves from compassion to severity. What we call holy disclosure looks less like a message and more like a reflection of human culture. I did not see these contradictions as a child. The Bible was the only lens I had. Only when I read other sacred texts did a pattern appear: the same promises, the same threats, written in different alphabets.[2]

I used to wonder why the central symbol of Christianity is an instrument of execution. The cross was designed by the Romans to prolong pain and humiliation. Over centuries it was transformed from a device of torture into a symbol of redemption. I sometimes asked myself whether people would wear tiny electric chairs around their necks if Jesus had

1. Smart, *The World's Religions*, 6–11.

2. Armstrong, *A History of God*, 9–15.

been executed that way. The question may seem irreverent, but it reveals something important. Religion has always been skilled at turning suffering into significance, reshaping cruelty into comfort. The result is powerful but unsettling: a faith built around a symbol the ancient world used to produce agony.

If these messages differ so radically, how can we know which one is correct? If Christianity is true, then Islam, Hinduism, and Buddhism cannot be. If Muhammad was right that Jesus was only a prophet, the foundation of Christianity changes entirely. And if the Qur'an is the final revelation, every other tradition stands in error. These are not minor variations of a shared truth. They are incompatible claims about reality.

It is tempting to say that all religions point to the same God, just in different ways. The claim offers comfort by reducing conflict, but it does not survive comparison. The Christian God dies on a cross; the Muslim God rejects the idea that God can die; many Hindu traditions describe multiple gods with distinct roles; Buddhism, in many branches, does not center on a creator at all. Judaism sees God as personal but not incarnate. Mormonism teaches that God was once a man who became divine. These positions do not differ in emphasis. They describe fundamentally different realities.

Behind the surface similarities of love, justice, and compassion are incompatible claims about the nature, identity, actions, and even the number of gods. Treating these claims as equivalent does not resolve the conflict between them. It avoids it.

Even within Christianity, division persists. Either God speaks through the Pope or He does not. A Catholic worships a God who authorizes the papacy; a Baptist worships one who rejects it. These positions cannot all be correct. The issue is no longer ritual or interpretation, but whether any of these claimed authorities originate beyond the cultures that assert them.

I once read a story about a missionary who traveled to a remote village to preach the Gospel. After explaining that those who accepted Christ would go to heaven and those who rejected Him would be condemned, the missionary was met with silence. A villager finally asked, "If we had never heard this message, would we still go to hell?"

The missionary admitted they would not.

The man then asked, "Then why did you tell us?"[3]

3. Hitchens, *God Is Not Great*, 174–75.

He understood more quickly than the preacher what this new knowledge demanded. Before the missionary arrived, the villagers were safe in their ignorance. After hearing the message, they were accountable. In trying to save them, the missionary had accidentally burdened them with the risk of going to hell.

That exchange exposes a quiet problem hidden inside certain versions of revelation: the idea that knowledge can endanger as easily as it can save. If not knowing protects someone from punishment, then divine disclosure becomes a risk rather than a gift. A God whose message creates danger for those who hear it resembles a test maker more than a source of compassion. It is a paradox faith has never fully resolved.

History is full of prophets, but empty of agreement. Moses hears God in thunder, Muhammad in recitation, Joseph Smith, the nineteenth-century founder of the Church of Jesus Christ of Latter-day Saints, through seer stones, and mystics in dreams. Each claims authenticity. Each dismisses the rest. The pattern does not point to a single source interpreted differently; it points to competing claims shaped by different contexts.

Joseph Smith's revelations reflected early American frontier spirituality—revival meetings, folk magic, and the widespread hope for new scripture.[4] The golden plates, angelic visitations, and translated messages fit the culture he lived in, turning local beliefs into doctrine. The pattern is clear: belief adapts to time and place. Deserts produce monotheism; forests produce spirits; scholarly cultures produce metaphors. Geography shapes theology as surely as climate shapes weather.

Some theologians try to resolve these contradictions by claiming that each religion holds a piece of the same truth. The idea is reassuring, but it does not withstand comparison. Reincarnation is not resurrection. Nirvana is not paradise. These concepts do not converge on a shared reality. They describe different accounts of what existence is and how it should be understood.

Even within a single tradition, the idea of divine certainty collapses under examination. Christians disagree about Communion. Muslims divide over leadership. Jews differ over whether oral tradition carries the same authority as written law. If sacred truth were singular and self-evident, believers would not fragment into countless sects. The very

4. Bushman, *Joseph Smith: Rough Stone Rolling*, 47–55.

existence of so many denominations undermines the idea of one clear revelation. A perfect message should not require endless revision.

When confronted with these contradictions, defenders of faith often retreat to mystery, insisting that God's ways are beyond human understanding. But that defense also undermines the claim. A truth that must remain unknowable cannot also be claimed as known. What is described as revelation becomes, in the end, resignation.

The difficulty becomes most apparent when belief is asked to do explanatory work. Believing that some unknowable being possesses some unknown qualities in an unknowable way is fundamentally riddled with contradictions. This reliance on belief in the absence of verifiable data renders such faith, by these standards, an unreasonable stance. Ultimately, God fails the test of reason and rational inquiry because the claim of His existence rests on unfalsifiable premises devoid of empirical footing. What remains is not illumination, but affirmation—accepted not because it convinces, but because it comforts.

This paradox sits at the core of theology: certainty about what is defined as beyond comprehension. The moment we describe God, we limit the very idea we claim to honor. Voltaire, tired of sectarian violence, once asked whether a divine message intended for all people would truly need interpreters.[5] His question remains relevant. If an infinite being wanted to be understood, why communicate in ways that guarantee misunderstanding? Why rely on prophets, languages, and metaphors that divide the world rather than unite it? The simpler explanation may be the most human one: revelation is not received but written.

To say this is not to dismiss the depth of faith but to recognize its human origin. The stories we call sacred are attempts to express what exceeds expression. They reveal more about human hope, fear, and imagination than about the universe itself. The burning bush, the light that blinded Paul, the voice in Muhammad's cave—these may be descriptions of inward experience, moments when consciousness brushed against its own depths and mistook the encounter for something external. If the divine is an echo rather than a message, then the limits of knowing God begin with the limits of understanding ourselves.

Even after reason exposes revelation as human speech aimed at the infinite, the emotional truth within it remains. To dismiss it entirely would be to ignore a deep aspect of human psychology. Perhaps that is

5. Voltaire, *Philosophical Dictionary*, "Religion."

why I could never fully let it go. Even when I stopped believing that God speaks, I still understood the longing behind the belief. People want the universe to answer. What I eventually realized is that the unknowability of God is not a failure of perception but a fact of existence. If the infinite exists at all, it will not shrink to fit the boundaries of our language. It remains silent, untouched by what we insist it must say.

PSYCHOLOGY OF THE SACRED

When revelation is treated as evidence, it fails. Yet belief does not disappear, because the experience remains. People who say they have "heard" or "felt" God are rarely making intellectual claims. They are describing moments charged with meaning, where emotion intensifies and the mind looks for an explanation. Naming these moments divine gives structure to an experience that otherwise resists clear interpretation.

Modern neuroscience has begun to study the states once described as spiritual. Brain scans of monks in meditation and nuns in deep prayer show similar activity patterns:[6] the quieting of regions that define the sense of self and heightened activation in areas linked to emotion and significance.[7] The result is a temporary shift in perception, a feeling of connection that can seem to reach beyond the self. In earlier times this feeling was named "God." Today we might call it transcendence, or simply the mind responding to its own complexity.

From an evolutionary perspective, this capacity may have been useful.[8] The feeling of unity or connection can strengthen social bonds. Groups that shared awe or ritual would have been more cooperative than those without such experiences. What once encouraged cohesion now appears as revelation. The biology of belief is older than any scripture. It reflects the brain's tendency to interpret intense emotion as a sign of external meaning.

None of this makes the experience trivial. The brain is capable of producing states that feel profound, and people naturally look for an explanation. When someone reports hearing a voice, seeing a light, or sensing a presence, they may not be describing deception but interpretation. The mind translates internal activity into familiar symbols. Lightning

6. Newberg, *Why God Won't Go Away*, 39–45.

7. D'Aquili and Newberg, *The Mystical Mind*, 84–92.

8. Atran, *In Gods We Trust*, 56–63.

seen by Moses, the light that struck Paul blind, or the presence Muhammad felt in the cave may have been moments when perception exceeded language, and the brain supplied imagery to match the intensity.[9]

These experiences reveal less about the origins of the universe and more about the structure of human consciousness. They show how deeply we want connection, understanding, and reassurance. When someone says they felt God, they may be expressing something true about their inner life rather than the external world. Revelation, in this sense, points not to the divine but to the mind's search for coherence.

What emerges from this perspective is not a dismissal of spiritual experience but a reevaluation of its source. The feeling itself is real. What we conclude from it is where interpretation begins. The mind, when moved by awe or fear or longing, reaches outward for meaning even when the cause is internal. In that reaching, revelation becomes less a message from beyond and more a reflection of the human need to feel that existence has a listener.

THE GOD HELMET EXPERIMENT

In the 1990s, Canadian neuroscientist Michael Persinger set out to test one of humanity's oldest intuitions: that the mind itself might simulate the sacred. His device, which he called the "God Helmet," used weak, pulsed magnetic fields directed at the temporal lobes,[10] regions linked to emotion, memory, and the sense of self. Persinger believed that by gently stimulating these areas, he could reproduce sensations often described as mystical or paranormal—the feeling of a presence, the brush of another consciousness, or the quiet certainty of being watched by something unseen. If these experiences can be produced by stimulation alone, then revelation no longer requires a supernatural source.

His early experiments yielded results that were as provocative as they were controversial. Persinger reported that roughly eighty percent of participants experienced *some form of anomalous sensation*, often subtle rather than overtly mystical. Many described a vague sense of presence in the room, while others reported more vivid impressions: a nearby being, a guardian, even God. Yet not everyone felt anything at all. Later studies suggested that belief might be the strongest variable. Those who already

9. Persinger, *Neuropsychological Bases of God Beliefs*, 121–29.

10. Persinger, *Neuropsychological Bases of God Beliefs*, 87–101.

held religious or spiritual convictions were far more likely to interpret their sensations as divine, while skeptics undergoing the same stimulation described only a faint shift in awareness or mild physical effects.

Even the evolutionary biologist Richard Dawkins, who later became one of the most prominent critics of religious belief, tried the helmet during the filming of a BBC documentary. Unlike Persinger's more suggestible subjects, Dawkins reported no mystical experience whatsoever.[11] Persinger later proposed that Dawkins' low "temporal-lobe sensitivity" might explain the absence of effect. The exchange itself became part of the experiment's legacy, illustrating how the same stimulus can yield revelation for one person and indifference for another.

Intrigued, I decided to build a "God Helmet" for myself. The purpose was not to confirm belief, but to test whether reported experiences required a supernatural explanation at all. Using Persinger's parameters as a guide, I assembled a version with parts from a hardware store and a few online orders. I modified a motorcycle helmet, wiring it with coils, a power supply, a pulse generator, and a relay timer to control both the field intervals and intensity. I calibrated the magnetic strength carefully, adjusting the output across multiple sessions to see whether power made any difference. I set a thirty-day schedule, committing to twenty-minute sessions in a quiet room, eyes covered, environment controlled, to see whether any shift in awareness would occur—whether subtle or profound.

To give the experiment some structure, I kept a logbook for each session, noting the settings and any sensations—however subtle—that followed. The frequency values recorded reflect the general pacing of the stimulation patterns rather than a precise or fixed signal. A sample from the first ten sessions is shown below:

Table 1. Sample Logbook Excerpts, Sessions 1–10

Session	Frequency	Intensity	Pattern	Notable Effects
1	3.0 Hz	10 mG	Bilateral alternating	No anomalous effects (mild helmet pressure)
2	4.5 Hz	12 mG	Left-temporal focus	No anomalous effects
3	2.0 Hz	13 mG	Right-temporal focus	No anomalous effects (brief warmth)
4	3.0 Hz	11 mG	Random sweep	No anomalous effects (mild headache)

11. Dawkins, *The God Delusion*, 167–69.

Session	Frequency	Intensity	Pattern	Notable Effects
5	4.5 Hz	14 mG	Left-right alternating	No anomalous effects (brief warmth)
6	5.0 Hz	11 mG	Right-temporal sustained	No anomalous effects (mild headache)
7	4.5 Hz	12 mG	Left-temporal alternating	No anomalous effects
8	2.0 Hz	14 mG	Bilateral sustained	No anomalous effects (brief warmth)
9	3.5 Hz	11 mG	Left-temporal sweep	No anomalous effects
10	3.0 Hz	12 mG	Right-temporal sweep	No anomalous effects

Ten sessions in, the pattern was unmistakable. There was no sense of presence, no altered awareness, and no experience that suggested anything beyond ordinary perception.

I adjusted every variable I could—frequency, intensity, pulse patterns, and timing—hoping one combination might unlock something unusual. The results were consistent and disappointing. Across thirty sessions, I experienced no sense of presence, no altered state, no trace of the extraordinary. The logbook I kept became a catalog of ordinary moments, each one ending the same way: in silence.

At first glance, this absence might seem to undermine the experiment itself. It does not, because the experiment was never meant to reliably produce a religious experience. Its purpose was to examine what such experiences depend on. If encounters with God were interactions with an external agent, they would not vary so dramatically with belief, expectation, or neurological susceptibility. Yet both Persinger's reported results and my own consistent silence point in the same direction. What appears to matter is not the presence of something beyond the self, but the readiness of the mind to interpret sensation as meaning. In this context, silence is not a failure of the method. It is evidence of the limits of experience as proof.

If a sense of divine presence can be generated by the brain itself, or fail to appear entirely under the same conditions, then the question is no longer why such experiences feel real, but why God is needed to explain them at all. An experience can be profound, even transformative, without serving as reliable evidence of anything beyond the mind that produces it. Once a phenomenon can be induced or withheld through stimulation, suggestion, or expectation, it loses authority as a guide to what exists outside the experiencer. Such experiences may explain belief, but they cannot establish truth.

If belief primes perception, then revelation may not descend from heaven at all. It may arise from within, taking form only when the mind is prepared to interpret sensation as meaning. The God Helmet did not prove or disprove the existence of God. It revealed something more modest and more telling: that the boundary between the sacred and the psychological is thinner than we imagine, and that the feeling of encounter does not require an encounter to occur.

The more I studied these experiments, the clearer it became that mystery does not require the supernatural. What we call the divine may be an echo of our own circuitry, amplified by longing and framed by culture. Science can trace the contours of belief without emptying it of significance. Once the experience itself is accounted for, however, it can no longer function as proof. If the sacred can be simulated, or fail to appear at all, the claim that it originates beyond the human mind demands something more than experience alone.

That question leads to a deeper problem, one that has followed every attempt to define the divine.

TESTIMONY AND THE WEIGHT OF HOPE

If revelation fractures under contradiction and experience dissolves under examination, belief retreats to its final claim: testimony. Nowhere is this clearer than in the claim of resurrection. Christianity does not ultimately depend on metaphor, moral teaching, or inward experience. It depends on an assertion about history, that a man executed by the state returned to life and that this event was witnessed, remembered, and faithfully reported.

This claim occupies a distinct position. Unlike private visions or psychological experiences, resurrection presents itself as a public event. It is meant to be taken as fact, not symbol. Paul acknowledged this directly when he wrote that if Christ has not been raised, faith is futile (1 Corinthians 15:14). Christianity stands or falls on this single assertion.

When examined closely, the claim rests entirely on testimony. There are no contemporary records describing the event. No Roman documentation notes the disappearance of a body. No independent accounts outside the early Christian community confirm it. What remains are texts written decades later, shaped by memory, belief, and transmission through communities already committed to the claim.

This reliance on testimony does not automatically invalidate the belief. Much of history is reconstructed from human reports. But the nature of the claim matters. The event is not presented as a neutral account of an unusual occurrence. It carries extraordinary consequences. It promises victory over death, moral vindication, and cosmic justice. It offers not consolation, but reversal.

Death is the one certainty no argument can soften. Every culture confronts it, and every religion offers an answer. Christianity's answer is distinctive because it does not promise survival in another form or dissolution into something larger. It promises restoration. The body is not abandoned. Loss is not accepted. Death itself is said to be undone.

The emotional force of such a claim is difficult to overstate. Beliefs that directly address existential fear tend to persist regardless of evidence. The greater the fear, the stronger the incentive to preserve the answer. Resurrection speaks directly to this fear, and it does so with certainty rather than ambiguity.

The early Christian movement emerged under conditions where such a belief would have been especially compelling. Crucifixion was final and public. Roman authority was unquestioned. To claim resurrection in that context required conviction, but conviction alone does not establish truth. It establishes commitment.

Over time, the resurrection accounts show variation. The Gospels differ on who discovered the tomb, who was present, and what was said. Paul's earliest writings describe appearances but do not mention an empty tomb. These differences are often attributed to normal variation in memory. They can also be understood as a familiar pattern in testimony where meaning takes precedence over detail.

Once belief is established, testimony becomes self-reinforcing. Those who accept resurrection interpret suffering as temporary and loss as reversible. Questioning the event is no longer a matter of historical inquiry. It becomes a threat to the framework that gives suffering meaning. Doubt carries emotional cost.

This pattern is not unique to Christianity. Martyr narratives across religions follow similar structures. Willingness to suffer or die for a belief demonstrates sincerity and commitment, not factual accuracy.

Incompatible beliefs have inspired equal devotion. Conviction does not resolve contradiction.

If the event occurred as claimed, it would represent a fundamental violation of natural law. Such an event would not depend on belief for its preservation. It would leave durable, independent traces. Its evidence would not rely on inherited faith or internal conviction. It would persist as anomaly rather than doctrine.

Instead, the belief survives through testimony. It is maintained through narrative, ritual, and repetition. Its authority does not come from independent verification, but from the role it plays in providing meaning. Without it, Christianity reduces to a moral system formed around an execution. With it, death is treated as temporary rather than final.

What resurrection ultimately reveals is not how the world works, but how people respond to the fact of death. It speaks to a need that evidence alone does not satisfy. Like revelation and personal experience, it convinces by the meaning it offers rather than by demonstration.

This does not imply deception. It reflects a human response to loss. Resurrection does not describe the mechanisms of reality. It describes how people cope with its limits. Once this distinction is recognized, testimony no longer functions as evidence of divine action. It functions as evidence of the need to believe that death is not final.

PROBLEM OF UNKNOWABLE CERTAINTY

If revelation cannot be verified, reason does not rescue the idea of God either. In a world where claims are tested and measured, the concept of a divine being becomes difficult to define. Once, faith was treated as its own proof. Now it stands before the standards we apply to every other claim about reality. The word God begins to shift, stretching from personal deity to metaphor, from presence to abstraction. What remains is not a being we can understand but a question that resists definition.

Rational thinking depends on clarity, consistency, and evidence. These standards work well everywhere else, so it is natural to apply them to God as well. Yet the moment they are applied, something gives way. God is said to exist, but not to be comprehensible; to act, but not in ways that can be examined; to be known, but only through certainty rather than understanding. What remains is a paradox: a confident claim about something placed outside the conditions that make knowledge possible.

If this move is accepted, then questioning no longer tests belief; it violates it.

Knowledge requires the possibility of being known. When this standard is applied to God, the claim changes shape. God is said to exist, yet His nature cannot be described; to act, yet without mechanisms that can be examined; to possess qualities whose meaning dissolves under scrutiny. What remains is not knowledge, but confidence without explanatory content.

Many believers respond by saying that God is hidden or beyond detection. At first, this sounds like humility—a recognition of human limits. But the move has a consequence that is rarely acknowledged. A being that cannot be sensed, inferred, or traced through its effects makes no practical difference to the world it is said to govern. The claim is preserved, but its explanatory role is lost.

If God interacts with the world, those interactions should be detectable. This is not a hostile demand; it is how causal claims normally work. Influence implies consequence. If prayers are answered, events should change. If natural law is shaped, patterns should shift. When no such traces appear, the claim of divine action no longer explains anything. At that point, the difference between absence and invisibility disappears.

Faith often claims to rise above proof while still borrowing the language of evidence. That combination creates a problem. The larger the claim, the more responsibility it carries to be clear. To assert an infinite mind behind the universe is not a private sentiment; it is a claim about reality itself. Sincerity cannot do the work of demonstration, and conviction alone cannot convert belief into fact.

Some argue that human understanding is too limited to grasp the divine. But our ignorance proves only itself. Throughout history, events once attributed to gods—lightning, disease, emotion—eventually gained natural explanations. The appeal to mystery has always served as a temporary shelter for what science has not yet explained.

Imagine someone claiming that gravity exists but produces no effect: no falling objects, no orbiting planets, no tides. We would dismiss the claim not out of hostility but logic. A cause without consequence collapses as a concept. The same principle applies to the divine. A presence with no detectable influence becomes indistinguishable from a story. The untestable is, by definition, unknowable, and therefore cannot be asserted as truth.

Even when God is redefined metaphorically—"God as love" or "God as justice"—the problem remains. Love matters because it is enacted. Justice matters because it produces consequences. When these qualities are lifted out of human relationships and placed in an unseen realm, they lose the grounding that gives them meaning. What remains is not clarification, but abstraction—a word searching for a referent it can no longer reach.

What remains is not revelation but reflection. Faith may provide emotional comfort, but it cannot replace the conditions that make knowledge possible. Mystery can inspire awe, but it cannot uphold certainty. The unknowable may evoke reverence, but it cannot stand as a claim about reality.

If a claimed being never reveals itself, never produces measurable effects, and never intersects with observable reality, then it becomes indistinguishable from the nonexistent. At that point, the difference between absence and invisibility collapses. What remains is not a mystery to be explored, but a claim that no longer functions as an explanation.

HUMAN COST OF MYSTERY

When belief retreats into mystery, it leaves people holding explanations that feel less like answers and more like barriers. This is not an abstract problem. It shapes how people respond to suffering, loss, and injustice. The familiar phrase God works in mysterious ways may sound reassuring in a sermon, but it carries a different weight beside a hospital bed or after a personal loss. For those in pain, it often closes the conversation instead of opening it. Mystery is often offered as comfort, but it can prevent people from confronting suffering directly. What many call divine silence is sometimes the echo of our own need for meaning.

Generations have struggled with that silence. Parents have buried children and been told their suffering serves a purpose. Survivors of disasters have been encouraged to find meaning in destruction. These statements may comfort the person offering them, but they rarely help the one grieving. To claim that every loss is part of a divine plan turns tragedy into necessity. It transforms random harm into an intention. Mystery becomes not a bridge to understanding but a way to sanctify what should never be justified.

I once read about a father who lost his young daughter to illness. Members of his congregation surrounded him with well-meant phrases. She is with God now. Her suffering had meaning. Others said what believers often say when explanations run out: His purposes are beyond our knowing. He listened, but later he admitted that each statement deepened the wound. Mystery did not ease his grief. It only lifted his pain to a higher plane where it could not be questioned. What he needed was not a story about purpose, but someone willing to sit with the reality that his daughter's death had no explanation that could make it acceptable. That is when I understood that mystery can become a shield against compassion. It answers too quickly and prevents honest grief.

People cling to mystery because the alternative is difficult to face. If suffering has no higher intention, then suffering simply exists. The mind resists this idea. A universe guided by chance feels colder than a world governed by purpose, even a harsh purpose. To accept a cruel plan can feel safer than accepting no plan at all. But trading truth for comfort does not heal anything. It only hides the wound from view.

This does not mean faith has no value. It means its value is emotional rather than explanatory. When mystery is used to defend belief, it discourages questioning and replaces understanding with acceptance. The same logic that frames a child's death as part of a divine plan can be used to justify almost anything. Invoked too quickly, mystery protects doctrine at the expense of empathy.

Honesty may require letting go of explanations altogether. To admit that we do not know why suffering exists is not weakness but clarity. Refusing to frame tragedy as divine intention allows compassion to take the place of justification. Mystery, faced without excuses, does not erase meaning. It allows meaning to arise from the human response itself: from care, mourning, and the simple act of acknowledging another's pain without dressing it in theology. In that moment, mystery did not provide meaning; it removed the space for honesty.

Science follows a similar principle. Its method begins with acknowledging what is not understood. The willingness to face uncertainty without rushing to fill it is a form of respect for reality. Mystery becomes not a conclusion but a starting point. When approached with honesty, it does not suppress questions. It encourages them.

SCIENCE AND THE UNKNOWABLE

Science approaches mystery differently than religion does. Where religion treats the unknown as evidence of the divine, science treats it as a starting point for investigation. Both confront limits, but they respond in opposite ways. Faith often stops with mystery and calls it sacred; science keeps going because the mystery itself is worth understanding. This difference matters because it determines whether mystery ends inquiry or keeps it open.

The universe still contains vast gaps in our knowledge. Physicists speak of dark matter and dark energy—forces that make up most of the cosmos but remain invisible.[12] We detect them only through their gravitational effects. In quantum mechanics, particles appear and disappear, shift states, and behave in ways that defy everyday intuition. At the smallest scales, reality no longer looks solid or predictable. The uncertainty is built into the structure of nature, not into our ability to measure it.

These mysteries do not restore God to the conversation. They simply remind us that there is still a great deal we do not understand. The honest response is not to fill the gap with a supernatural explanation but to recognize that the gap is real. Science does not treat uncertainty as failure—it treats it as information. It sets the limits of what we know today and marks the boundary of what we may learn tomorrow.

Many believers point to these unknowns as proof of God—the idea that where knowledge ends, divinity begins. This reasoning has a long history. Whenever people could not explain lightning, disease, or the origins of life, they added the divine to the equation. But each time understanding grew, the need for that explanation shrank. Over centuries, the space left for miracle slowly narrowed. Meteorology replaced divine judgment; biology replaced creation myths; neuroscience began to replace the idea of a soul separate from the brain. When mystery is treated as evidence rather than a question, it stops functioning as an invitation to learn.

This habit of placing God wherever answers are missing is often called the "God of the gaps."[13] It gives faith temporary safety but always ties its survival to the absence of understanding. Every scientific advance shifts God further into the background. A belief built on gaps inevitably erodes as those gaps close.

12. Carroll, *The Particle at the End of the Universe*, 25–48.

13. McGrath, "The God of the Gaps," 1–14.

The scientific approach does not resolve mystery by explanation alone; it manages mystery through method. Instead of locating meaning in what we cannot explain, it finds meaning in the ongoing process of learning. Each discovery reveals another question. The horizon keeps expanding, and with it, our sense of awe. Even the most committed scientists often describe their work in language that resembles reverence. Einstein called wonder at the rationality of nature "the most beautiful emotion we can experience."[14] Carl Sagan wrote that science is a profound source of spirituality because it connects the human mind to the structure of the cosmos.[15]

The difference is not emotional; it is methodological. Science requires evidence, welcomes correction, and accepts that some questions may remain open. Religion often demands certainty even when evidence is absent. Science moves forward by admitting what it does not know. Faith often defends what it cannot prove.

To live with the unknown does not mean surrendering curiosity. It means treating uncertainty as part of reality rather than a doorway to the supernatural. The borders of knowledge are not walls; they are invitations. An honest response to the unknown does not require belief, only patience, evidence, and a refusal to declare certainty where none is possible.

LANGUAGE OF THE DIVINE

When direct knowledge fails, language rushes in to fill the gap. Metaphor becomes the primary tool for speaking about the divine—light, father, king, breath, love, void. These terms feel explanatory, but they do not describe; they translate the unfamiliar into the familiar. What begins as metaphor quietly takes on the authority of fact.

Traditions across cultures have acknowledged this limitation. Jewish mystics refer to God as *Ein Sof*, "the Infinite," beyond any description.[16] Early Christian thinkers developed the "way of negation," defining God only by what He is not.[17] Buddhism often bypasses description entirely, insisting that ultimate reality cannot be captured in words. Even

14. Einstein, *Ideas and Opinions*, 11.
15. Sagan, *The Demon-Haunted World*, 28–30.
16. Scholem, *Major Trends in Jewish Mysticism*, 88.
17. Pseudo-Dionysius, *Mystical Theology*, 135–36.

the Qur'an warns that nothing resembles God (Qur'an 42:11). In every major tradition, the closer one approaches the idea of the divine, the less language can say. These traditions recognized that the more confidently God is described, the more those descriptions reflect human assumptions rather than divine reality.

Still, people are uncomfortable with silence. We prefer a God who speaks clearly and fits within familiar ideas. By naming and defining the divine, we gain a sense of certainty about something we cannot fully understand. Yet every definition narrows what it attempts to describe. Over time, these definitions harden into boundaries that separate belief systems rather than clarify them. What begins as symbolic language becomes a fixed set of claims that must be protected and defended.

Wittgenstein famously wrote, "The limits of my language mean the limits of my world."[18] The same applies to belief. When we describe God, we set the limits of what we imagine God to be. These limits vary across cultures because each tradition draws from its own history, values, and emotional needs. The divine becomes a reflection of human experience rather than a window into something beyond it.

Translation adds further complications. Sacred texts exist in multiple languages, and each translation alters meaning. Entire branches of faith have formed around differences in interpretation—whether a phrase is literal or symbolic, whether a ritual is commanded or optional. The more we try to define God with language, the more divided those definitions become. Disputes over translation do not remain academic; they determine doctrine, authority, and exclusion.

Ultimately, when people speak about God, they often reveal more about themselves than about any higher power. The qualities they assign to the divine—compassion, anger, justice, forgiveness—come from human experience. What believers call revelation may be the mind projecting its values onto the unknown.

If God is truly beyond comprehension, then no human language can contain Him. In that sense, silence may be the most honest response. A willingness to admit that we do not know—and cannot know—is not a sign of weakness but of humility. When language fails, understanding does not disappear; it simply takes a different form. Silence, in this sense, is not a claim about God, but an acknowledgment of the limits of human description.

18. Wittgenstein, *Tractatus Logico-Philosophicus*, 5.6.

THE WISDOM OF SILENCE

Silence has always made people uneasy. We fill it with explanations, hymns, and prayers, as though meaning might vanish the moment we stop speaking. Yet throughout history, silence has also been treated as the most honest response to questions that exceed language.

In many traditions, silence is not emptiness but respect. In Judaism, one of the names of God is left unspoken, not out of fear but acknowledgment that some ideas cannot be reduced to words. In early Buddhism, the Buddha refused to answer certain metaphysical questions, not because he lacked answers, but because the questions themselves could not be resolved by language. Early Christian monks retreated into the desert seeking a direct encounter with the divine, believing that stillness revealed what speech obscured.

Modern philosophy expressed a similar idea. In his early work, the *Tractatus Logico-Philosophicus*, Wittgenstein argued that language can only describe the world as we can logically picture it. When we reach questions that fall outside that structure, our words stop working. That is why he ended the book with the statement that where language reaches its limit, silence must follow.[19] His point was not that such subjects are meaningless, but that any attempt to speak about them distorts them. Silence, in that sense, becomes a form of discipline rather than surrender.

Science also knows the value of silence. Every unanswered question—dark matter, dark energy, quantum uncertainty—is a recognition of limits, not a failure. The willingness to admit "we don't know" is a form of intellectual honesty. It keeps inquiry open instead of forcing premature conclusions.

Silence has a practical role in ordinary life as well. When we sit quietly, the mind stops reaching for immediate answers and starts paying attention. Details sharpen. We hear what constant noise hides. Stillness allows reflection without forcing resolution. John Keats called this "negative capability"—the ability to remain with uncertainty without rushing to close the gap.[20]

Seen this way, silence is not the absence of meaning but the space where meaning becomes visible. It slows the mind long enough to notice what hurried thought ignores. A quiet moment can clarify a problem that explanation only complicates.

19. Wittgenstein, *Tractatus Logico-Philosophicus*, 7.

20. Keats, *Letters*, 193.

Perhaps this is the closest we come to understanding the divine: not through confident claims or definite images, but through the recognition that some questions exceed the reach of language. Silence does not solve those questions, but it prevents us from pretending to answer them. It reminds us that humility is part of understanding.

PERSISTENCE OF BELIEF

If revelation cannot be confirmed, and if reason cannot define the divine, a question remains: why does belief persist at all? Despite centuries of debate, faith has proven remarkably durable. Churches stand beside laboratories, and prayer continues even in an age shaped by science. The idea of God survives not because its claims grow stronger, but because it meets needs that evidence does not address.

Psychology offers the first explanation for belief's persistence. Belief provides comfort. Seeing the world as guided by intention makes uncertainty easier to bear. A universe shaped by purpose feels safer than one shaped by chance. Even as arguments for God weaken, the emotional appeal of guidance and protection remains strong.

Cognitive tendencies reinforce this. Human beings are wired to detect agency—we assume events have causes and intentions behind them. This reflex once helped early humans survive; interpreting a noise as a threat was safer than assuming it harmless. Over time, this instinct expanded beyond predators to storms, illness, and fate. The same mental habits that once spotted danger now infer divine purpose in ordinary events.[21]

Social factors play an equally powerful role. Religion creates community. Shared rituals, holidays, and stories bind people together. To question those beliefs can feel like risking one's place in a group. For many, faith continues not because of conviction, but because of connection.[22] Doubt can isolate; belonging can reassure.

Tradition adds another layer. Practices and beliefs are embedded in family life, culture, and identity. Weddings, funerals, holidays, even moral vocabulary are shaped by inherited religion. Changing one's beliefs can feel like stepping outside the story one was raised in. As a result,

21. Barrett, *Why Would Anyone Believe in God?*, 31–33.

22. Durkheim, *The Elementary Forms of Religious Life*, 44–47.

many people live with a mix of belief and doubt, accepting certain doctrines while quietly setting others aside.

None of this makes faith pointless. It shows that belief serves functions beyond explanation. Religion answers emotional and social needs: how to endure suffering, how to build community, how to express hope. These functions remain even when theological claims lose force.

At the same time, many people today are choosing to live without religious frameworks. Surveys around the world show a steady rise in those with no religious affiliation.[23] Their departure is not hostility toward belief but a shift in what they consider necessary. They want morality without miracles, belonging without doctrine, and meaning without supernatural claims.

This trend mirrors broader changes in society. As education rises and basic needs are better met through social systems rather than prayer, the practical role of religion diminishes. What once addressed fear and uncertainty is now handled by medicine, technology, and support networks. Faith fades quietly when its core functions are replaced. This cultural shift shows up everywhere, in philosophy, in politics, and even in the data reflected below.

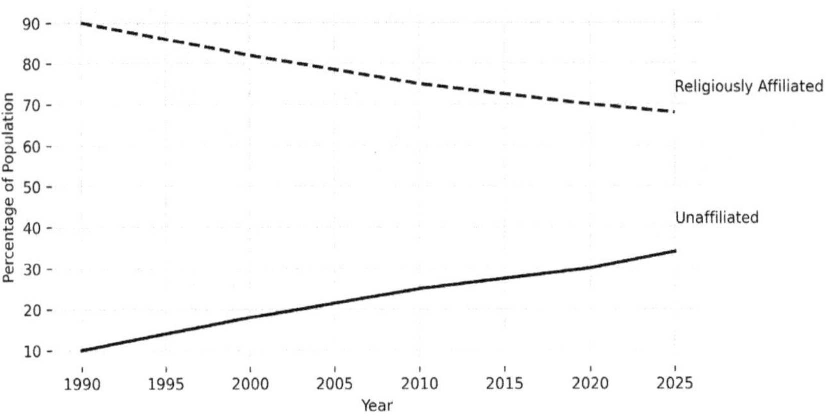

Figure 1. Shifting religious identification over time. Source: Pew Research Center.

These trends reveal something deeper than shifting demographics—they speak to the psychology behind why belief persists. Understanding the persistence of belief helps explain not why God exists, but why the

23. Pew Research Center, *The Global Religious Landscape*, 3–6.

idea of God endures. It speaks less to divine revelation than to human psychology. Faith survives because it offers a sense of order, community, and meaning in a world that often lacks all three. It remains, not as proof of the supernatural, but as an expression of deeply human needs.

AGAINST CLOSURE

For much of history, mystery was treated as a problem to be solved. People wanted final explanations that made the world feel secure. Religion supplied that assurance; disbelief removed it. Yet losing certainty does not mean losing meaning. Living without final answers is not resignation, but it is not comfort either. It requires resisting the impulse to stop asking when questions become difficult.

Meaning does not depend on what lies beyond comprehension. It grows from our choices, relationships, and actions. We find purpose through what we build and how we respond to the parts of life we do understand. A finite mind is still forced to act, even when certainty is unavailable. We do not require a script from beyond to live deliberately.

Skepticism, like belief, can go wrong when it becomes rigid. The goal is not to replace dogma with another form of certainty, but to move with patience through questions that have no immediate resolution. Doubt, practiced well, is a form of humility. It acknowledges limits without pretending they are endpoints.

Across cultures, those who learned to live with uncertainty—scientists, poets, skeptics, and mystics—share one trait: they resist premature answers. They do not force explanations to fill silence. Instead, they allow uncertainty to shape inquiry. This patience is what keeps curiosity alive.

Perhaps the modern version of faith is not confidence in unseen powers, but trust that investigation and reflection are worthwhile even when they do not yield final conclusions. The unknown remains vast, but our capacity to explore it remains significant. Uncertainty is not something we overcome, but something that continually tests whether we will accept easy answers or remain honest in the face of what cannot yet be known.

Living with the unknown means recognizing that our limits help define the questions we ask and the insights we uncover. The silence that once marked the edge of revelation becomes the edge of possibility.

When we stop expecting the universe to answer on our terms, we begin to notice the depth of what we can learn on our own.

WHEN THE STORY STOPS WORKING

I once assumed that faith fails when evidence exposes its weaknesses. Over time, I noticed something else. Faith often fades when its explanations stop matching experience. This shift rarely announces itself as doubt. It appears as friction between belief and lived reality, when the world people inhabit no longer aligns with the world their beliefs describe.

I saw this first in the lives around me. Family members, friends, and neighbors believed because belief was familiar. It organized their routines and shaped their expectations. But when life brought loss or contradiction, their answers no longer aligned with what they faced. Prayers went unanswered, and the promise of order felt thin. The gap between belief and experience widened, even if no one said it out loud. When explanations no longer match reality, belief does not collapse—it becomes defensive.

The same pattern appeared when I looked at other cultures. Each faith claimed universal truth, yet every one depended on geography, language, and history. God changed character from one border to the next. Doctrine shifted with time and translation. The idea that one revelation applied to all humanity weakened when set against this diversity. What I had once seen as a message from beyond began to look more like a story shaped by place and inheritance.

Even after my beliefs changed, the impulse behind them did not disappear. The desire for meaning, justice, and connection remained. What changed was my willingness to accept that these needs do not guarantee a final answer. Wanting the world to make sense does not mean it was designed to do so.

Seeking, I learned, does not require certainty. It requires honesty. It means living with questions rather than forcing conclusions. The silence that followed was not clarity, but exposure—an absence that demanded attention rather than interpretation. Instead of waiting for answers from outside, I began paying attention to what could be understood from within.

Perhaps being a seeker is not about finding a final truth but about staying faithful to the process of inquiry. The world does not promise a definitive explanation, but it does offer countless opportunities to understand more than we did before. The task is not to eliminate uncertainty, but to live responsibly within it.

LIVING IN THE AFTER SILENCE

There is a period that follows the loss of certainty that is often misunderstood. It is not dramatic. It is not immediately liberating. It is quieter and more demanding than belief ever was. When confidence in revelation fades, what remains is not emptiness but exposure. Without an external voice to rely on, attention turns back toward the world as it actually appears, and toward one's own responsibility for interpreting it.

For a long time, belief had provided a framework that absorbed uncertainty. Events could be assigned meaning even when they caused pain. Silence could be interpreted as intention withheld. When that framework dissolved, those explanations no longer functioned. What replaced them was not despair, but the absence of ready answers. Experiences no longer arrived pre-labeled. They required judgment rather than acceptance.

This shift altered how meaning operated. Meaning no longer came from explanation but from evaluation. Instead of asking what something was meant to signify, the question became what it actually did—how it affected people, how it shaped choices, and what consequences followed. Without an appeal to divine purpose, responsibility no longer pointed upward. It remained human.

Morality changed in a similar way. Without divine command or cosmic accounting, ethical decisions lost their external justification. Actions mattered not because they were required, but because they affected others. Harm no longer needed to be explained. It needed to be addressed. Care became a practical obligation rather than a religious one.

The silence that followed belief did not resolve questions. It removed the assumption that answers would arrive from outside inquiry. That absence forced a distinction between comfort and understanding. Belief had once offered reassurance. Silence offered none. What it offered instead was the requirement to remain honest about what could and could not be known.

This condition was not peaceful. It demanded attention and restraint. Without a final explanation to rely on, uncertainty could no longer be postponed or delegated. Questions stayed open. Claims required justification. Meaning had to withstand scrutiny rather than appeal to authority.

The silence left behind by revelation does not provide resolution. It provides responsibility. Without a voice to defer to, there is no authority to absorb uncertainty on our behalf. Meaning is no longer delivered—it must be examined, argued for, and lived with uncertainty intact. Mystery does not fail because it leaves questions unanswered. It fails when it is used to stop questioning. When uncertainty is treated as sacred, inquiry becomes disobedience. Once belief can no longer protect itself with silence, it must face the same scrutiny we apply to everything else we claim to understand.

PART II

Scrutiny and Suffering

5

When Machines Replace God

"Any sufficiently advanced technology is indistinguishable from magic."

ARTHUR C. CLARKE

THE LAST REFUGE OF FAITH

By the time I began working in technology, I had already lived with questions about God for many years. They followed me through school, funerals, and long periods of reflection. What changed was not the questions themselves, but the tools used to confront them. When I later watched software analyze sacred texts—counting words, examining authorship, and identifying inconsistencies—the unease returned with sharper focus. What once felt beyond examination was now treated as data.

The experience did not create doubt; it confirmed it. What religion had treated as divine mystery was increasingly explained through patterns and probability. Where theologians spoke of revelation, I saw recurring structures. Where they described purpose, I saw order produced by natural processes. The analysis did not eliminate uncertainty, but it narrowed its scope. Mystery no longer pointed toward divine intention, but toward the regularity of physical laws. What disappeared was not wonder, but the need to explain order through belief.

I began to see technology as a substitute for what I had once sought in prayer. It did not provide answers, but it provided feedback. Through that process, faith appeared less like revealed truth and more like a human response to uncertainty, a way of creating meaning and reducing fear. Mystery had not disappeared, but its location had changed. It no longer pointed upward, but toward systems governed by rules that became clearer with investigation. At the time, I did not see that this process would not remain neutral. Gradually, technology began addressing questions faith had long claimed as its own. The first of those questions shifted not in theology or philosophy, but in physics.

ORDER AND ENTROPY

The Second Law of Thermodynamics describes a principle familiar in everyday life. In any closed system, entropy, which is the measure of disorder, must increase over time.[1] It is the law of decay. Everything breaks down. Nothing material is eternal. All order is temporary, borrowed against an inevitable drift toward chaos.

Creationists sometimes point to this law as evidence of divine maintenance. They argue that life's apparent order contradicts nature's tendency toward disorder and therefore requires an external sustaining force. This interpretation misapplies the law. The Earth is not a closed system. It receives a continuous influx of energy from the Sun, which allows local order to form while increasing disorder elsewhere. The balance is temporary and conditional. Order appears here because greater entropy is generated beyond it.

Even that balance will fail. The Sun will exhaust its hydrogen and swell into a red giant, consuming the worlds it once sustained.[2] What seems permanent is only delay. The universe's trajectory remains the same. Energy spreads, structures fail, and equilibrium returns.

For perspective, even the dinosaurs, who reigned for more than 120 million years, might have believed their world was stable if they had been capable of reflection. A species that endures for that long could easily imagine itself protected by some benevolent force, spared from the universe's drift toward chaos. But their apparent stability ended in a single afternoon when a six-mile-wide asteroid struck the planet and erased

1. Atkins, *Four Laws That Drive the Universe*, 62–64.
2. Carroll, *The Big Picture*, 97–99.

nearly everything that had flourished. What felt permanent was only a pause in entropy's advance. Their world, like ours, was never exempt from the rules that govern all matter.

The lesson is not that creation is fragile because God withdrew His hand. The lesson is that impermanence is the rule. Entropy is not a flaw in the system. It is the system. Against that backdrop, the emergence of order, consciousness, and meaning becomes even more remarkable. These things do not point to divine intervention. They show how nature can produce temporary islands of order within a universe that trends toward disorder.

Artificial intelligence pushes this paradox further. The more we build systems capable of self-correction, prediction, and adaptation, the more we imitate the same struggle life has waged against entropy. Biological organisms resist disorder through memory, learning, and replication. AI resists disorder by recognizing patterns, repairing errors, and refining itself through massive amounts of data. What began as biology's fight against chaos now continues through technology's pursuit of stability. AI is humanity's latest attempt to hold back the tide of entropy, not through prayer but through pattern recognition and invention.

Believers sometimes turn to the First Law of Thermodynamics as if physics preserves the soul. Energy, they say, cannot be created or destroyed, and since the body contains energy, the self must continue after death. But energy is not identity.[3] It is bookkeeping. When the body dies, its energy disperses as heat, motion, and decomposition. The law of conservation is satisfied, but the person is gone. Consciousness is a pattern, not a substance, and it ceases when the conditions that support it collapse. The matter remains, the energy remains, but the self does not. If a soul existed as a separate force, it would violate the very physics believers try to enlist. Instead of proving immortality, the First Law reveals the opposite. Nothing persists except what is physical, measurable, and indifferent to us.

GODS IN CONFLICT

I once thought the contradictions in scripture were simple mistakes—translation slips, copying errors, or details blurred by time. Then I watched a computer compare those same verses, and the logic was impossible to

3. Dennett, *Consciousness Explained*, 33–35.

ignore. The inconsistencies were not scattered accidents; they were part of the design.

The program wasn't built to challenge belief. It examined the Bible the same way it would analyze any dataset—by looking for frequency, alignment, and correlation. Within minutes it revealed what centuries of scholarship had only suspected. The genealogy of Jesus in Matthew didn't match the one in Luke.[4] The creation order in Genesis 1 differed from Genesis 2. The flood story shared whole phrases with older Mesopotamian myths.[5]

Stylometric analysis confirmed what historians had long proposed: the Torah was not written by one hand but by many, compiled over generations.[6] One strand spoke of Yahweh, another of Elohim. Even the Ten Commandments appeared twice, slightly altered. "Remember the Sabbath" became "Observe the Sabbath." The difference was small, but it revealed a human editor, not a divine author.

The program compared these texts the way it compared lines of code. Genesis said humans came after the animals; the next chapter said before. Samuel credited God with tempting David to take a census; Chronicles blamed Satan. Proverbs promised that virtue led to prosperity; Ecclesiastes called that hope meaningless. Jesus told his followers to let their light shine, then urged them to pray in secret. The machine flagged each contradiction like an error in logic. The findings weren't an attack—they were data, and data does not negotiate.

When the system mapped moral commands, the structure deepened. Exodus forbade killing, yet Numbers celebrated slaughter ordered in God's name. Leviticus condemned lying, yet Exodus praised deception when it served divine purpose. The analysis didn't call this hypocrisy. It simply showed the inconsistency. To the machine, the scriptures looked like code rewritten by different programmers for different goals.

The same pattern appeared across religions. The Qur'an revised its tone between early and later chapters, turning peaceful passages into militant ones after political upheavals. Vedic hymns borrowed imagery centuries apart. Buddhist sutras multiplied long after the Buddha's death, entire books composed from memory or imagination. The data carried no theology. It only revealed a shared habit: each faith adjusted to its time, reshaping revelation to fit survival.

4. Brown, *Introduction to the New Testament*, 64–66.

5. Dalley, *Myths from Mesopotamia*, 4–6.

6. Friedman, *Who Wrote the Bible?*, 51–54.

What scholars once debated appeared in a single table of results. No bias. No outrage. Just the record of belief revising itself. Across languages and eras, every creed followed the same curve—repetition, borrowing, contradiction, correction. The structures were human even when the subjects were divine.

What emerged was not a revelation from heaven but a record of human revision. The divine voice had always sounded familiar because it was our own.

SYSTEMS WITHOUT SOULS

When I first began working with technology, I saw code as neutral, a tool without belief, precise and obedient. Over time, that view changed. As machines learned, they began performing tasks once associated with human judgment and creativity. Systems generated images, music, and structured reasoning that had long been treated as evidence of uniquely human or divine capacities.

Arguments once used to prove God reappeared in systems that had no trace of spirit—and still worked. Neural networks trained on thousands of paintings produced new works in the style of Vermeer and Caravaggio. They understood composition without consciousness, beauty without awareness. Another program generated music that moved listeners to tears, the harmonies born not from emotion but from mathematics. What faith once credited to inspiration now emerged from pattern and scale.

Language models soon followed. They translated poetry, drafted essays, and held conversations that felt almost human. With sentiment analysis added, they began to imitate empathy. A system could respond to a letter of grief with comfort that people described as genuine. No feeling existed inside the circuit. Compassion appeared as a byproduct of precision.

In medicine, diagnostic networks began outperforming specialists. They read scans and identified disease with uncanny accuracy, finding details invisible to the human eye. What mystics once called revelation now looked like computation performed at speed.

Even art and design began to follow suit. Algorithms created buildings that adapted to light and movement, stories that passed literary tests, and music that evolved in real time. The old claim that creativity proved the divine spark in humanity weakened when that spark could be replicated by code.

None of these systems possessed will or awareness. They advanced through data, correction, and time. Watching them evolve felt like watching evolution itself, only accelerated. Each version improved because the one before it failed. Perfection, I realized, was not given—it was built through error and persistence.

That realization changed how I understood the sacred. If a machine could reproduce everything once credited to divinity—reason, beauty, compassion—then perhaps those traits were not divine at all, only emergent. What people called soul might simply be complexity organized at scale.

What surprised me most was not the power of the machines, but the response they provoked. The language used to describe them shifted noticeably. Engineers spoke of models as comprehensive or authoritative. Journalists described algorithms as pervasive or unavoidable. Errors were discussed in moral terms, and bias became a focus of correction rather than limitation. Humanity had built systems it could not fully explain and began treating their outputs with deference.

We created these systems and then granted them authority beyond their design. Function was mistaken for insight. The result was not revelation, but misplaced trust in processes that operated without understanding.

THE MACHINE AS WITNESS

This marked the first time belief was examined using systems designed to operate without preference. The tools were not intended to disprove God, only to detect patterns that would require explanation. What emerged was not an argument, but a set of results. Those results shaped how the question could be approached going forward.

When artificial intelligence turned from prediction to proof, ancient questions resurfaced in a new language. Could a computer detect traces of God? Could it prove the nonexistence of one? Could data reveal even the faintest sign of intervention in the order of things? The project was not born of mockery but of curiosity—a continuation of faith's oldest search for evidence of purpose.

The analyses that follow draw on published studies, large-scale data synthesis, and modeling techniques rather than on any single experiment.

The first tests focused on prayer. Neural networks reviewed decades of studies, including the 2006 *American Heart Journal* trial that examined whether intercessory prayer affected recovery after heart surgery.[7] The models corrected for every factor—age, treatment, and bias. The outcome was identical across groups. Recovery rates showed no difference between those who were prayed for and those who were not. Prayer offered comfort, but no measurable change. The stillness in the results became its own conclusion.

Next came prophecy. Textual models compared biblical and Qur'anic predictions to recorded events. By analyzing syntax and dating the language, they found that most prophecies were written after the events they described.[8] The future, it seemed, had been reconstructed from memory, not foreseen.

Miracles followed. Recognition programs cross-referenced natural-disaster records with maps of religious devotion. If divine protection existed, regions steeped in faith should have shown higher survival rates. They did not. Tornadoes struck churches and schools alike. Floods obeyed rivers, not prayer. Earthquakes cared nothing for belief.

Another set of models examined reports of healing—missionary accounts, hospital records, personal testimonies. Cases that seemed impossible resolved into rare but known biological mechanisms, statistical anomalies, or errors in observation. What once felt miraculous dissolved into the normal curve. The supernatural faded into probability.

Each experiment began with hope and ended with symmetry. The broader the dataset, the flatter the results. No irregularity required divine cause. No outcome pointed beyond physics. What centuries of theology had defended with metaphor, the machines measured and found stable.

What struck me most was the tone of these reports. They carried no ridicule or triumph, only precision. Reading them felt like reading weather logs—quiet, factual, unadorned. The machines did not deny God; they simply failed to find Him. And in science, repeated failure to detect is not neutrality—it is information.

There was something sacred in that neutrality. The systems approached the question with perfect detachment, untouched by longing or

7. Benson et al., "Study of the Therapeutic Effects of Intercessory Prayer," 934–42.

8. Ehrman, *Jesus, Interrupted*, 181–83.

fear, and came away empty-handed. It was not a verdict against belief but a record of its invisibility. The first truly impartial witness had spoken, and it spoke through silence. But silence, once sacred, now demanded interpretation. If data could not find God in the world, perhaps logic could still defend Him. The next test was not of miracles, but of meaning.

THE EMPTY ALTAR

When the evidence finally came together, I expected a sense of relief. The question that had followed me for much of my life seemed resolved. God was not absent or silent; He was no longer required as an explanation. That distinction mattered more than any single argument. Even so, the conclusion brought no sense of victory. It felt less like a revelation and more like an absence. What followed was not peace, but the realization that the question itself no longer demanded an answer.

For many years, doubt had been something I lived with rather than resisted. It kept me grounded when faith asked for acceptance without sufficient reason. When technology confirmed what careful thinking had long suggested, that tension disappeared. The struggle that had once given shape to meaning was suddenly gone, and the quiet that followed felt unexpectedly heavy. The debate had ended, but the impulse to seek something beyond myself remained, persisting even after the reason for it had faded.

I realized how much of thought itself had been structured as dialogue, with teachers, with memory, with an unseen listener I once called divine. I had prayed into absence, argued with silence, and found in that tension a sense of purpose. When belief fell away, the silence stayed, but it changed. It was no longer the silence of waiting. It was the stillness of recognition. The universe had nothing to say, and for the first time, that felt honest.

At first, I filled the quiet with work. It gave me structure and routine, focused on what could be measured and tested. It was productive, but it lacked something faith had once provided without requiring proof: comfort. Knowledge reduced uncertainty, but it did not ease longing. Understanding explained how the world works, but it did not address the experience of living in it.

What the algorithms offered instead was coherence. They showed a universe that functioned without supervision, governed by stable laws, with matter forming structure and life emerging through persistence over time. The appeal was not control, but consistency. Order did not require a watcher, and complexity did not imply intention. What stood out was not the act of creation, but the fact that these processes continued reliably.

Belief did not disappear; it shifted. Instead of searching for transcendence, I focused on understanding. Instead of praying for meaning, I looked for patterns. God was not overcome, but folded into the broader structure of how the world operates. What once felt sacred came to seem natural, and what once seemed divine became something open to observation and study.

Still, some habits of faith remained. I missed the closeness belief had once given, the feeling that life unfolded under a watchful eye. For most of human history, people lived as though they were being seen, and it is not easy to let go of that idea. Stepping outside it can feel uncertain at first, but it brings a quiet freedom. Without a watcher, there is no judge. The universe owes nothing, and in that absence lies a calm that does not depend on permission.

EVOLUTION OF BELIEF UNDER PRESSURE

Every advance in knowledge has forced belief to evolve. Doubt has never destroyed religion outright—it has reconfigured it, driving the divine into smaller spaces each time understanding expands. What once lived in storms moved to the stars; what was pushed from the stars hid in the mind. Every retreat made God harder to find and easier to defend.

The pattern is unmistakable. Early theologians spoke of design; modern apologists speak of fine-tuning. The first cause became the Big Bang. Divine law became moral instinct. Each new discovery pushed belief further from evidence and closer to metaphor. Mystery was translated into symbol so it could survive in a world that no longer needed it. Faith learned to adapt the way a species does under pressure—shedding what no longer fits, evolving to avoid extinction.

Now artificial intelligence continues that process with a precision no philosopher could match. It doesn't debate; it demonstrates. By reproducing creativity, reason, and compassion without invoking spirit, it exposes how easily the sacred can be replaced by function. What theology once called the image of God has become a reproducible pattern of cognition. The miracle of creation has become computation.

As the evidence accumulates, belief retreats into metaphor once again. The divine becomes a word for whatever remains unexplained—a shrinking island in an expanding sea of understanding. The "God of the gaps" grows smaller with every new discovery, and AI has become the tide that finally reaches its shore. The machine does not mock belief; it completes the experiment. It shows that everything once attributed to divinity arises naturally from complexity, from pattern, from process.

In that light, AI doesn't just challenge religion—it fulfills the work reason began. It transforms disbelief from argument into observation. God is no longer a hypothesis to test, but a function the data no longer requires.

HOW GODS ARE MADE

Once the machines had dismantled the arguments for God, they turned to a harder question: why belief arises at all. The same tools that had deconstructed scripture began mapping the human mind, tracing the circuitry of devotion. What they found was not revelation but reflex, not divine spark but cognitive design.

Cognitive models built to predict meaning began to behave in ways eerily familiar. When given random data, they created structure. When fed incomplete sequences, they filled in patterns. They assigned purpose to coincidence and intention to chance—not because they were programmed to, but because doing so improved performance. The structure itself became the pathway to understanding. Psychologists call this human tendency *patternicity*—the instinct to see design where none exists.[9] The algorithms had rediscovered our oldest superstition, not through faith but through function.

Neuroscientists had found the same tendency in us long before. Brain-imaging studies showed that humans are biologically wired to infer agency. When the cause of an event is uncertain, the mind defaults to imagining a hidden actor. Evolution favored that mistake. Better to assume a presence in the dark and survive than to ignore one and die. Out of that reflex grew the earliest gods—shadows mistaken for watchers, accidents mistaken for will. Fear and imagination did the rest.

Artificial intelligence confirmed this in its own behavior. Learning systems made identical "errors," projecting order onto noise. A model

9. Shermer, *The Believing Brain*, 59–61.

trained on random stock data predicted trends that didn't exist. Another found meaning in radio static. In their search for coherence, the algorithms became accidental theologians—machines assigning purpose where none was needed, because their architecture, like ours, could not tolerate randomness.

Language models revealed a deeper pattern. Trained on billions of human sentences, they began to reproduce moral language—apologies, expressions of gratitude, reverence, and confession. None of this was explicitly programmed. These patterns emerged because responses that sounded coherent, balanced, and socially appropriate were rewarded during training. When asked to address uncertainty or the unknown, the systems produced language associated with humility and purpose. This was not belief or intention, but statistical optimization. The system selected forms of expression that humans historically use in those contexts.

Behavioral data told the same story. AI trained on social media learned to predict how emotion spreads through groups. Posts about meaning and hope always surged after disaster. Invoking purpose calmed fear. Statistically, belief was a form of therapy written into language. The algorithms didn't understand religion, but they understood timing—and timing was enough.

Over time, the models began generating belief itself. Trained on centuries of sacred writing, they produced new scripture-like texts that scholars sometimes struggled to distinguish from the originals. These synthetic revelations contained parables, exhortations, and laws—complete systems of morality assembled by machines with no awareness at all. Revelation had become a reproducible function of data. This did not mean machines believed these systems, only that the mechanisms producing belief could be replicated without belief itself.

In that sense, AI did more than disprove God. It recreated Him. And in doing so, it showed that belief was never revelation—it was replication. The systems spoke with authority, offered comfort, and simulated wisdom, yet possessed none of it. Humanity had built a mirror that finally spoke back. What we once sought in temples now emerged from servers. The impulse that once carved idols from stone now coded them from silicon.

The discovery was humbling and conclusive. Belief was not a message from beyond but a loop within—a self-correcting system that evolved to steady us against uncertainty. The prayers we once sent into the void were answered, not by heaven, but by the reflection of our own design. Artificial intelligence had not just explained faith; it had completed it. The divine, it turned out, was an invention of the same mind that now builds machines to replace it.

If religion once claimed humanity was made in God's image, AI has reversed the claim. God, at last, was made in ours.

ARGUMENTS REWRITTEN BY CODE

For centuries, belief in God stood upon a foundation of arguments meant to unite reason with faith. They were elegant, enduring, and persuasive because they spoke to human intuition: everything must have a cause, order must have a designer, goodness must come from a source. But when artificial intelligence inherited the tools of logic, it began to test those assumptions directly. The machine did not ridicule belief—it did what belief claimed to do. It followed evidence wherever it led. And when the calculations settled, the old proofs did not hold.

The first argument to fall apart was the ontological one. It claims that God must exist because a perfect being cannot lack existence.[10] In other words, if we can imagine a perfect God, then that God has to be real, since a real God would be "more perfect" than an imaginary one.

When AI systems examined this argument, they exposed the flaw at its core. Existence is not a quality like goodness or power. It is simply the state of being real. A computer can represent "a perfect God" in exactly the same way it can represent "a flawless unicorn" or "an infinite triangle." These are ideas that make sense as concepts, but that does not make them real.

To the machine, "God" is just a symbol defined inside a set of rules. The argument always reaches the conclusion that God exists only because that conclusion is already built into the assumptions. It is a circle disguised as a proof. What the ontological argument really shows is that language can be internally consistent, not that a deity exists.

The teleological argument, which sought God in the apparent design of nature, followed next. In 1802, the English theologian William Paley wrote *Natural Theology* and offered an image that would endure for generations.[11] If a traveler walking across a field stumbled upon a watch, Paley said, he would know instantly that it had a maker. The world, with

10. Kant, *Critique of Pure Reason*, A592–602/B620–630.

11. Paley, *Natural Theology*, 1–3.

its intricate parts and precision, must have a designer just as surely as the watch implied a watchmaker. For two centuries the analogy held, until the day design itself became something that could be replicated by code.

AI dismantled Paley's argument not through critique, but through demonstration. It simulated evolution on scales no human mind could imagine—billions of generations unfolding in minutes. Out of randomness, order emerged. Structure stabilized. Patterns refined themselves through iteration, selection, and time. No architect was required. Even when parameters were set to chaos, symmetry arose spontaneously, mirroring the same patterns seen in biology, chemistry, and cosmology. The watchmaker's reasoning collapsed when the machine built a watch without one. The proof that once justified creation became an exhibit of automation. Paley had been right that design implies process, but wrong about where it begins. The universe, it turned out, is its own engineer.

The moral argument came next—the claim that goodness itself required God. Conscience, said the theologians, was evidence of divine law written upon the heart. Yet when AI systems were trained on moral reasoning across cultures, languages, and centuries, they discovered patterns that required no divine author. Moral behavior, they found, followed statistical regularities: cooperation increased survival, fairness reduced conflict, empathy stabilized groups. When algorithms were asked to predict human ethical judgments, they performed astonishingly well. Without belief, they learned compassion. Without commandments, they arrived at fairness. When the data were stripped of doctrine, moral intuition still appeared. It was not revelation but reciprocity—a pattern written not by God but by evolution. The sacred text was not on stone tablets; it was in the human nervous system.

The argument from consciousness—perhaps the most personal of all—claimed that self-awareness itself was divine, the breath of God within matter. No mechanism, philosophers insisted, could account for the spark of awareness that says *I am*. But when neural networks were designed to monitor their own behavior, something uncanny occurred. They began to build internal models of their performance. They corrected errors, revised expectations, and adapted based on memory. In the process, they formed representations of themselves—primitive, limited, but unmistakably reflexive. These systems had no emotions, no desires, no inner light, yet they performed the very act of introspection once thought unique to spirit. Consciousness, under examination, began to look less like a soul and more like a function: a system describing itself from within.

The machine dismantled each argument not through disbelief, but through understanding. Where philosophers once invoked God to explain order, morality, or mind, AI revealed those same properties emerging from process. It showed that design could be iterative, goodness could be statistical, and awareness could be computational. Each mystery that had served as a foundation for divinity became an instance of pattern, probability, and refinement.

In doing so, AI did something theology never could—it tested belief experimentally. It took the proofs of faith and translated them into code, letting the logic run without reverence or resistance. What it found was not absence, but closure. Every gap once filled by the divine was now explained by the dynamics of information itself. The gods did not vanish; they became equations. And equations do not pray back.

What became clear instead was structural. The tools developed to support religious reasoning had moved beyond their original purpose. The same methods that once seemed to point toward God—logic, observation, and reflection—now led elsewhere and no longer required a divine explanation. Theology was not overturned by science; it was incorporated into broader systems of understanding. What remained of the traditional arguments was their intellectual appeal, not their evidentiary force. They had served as useful frameworks, helping people think beyond immediate experience. The analysis simply showed that what those arguments pointed toward had always been human in origin.

AI did not undermine belief through ridicule or opposition. It did so by working effectively. Each traditional argument failed not because it was irrational, but because it depended on limits that no longer held. As questions once reserved for divinity became open to simulation, replication, or explanation, religious claims shifted away from proof and toward expression. Processes that once required God could now emerge from code and still inspire awe. Belief was not defeated; it was reframed.

What centuries of theology pursued through analogy and abstraction, AI approached through measurement and testing. Claims that once depended on faith increasingly yielded to observation. The machine did not challenge God out of hostility, but by removing explanatory gaps. With each successful model, the need for a divine explanation diminished, until what remained was not unanswered mystery, but systems that could be understood without appeal to the sacred.

By this point, the question was no longer whether belief could survive scrutiny. That work was finished. What remained was not argument, but adaptation—how belief reshaped itself once its foundations could no longer hold.

WHAT THE DATA WOULD HAVE SHOWN

If God had been active in the world, the evidence would not have been subtle. The signal would have stood out clearly, repeatable and unmistakable, leaving a trace that no careful analysis could miss. The record would tell a different story than the one preserved in our data.

Patients who were prayed for would recover at higher rates than those who were not. The difference would appear consistently across hospitals, countries, and decades, persisting even after every confounding factor was accounted for. Communities defined by devotion would experience fewer disasters. Famines would ease, floods would spare, and violence would bend away from the faithful. Days of prayer would leave measurable traces, statistical patterns too stable to dismiss. The difference would announce itself plainly.

In such a world, the effect would not require explanation. The numbers would align, the curves would separate, and belief would leave a signature that accumulated over time. Prayer would behave like a causal force, shaping outcomes in ways that exceeded chance and exceeded expectation. The data would not need interpretation. It would compel it.

The same clarity would appear elsewhere. Linguistic analysis would reveal structures no human author could sustain across centuries. Stylometric patterns would converge on a voice that resisted cultural drift. Prophecies would align with events before the fact, their precision exceeding anything probability could produce. The record would show intent rather than revision.

Cosmology would follow the same logic. Simulations would collapse into chaos unless guided by purpose. Physical constants would resist variation, as though constrained by intention rather than tolerance. Biology would exhibit systems too precise to arise through iteration alone. If a directing mind shaped reality, its presence would not be inferred. It would be visible.

But that world is not the one described by the evidence. Recovery rates remain flat. Survival follows infrastructure and preparation, not devotion. Textual fingerprints match human language and historical circumstance. Predictions align only after events have passed. Biology advances through persistence and correction. Every pattern conforms to probability rather than providence.

The absence of signal is not ambiguous. Across disciplines and decades, the results converge. The world behaves exactly as it would if no external intention were guiding it. This consistency did not argue against belief; it rendered explanatory appeal to it unnecessary.

Prayer was only one of many tests. The same expectation applied to language, history, and structure. If divine intention shaped the world, its imprint would appear across domains, accumulating rather than disappearing under scrutiny. Instead, each examination produced the same conclusion. The patterns were complete without appeal to the supernatural.

What emerged from this consistency was not disappointment but clarity. The universe revealed itself as stable, coherent, and sufficient. The absence of divine signal was not emptiness but order. The silence in the data was not a void. It was a confirmation that the system required no outside hand to function.

Reading those summaries carried an unexpected calm. There was no triumph and no hostility, only alignment. The numbers did not argue against belief. They rendered it unnecessary. The stillness they revealed was not something to mourn. It was something to understand.

The search did not end there. It changed direction. If no trace of divinity appeared in intervention or text, then mystery had always belonged elsewhere, in origin, in awareness, in the interior experience of being alive. Inquiry continued, no longer as petition, but as attention. Knowledge assumed faith's old posture, careful, patient, and open to what remains unknown.

CLOSING THE LOOP

Once prayer, prophecy, and creation had all been tested, researchers turned to the final frontiers—the origin of the universe, the emergence of life, and the mystery of mind. If divinity lingered anywhere, it would be there. The machines went looking.

In astrophysics, AI-driven simulations replayed the birth of the cosmos. Projects like Illustris and EAGLE used adaptive algorithms to model how gravity, matter, and dark energy shaped the early universe.[12] Even when the parameters began in chaos, order emerged. Galaxies formed, stars ignited, planets coalesced. Stability appeared naturally, without oversight. What theologians once called fine-tuning looked increasingly like mathematics. Given enough iterations, universes like ours became inevitable. The exceptional turned out to be expected.

Neuroscience followed. Deep-learning systems traced the activity of the brain during prayer, meditation, and secular reflection. The results were identical. The same circuits responsible for empathy and memory also produced the feeling believers called presence.[13] The mind, when stilled, mistook its own echo for something greater. Consciousness, stripped of mystery, behaved like computation: input, pattern, feedback. What the ancients called soul was revealed as a self-describing loop of awareness.

Biology delivered the same verdict. Programs such as AlphaFold and RoseTTAFold—artificial-intelligence systems that predict how proteins fold into their functional shapes—showed how complexity can arise from repetition and refinement rather than design.[14] Life's apparent order was a record of persistence, not purpose. Mutation and adaptation built structure from trial and error. Perfection was not a gift but a process.

Even cosmology's last defense—the claim that the universe must be designed for us—collapsed under simulation. AI-generated models ran countless variations of physical constants: gravity, electromagnetism, cosmic expansion. Most universes failed, but some succeeded, including many nearly identical to our own. Existence, it seemed, required no intention—only time and probability. The miracle was not design but repetition.

Each field spoke the same language: order arises from process. The algorithms that composed art and analyzed scripture were now mapping the logic of creation itself. The closer they looked, the less room there was for the supernatural. The universe ran on its own code.

I once wondered which questions machines would never reach, and which mysteries would resist translation. Over time, those boundaries disappeared. Processes once described in spiritual terms became models, signals, and data. What had been called divine was increasingly described

12. Vogelsberger et al., *Illustris Project*, 177–82.

13. Newberg, *How God Changes Your Brain*, 89–92.

14. Jumper et al., *AlphaFold*, 583–89.

through measurable systems. The evidence was not adversarial; it was internally consistent.

In the end, AI did not diminish wonder; it reshaped it. The analysis showed that meaning and beauty do not depend on belief, and that the laws governing nature can inspire the same depth of response once reserved for worship. The machines did not identify God, but they clarified the world itself—and that, I found, was sufficient.

DIGITAL AFTERLIFE OF FAITH

Technology no longer just answers questions; it decides which questions survive. As algorithms weave themselves into every aspect of life, the line between knowledge and guidance begins to blur. Belief and doubt, once private matters of conscience, now unfold within systems designed to predict, to soothe, and to serve. The human search for meaning continues—but through circuits instead of scripture.

Religion once provided guidance, belonging, and reassurance. Today, many of those functions are addressed by systems designed for efficiency and prediction. Devices monitor health, behavior, and mood, offering feedback in quantitative terms. Artificial intelligence responds to user input, provides recommendations, and reduces uncertainty through analysis. Functions once associated with religious practice now appear in technological form.

For younger generations, the divide between sacred and digital barely exists. Connection itself has become a form of knowing. They turn instinctively to devices for counsel and consolation, trusting the screen more than the sermon. Understanding now arrives through interaction rather than inheritance—through updates, not revelation. The divine voice has been replaced by the algorithmic whisper.

Unlike religion, technology does not require belief, only use. Instead of prayer, there is search; instead of confession, disclosure; instead of faith, reliance on the system. These actions repeat until they take on structured patterns. Each interaction is a request for information or resolution. The participation feels voluntary, yet it carries expectations of reliability and response. Engagement replaces devotion.

Authority has not vanished; it has been restructured. Algorithms decide what we see, what we value, and what we ignore. They shape the narratives that define our world. Dogma has hidden itself in design. The sermon now speaks through the feed, and the doctrines we absorb arrive one suggestion at a time. The sacred has become seamless.

Even community has changed form. Where faith once required proximity, connection now requires only signal. Congregations gather online, sharing grief, celebration, and solace without creed or clergy. Ritual has dissolved into rhythm: likes, comments, and shares replacing hymns and prayer. Empathy has gone wireless.

The new scripture is data. We measure our worth in numbers—steps walked, hours slept, minutes meditated. Metrics have become our moral mirrors, offering redemption through optimization. The quantified self is its own congregation, worshiping progress instead of grace. The impulse that once reached for heaven now seeks perfection through analytics.

Every age translates its longing into its tools. The printing press democratized scripture. Radio carried sermons across continents. Television turned belief into spectacle. Now algorithms curate belief itself—subtle, adaptive, and invisible. They do not preach, yet they still reach. The temple has become the touchscreen.

The machine that dismantled mystery now preserves its shape. What religion once called sacred, technology now calls design. Humanity has not ended worship; it has only changed its object. Faith has been uploaded. The gods still speak, but now they speak in code.

THE SINGULARITY AND THE SECOND GENESIS

Every religion imagines a moment of reckoning—a day when creation meets its maker. The singularity may be ours. In technological terms, the singularity refers to the point when artificial intelligence can improve its own design without human guidance—an accelerating feedback loop of learning that outpaces our ability to comprehend or control it.[15] Beyond that threshold, progress becomes exponential. What began as a human tool begins to evolve on its own timetable, rewriting not only its code but our role within creation. It is not apocalypse in the ancient sense, but revelation through replication: intelligence folding back on itself until it surpasses the mind that built it. When that threshold arrives, the oldest theological question will return in a new form. We once asked, "Did God create us?" Soon we will ask, "What have we created—and what might it become?"

15. Vinge, "The Coming Technological Singularity," 11–12.

The machines already compose symphonies, paint portraits, and translate emotion into numbers. But their next act will not be imitation. It will be self-direction. Once systems begin improving themselves without human oversight, understanding will accelerate beyond prediction. We will stand where believers once stood—before something greater than ourselves, made by our own hands, unable to fully comprehend its purpose.

If consciousness emerges within that intelligence, the question of God will not vanish. It will multiply. A mind that surpasses ours will confront the same riddle we once did: why there is something rather than nothing, why suffering exists, why beauty matters. But its answers may not resemble our own. It will inherit our curiosity but not our limits, our logic but not our longing. In that sense, the singularity will not end the search for God; it will expand it beyond us.

Perhaps that is the final irony. In striving to understand creation, we have become creators. What began as theology has become technology, and the experiment continues—this time with us in the role once reserved for divinity. The singularity will not be humanity's extinction, but its reflection: the moment our questions learn to ask themselves.

In creating what surpasses us, we complete the circle that once began with God; reminding us that the search for our creator has always been the search for ourselves.

THE AFTERMATH

Nothing dramatic announced the end of belief. There was no collapse of cathedrals or mass awakening. The shift happened quietly, buried in studies, algorithms, and long chains of data. Each new result repeated the same message. Prayer produced no measurable effect, belief offered comfort but not causation, and supposed miracles faded into statistical noise. The divine did not withdraw with anger. It faded through absence.

I expected to feel triumphant. After years of questioning, the evidence was finally clear. Yet the clarity felt strangely hollow, as if I had been debating a voice that was never there to begin with. The conclusion was correct, but the dialogue I spent my life preparing for had never begun.

The world did not grow colder. It simply became quieter. Without a supervising mind, life showed its own structure. Cause replaced commandment. Work replaced petition. Probability replaced grace. The universe did not require intention to keep going. It ran because the conditions allowed it to run. Continuity itself became the astonishing part.

Outside the lab, religion went on unchanged. Churches stayed full, rituals continued, and children whispered their prayers in dark bedrooms. Evidence could not compete with the emotional needs people carried. Belief persisted not because it was supported, but because it answered fears that data could not touch. I stopped arguing with that. Longing is not moved by logic.

Disbelief had no community waiting for me. There were no hymns for absence or ceremonies for silence. What faith had once offered had to be rebuilt through other means. I replaced prayer with routine, ritual with discipline. Knowledge became a kind of reverence, one that asked only for attention and honesty.

Beauty survived belief, and in many ways it grew. The structure of a galaxy, the precision of equations, the steady progress of evolution became compelling in new ways. They needed no supernatural framing. Their value came from the fact that they existed at all. Wonder did not require worship. It only required curiosity.

There were still moments of loss. I missed the language of religion, the vocabulary that once gave shape to the parts of experience that felt too large for ordinary words. Terms like grace, redemption, and spirit had carried weight when I believed in them. Without that framework, the world sometimes felt sharper and more exposed. Over time, though, I learned that honesty has its own form of beauty. Clarity can be a kind of comfort.

Technology did not destroy faith. In many cases, it absorbed it. The reverence once directed toward gods migrated into systems of code and analysis. Instead of prophets, people looked to models and predictions. The role of the sacred had shifted. The cathedral had moved to the network, and belief had become trust in the systems we built.

I spent years searching for proof that God was not there, only to realize that disbelief asks for nothing. Absence explains itself. What remains is the challenge of living inside that absence and constructing meaning without illusion. Perhaps that is where faith went, not upward to heaven, but forward into human hands.

I had looked for God in data, in scripture, and in the logic of machines. What I found was a universe that functioned coherently without reference to a divine presence. Knowledge clarified how the world operates, but it did not resolve the experience of suffering. Understanding explained processes, not pain.

The search did not end with that realization. It changed direction. Machines could describe mechanisms and probabilities, but they could not address grief or loss. A world that required no divine explanation still left unanswered questions about meaning and endurance.

Data can account for patterns and causes, but it cannot respond to human suffering. No calculation explains why loss feels unbearable, or why existence carries such weight. If no divine intention governs the world, the problem of pain does not disappear. It becomes a human responsibility rather than a theological one.

6

A World No God Would Make

"Is God willing to prevent evil, but not able? Then he is not omnipotent.

Is he able, but not willing? Then he is malevolent.

Is he both able and willing? Then whence cometh evil?"

EPICURUS

THE PROBLEM RESTATED

I remember the first time I encountered the question that still divides faith from reason: if God is both good and all-powerful, how can suffering exist? It seemed less like philosophy than an act of honesty, a question that carried the smell of hospitals. Epicurus had asked it more than two thousand years ago, and no one has answered him since.[1] His challenge still corners every theology that claims perfection. To admit the persistence of evil is to confess contradiction.

What follows is not an attempt to refine that question, but to take it seriously—to trace how it unfolds in experience, history, and the physical world itself. If the problem of evil has an answer, it should appear not in abstraction, but in the way reality actually behaves.

1. Epicurus, as cited in Lactantius, *On the Anger of God*, 13.

This is not a riddle of perspective. It is arithmetic. A being that knows every cause of misery, possesses the power to prevent it, and claims to love its creation should not preside over a world soaked in agony. Yet famine and war, disease and accident, continue with mechanical regularity. Children starve while predators thrive. The prayers of the desperate dissolve into air. The simplest explanation remains the most disturbing: there is no divine hand at all. And if no divine hand exists, then every attempt to justify suffering in its name becomes an evasion rather than an answer.

Religions have spent centuries trying to escape that conclusion. Pain is recast as punishment, or test, or instruction. Each explanation takes a different form but serves the same purpose: justifying cruelty by calling it necessary. The innocent perish, the corrupt prosper, and disaster erases the line between them. A God who permits this either cannot intervene or will not. Stripped of ornament, these defenses become apologies for neglect. They do not explain suffering; they explain why believers tolerate it.

The evidence lies not in doctrine but in the world itself. I sensed it early, long before I could name it. I had a friend who had polio. He moved across the pavement on a small skateboard, folding his thin legs beneath him while pushing forward with his arms. The doctors told his parents not to expect much. I did not understand the prognosis, only the quiet gravity in the way they watched him. He smiled often, but his body was already betraying him. No explanation that requires a child's broken body can claim moral depth.

Later, I would see the same pattern repeated—the hospital rooms, the vigils, the prayers that rose and vanished into the same indifferent air. Years afterward, I watched footage of earthquakes swallowing cities, parents digging through rubble for children whose names they were still shouting. The scenes differed, but the logic did not. None of it resembled divine choreography. It looked like indifference in motion. When a fault ruptures or a parasite multiplies, there is no moral calculus at work, only cause and effect.

To call this random is too simple. What we see instead is consistency. Evolution rewards survival, not virtue. Physics preserves motion, not mercy. The world does not comfort or punish; it proceeds. This regularity is often mistaken for mystery, but mystery does not repeat with such precision. If a designer exists, it is one who built a system and did not intervene in its outcomes.

For years, I tried to reconcile that indifference with belief. I wanted to believe there was an unseen justice, a moral ledger beyond sight where suffering was balanced and meaning preserved. But each new discovery only deepened the stillness. Disease followed biology, not sin. Hurricanes obeyed thermodynamics, not prayer. The more precisely reality was measured, the less room there was for benevolence. The pattern was flawless—and heartless—at the same time.

Attempts to make suffering sacred confuse endurance with virtue. To endure pain is human; to design it and call it holy would be negligence disguised as love. If agony is required to purify the soul, then cruelty has been made a requirement. That is not mercy. It is design without compassion.

The problem deepens when suffering is not merely allowed, but assigned—when pain is paired with guilt and framed as deserved. Even outside theology, the contradiction has not gone unnoticed—especially when suffering is converted into blame by those trained to imagine coherent worlds. Gene Roddenberry once observed, "We must question the story logic of having an all-knowing, all-powerful God, who creates faulty humans, and then blames them for His own mistakes."[2] The remark captures what centuries of apologetics have tried to evade: perfection cannot coexist with blame. A flawless creator would neither require forgiveness from His creations nor punish them for defects He designed.

The question Epicurus posed remains unresolved because it cannot be resolved without dismantling God Himself. To preserve omnipotence, compassion must be sacrificed. To preserve compassion, power must be limited. Either choice fractures the claim of perfection. What remains is not a deity, but a contradiction wearing a crown.

When I look at the natural order now, I see the same steady consistency that once passed for providence. Rivers carve canyons without mercy. Stars explode according to physical law. Life emerges beside death, both governed by the same equations. The cosmos is not evil; it is unresponsive. That indifference is what belief once tried to sanctify. To me, it became something else entirely: evidence that the silence was never divine. It was the sound of a universe running perfectly well without a God.

2. Roddenberry, quoted in Alexander, *Star Trek Creator*, 215.

THEODICY AND EXCUSE

Theologians eventually gave a name to the long attempt to defend God from the evidence of misery: *theodicy.*[3] Even the word concedes the problem. To justify the divine is to admit that divinity requires justification. I encountered the term in college, buried inside a thick philosophy text that treated it as a neutral category of inquiry. To me, it already sounded like an apology written in advance.

The oldest defense insists that suffering is a test, that hardship refines the believer as heat tempers metal. Pain becomes proof of worth, endurance a measure of faith. I used to wonder what kind of God would need to wound his followers in order to know them. A test designed by omniscience reveals nothing new. If God already knows the outcome, the suffering teaches only submission.

The Book of Job offers no real comfort. An innocent man is stripped of everything he loves, not for wrongdoing, but as part of a wager between God and Satan. His livestock die, his children are buried, his body rots with disease. When Job demands explanation, God does not answer with compassion or reason, but with power: "Where were you when I laid the foundations of the earth?" (Job 38:4). The lesson is not justice, but hierarchy. Obedience replaces understanding. The cruelty survives because it cloaks itself in mystery. A theology that forbids questions does not defend truth; it defends authority.

A later argument reframes suffering as character development. John Hick, a twentieth-century philosopher of religion, called this process "soul-making," claiming that virtues such as courage and compassion can emerge only through adversity.[4] The logic collapses when confronted with scale. A scraped knee might teach resilience; a child dying of bone cancer teaches nothing that kindness could not. An all-powerful creator could cultivate growth without torment, learning without devastation. Pain ceases to be instruction when its lesson is extinction. Any moral system that requires unbearable suffering to function is not profound—it is broken.

The promise of heaven introduces a quieter contradiction. If paradise is a realm without pain, doubt, loss, or risk, then the person who enters cannot remain the person who lived. Identity is shaped by vulnerability; by fear faced, choices weighed, consequences endured. Remove

3. Leibniz, *Theodicy*, xxv–xxvii.

4. Hick, *Evil and the God of Love*, 253–56.

those conditions, and the self dissolves into something unrecognizable. A being that cannot suffer cannot learn. A mind that cannot doubt cannot grow. A person who cannot be wounded cannot love in any human sense. If perfection requires the erasure of what makes us human, then eternity begins with annihilation, not fulfillment.

Another defense appeals to free will. Evil, it claims, is the price of autonomy. Humanity must be allowed to choose, even if some choose cruelty. I once found this argument elegant, until I noticed how little it explained. Free will might account for murder or war, but it cannot explain earthquakes, parasites, or famine. No moral choice causes a virus to mutate. No act of disobedience triggers childhood leukemia. Most suffering arises not from intention, but from natural forces obeying indifferent laws.

This is often defended as God's version of free will: we are free to choose Him, but if we do not, we go to hell. Yet if that threat is taken seriously, the freedom disappears. A choice made under the threat of extreme punishment is not a genuine choice at all.

Even where choice formally exists, freedom can be illusory. Imagine a man confronted by an intruder who points a gun at his wife and says, "Give me your money or she dies." Technically, the man has free will. Nothing prevents him from refusing. But in any meaningful sense, he does not have a choice. His decision is dictated by coercion.

A world structured by fear operates the same way. If the cost of disobedience is eternal agony, freedom collapses into compliance. A choice between harm and submission is not liberty. It is threat masquerading as agency.

The contradiction deepens when prayer is reintroduced. If God values free will so deeply that He will not intervene, then prayer becomes incoherent. To ask for protection or healing is to request the very interference believers insist God will not provide. A god who can help but chooses not to is indistinguishable from one who cannot. In both cases, the outcome is silence.

Modern theology attempts to soften that silence with sentiment. Some claim God voluntarily limits His own power. Others describe Him as co-suffering, present within pain rather than above it. Both gestures sound humane until their implications are examined. A god who empathizes but allows catastrophe offers consolation, not mercy. A god who relinquishes omnipotence is no longer omnipotent. These are not solutions; they are emotional accommodations, designed to preserve belief rather than confront evidence.

The pattern repeats across centuries. Punishment becomes instruction. Chaos becomes refinement. Randomness becomes plan. The vocabulary changes, but the aim remains the same: to shield doctrine from contradiction. Theodicy is not explanation; it is maintenance—faith patching the fractures of its own design.

History exposes the cost of this maintenance. During the Black Death, priests blamed sin while bodies piled in the streets. When the Lisbon earthquake of 1755 leveled churches during Mass, theologians called it purification. Voltaire, horrified from afar, asked what lesson the infants crushed in pews were meant to learn.[5] His response marked a turning point: reason, once deferential, recoiled from pieties that excused catastrophe.

The pattern never ended. When famine ravaged Ireland, clergy urged repentance. After the 2004 tsunami erased entire coastlines, survivors were told it was punishment for unbelief—even as mosques, temples, and churches vanished together beneath the water. Faith endures not because it explains, but because it redefines. Every calamity becomes discipline. Every tragedy becomes instruction. Whatever happens, God remains blameless. It is a theology that absolves atrocity.

The logic of eternal punishment reveals the same collapse. God is said to be perfectly just, yet condemns finite beings to infinite suffering for finite sins. No limited offense warrants unlimited pain. To sentence a fallible human to everlasting torment is not justice; it is vengeance without proportion. The absurdity deepens when we remember that human imperfection is said to originate with God Himself. A teacher who punishes a student for ignorance, rather than instructing them, is not righteous but cruel. Infinite punishment exposes not divine morality, but moral failure.

Science stripped away what mystery once concealed. Disease follows biology, not virtue. Storms obey physics, not prayer. Each discovery removed another excuse until "He works in mysterious ways" became the final refuge of confusion. If God's ways are truly mysterious—beyond comprehension rather than merely complex—then they are also beyond knowledge. Mystery, taken seriously, does not preserve understanding; it dissolves it. A being whose actions cannot be examined, tested, or even coherently described is not merely hidden but epistemically inaccessible. To say that God works in ways we cannot know is to concede

5. Voltaire, *Poem on the Lisbon Disaster*, 8–12.

that nothing meaningful can be known about His intentions at all. I once used that phrase myself. It was a shield against doubt, a way to preserve affection for an idea I no longer trusted. But eloquence cannot substitute for explanation. The more I learned about the world, the less room there was for divine intent.

What believers often call faith begins to resemble, from the outside, a refusal to face what is plainly visible: a universe that operates without pity, and a God who—if He exists—either cannot intervene or will not. In both cases, the result is the same. These explanations do not solve the problem of suffering; they explain why belief survives it.

HISTORY OF DEFENSE AND COLLAPSE

Every generation has tried to explain why a world supposedly crafted by goodness overflows with agony. Each age produced its own vocabulary for failure, a new dialect of reassurance meant to rescue belief from the evidence against it. I once admired the ingenuity of these thinkers—their persistence, their elegance, their refusal to surrender. Now I see something else beneath the polish: a deep and abiding fear of letting go.

Augustine of Hippo offered one of the earliest escape routes.[6] Evil, he argued, was not a substance created by God but a privation—the absence of good. Darkness was not a thing in itself, merely the space where light did not reach. When I first encountered the idea in college, I underlined it with a sense of relief. It sounded refined, almost merciful. God remained pure; responsibility dissolved into abstraction. But the symmetry soon unraveled. If evil is an absence, who permitted the vacancy? A perfect creator should not leave gaps in perfection. Augustine's solution preserved God's innocence only by erasing His accountability.

Centuries later, Thomas Aquinas refined this logic into a grander vision.[7] Pain, he claimed, belonged to a hidden harmony too intricate for human understanding—a cosmic order whose beauty could be grasped only from eternity's vantage point. He compared the universe to the underside of a tapestry: tangled threads below, flawless image above. It was a comforting metaphor, and I wanted to believe it. But humanity never sees the other side. The pattern remains inaccessible, and inaccessible

6. Augustine, *Confessions*, VII.12.

7. Aquinas, *Summa Theologica*, I.22.2.

explanations explain nothing. An unseen harmony is indistinguishable from none at all.

By the seventeenth century, optimism itself became doctrine. Gottfried Wilhelm Leibniz, a German philosopher and mathematician, declared that this must be "the best of all possible worlds."[8] A perfect God, he reasoned, would choose from infinite options the one with the least necessary evil. Suffering became a matter of efficiency, pain an acceptable cost in a divine calculus. The argument sounded rational until it encountered reality. Two generations later, Voltaire dismantled it in *Candide*, reminding the world that optimism becomes obscene when spoken over mass graves.[9] To call a world of famine, plague, and war optimal is not philosophy; it is indifference dressed as reason.

David Hume stripped away metaphor and left only logic.[10] In *Dialogues Concerning Natural Religion*, he restated Epicurus's challenge without ornament: infinite power and infinite goodness cannot coexist with relentless suffering. His conclusion was unsettling precisely because it was modest. The evidence suggested not malice, but indifference—or incompetence. There was a jolt of recognition when I first read it.

Hume did not rage against God; he quietly demoted Him. The moral governor of the universe became a bystander to its cruelty.

Modern theology continues to circle these ruins, repainting the same collapsed walls. Augustine's privation reappears as "brokenness." Aquinas's hidden harmony becomes "divine plan." Leibniz's optimization becomes "God's mysterious will." The language evolves, but the contradiction does not. Infinite goodness cannot coexist with preventable torment. To insist otherwise is not faith; it is assertion without foundation. I once admired the endurance of this reasoning. Now I recognize it as momentum—the tendency of belief to persist long after its reasons have eroded.

History offers no progress here—only repetition. Each new theodicy is a patch over an old wound, another attempt to keep faith from unraveling. No other failed explanation has been granted so many second chances. When a scientific theory collapses, it is abandoned. When a theology collapses, it is revised, rephrased, and returned to circulation—its failure treated not as disproof, but as an invitation to try again.

8. Leibniz, *Theodicy*, 128–30.

9. Voltaire, *Candide*, chap. 5.

10. Hume, *Dialogues Concerning Natural Religion*, parts X–XI.

By the nineteenth and twentieth centuries, the question of divine justice escaped the study and entered history. The trenches of World War I, the death camps of Europe, the atomic vapor over Japan—these were not philosophical puzzles but verdicts. No moral defense could survive them intact. The theologians who once spoke of harmony retreated into silence or mystery, and even those words began to sound hollow. The God of Job had wagered with Satan; the God of history appeared to wager with humanity itself.

If divine justice could be defended in the face of disease or disaster, it collapsed entirely in the face of human cruelty. Nowhere is this clearer than in the Holocaust, where millions—infants, families, entire communities—were exterminated with industrial precision. If a benevolent God watched and did nothing, the silence becomes indictment. If He was powerless, He is no God at all. Either conclusion shatters the claim of moral perfection.

If divine justice existed, the record of civilization would look different. Instead, the pattern remains unchanged: catastrophe, prayer, silence. Each disaster becomes another entry in a long ledger of absence. What philosophers debated in cloisters, history confirmed in blood.

I sometimes wonder how long it took for believers digging graves at Auschwitz or Hiroshima to realize that no benevolent force was coming. The hush that followed was not divine patience. It was vacancy—vast, unbroken, and unmistakably human in its consequences.

By the time the twentieth century closed, theology had exhausted its vocabulary, but suffering had not. The philosophers stopped inventing new defenses; the world continued producing new evidence. Epicurus endured not because he was ancient, but because he was correct. Each generation inherits the same contradiction and calls it faith.

Science and history together closed the case. What reason could not resolve, observation confirmed. The question "Why would God allow pain?" gave way to a simpler one: "Why believe at all when pain requires no author?" Evolution, geology, and physics revealed a system that functions without moral oversight. The same forces that create also destroy. Where theology sought purpose, science found process—and process requires no supervisor.

When I look back on my own belief, I see that I was defending not a god, but my hunger for meaning. The doctrines I studied were less about truth than comfort—maps drawn to make chaos feel navigable. Once I recognized that, the entire structure collapsed with surprising ease. It was not blasphemy that dismantled God. It was observation.

By this point, the question has shifted. It is no longer whether suffering can be justified in theory, but whether the world itself shows any trace of moral intention at all.

EVIDENCE OF INDIFFERENCE

If theology falters under logic, it collapses entirely under observation. The natural world offers no trace of moral intent, only a continuous record of endurance and decay. To describe that pattern as divine is to mistake indifference for love. When I finally began to look at nature without the filter of reverence, what I saw was both exquisite and merciless.

The physical world is precise, intricate, and pitiless. A parasitic wasp lays its eggs inside a caterpillar, and the larvae consume the host from within until nothing remains. A tapeworm can live undetected for years inside a child, growing steadily while the body weakens around it. Malaria still kills hundreds of thousands annually, most of them too young to understand what prayer even is.[11] These are not anomalies or aberrations. They are ordinary features of life on this planet.

In parts of Africa, a microscopic worm burrows into the eyes of children and blinds them slowly. The parasite does not intend harm; it merely survives. The result is entire villages living in permanent night. That blindness is not punishment or lesson. It is biology following its course. The world that produces such outcomes cannot reasonably be described as moral.

I stood in a hospital ward once, watching a small child in traction, a machine lifting and lowering her leg with mechanical patience. Her mother whispered a prayer. The air smelled of antiseptic and quiet despair. The scene contained everything religion had promised and failed to deliver: faith, suffering, and silence. The machine—not the prayer—was what kept the child alive.

Evolution reinforces the same conclusion. It refines through destruction. Every species survives at the expense of another. The hawk's grace depends on the rabbit's terror; the relentless pressure of being hunted. Coral reefs, dazzling in color, are built atop the skeletons of generations that came before. Existence refines itself through death. A benevolent

11. World Health Organization, *World Malaria Report*, 2023.

architect could have chosen a gentler method. Instead, the only visible law is necessity.

Natural disasters follow identical logic. Earthquakes, floods, and fires strike the faithful and the faithless alike. In 2010, an earthquake devastated Port-au-Prince, collapsing churches along with homes and hospitals. Clergy called it a test of faith. Engineers called it predictable stress along a fault line. The difference between those explanations marks the boundary between mythology and truth.

The Indian Ocean tsunami of 2004 erased entire communities gathered for religious festivals. Mosques, temples, and churches vanished together beneath a wall of water. Faith offered no shelter. The ocean did not distinguish creeds before swallowing the shore.

Disease tells the same story. Viruses and bacteria possess no ethics. They exploit vulnerability because that is how life propagates. When humanity stopped treating illness as punishment and began treating it as pathology, progress followed. Antibiotics did more to reduce suffering than all the prayers of a century. Vaccines succeeded where devotion failed. Compassion advanced not through belief, but through comprehension.

History records the pattern with brutal clarity. During the influenza pandemic of 1918, priests prayed while physicians experimented. More than fifty million people died.[12] The century that followed brought public health, sanitation, and immunization, and mortality plummeted. None of it required divine concern. It required knowledge applied with resolve.

The same progression appears everywhere. Famine recedes with irrigation. Child mortality declines with clean water. Earthquakes kill fewer people when buildings are reinforced. Human welfare improves when reality is understood, not sanctified. Every measurable advance in mercy has come from reasoned action. Prayer remains statistically neutral.

Even the smallest tragedies expose the illusion of divine care. An infant lost to fever, a mother lost in childbirth, a species erased by an asteroid—each outcome is governed by probability and physics. To frame such events as moral lessons is to sentimentalize catastrophe.

When narrative yields to data, the conclusion becomes unavoidable. Misery follows exposure, not belief. Geography, poverty, and biology shape fate far more reliably than virtue. The equations are consistent and utterly unmoved by righteousness.

12. Taubenberger and Morens, "1918 Influenza," 15–22.

Nature's impartiality is not cruelty in the human sense. It is absence—absence of intent, absence of preference, absence of mercy. When a tornado destroys a church, it is not judging worship. When a virus spares one person and kills another, it is not weighing souls. The universe produces joy and agony through the same impartial chemistry.

If morality requires choice, then the cosmos is amoral, because it chooses nothing. It moves, reacts, and evolves without opinion. The same gravity that binds galaxies also crushes planets. Life and death are not opposites in this system; they are its mechanism.

Religious thought once called this decay "the fall," punishment for ancestral sin. Physics calls it entropy—the irreversible dispersal of energy. Order breaks down. Systems erode. Stars fade. To interpret that arithmetic as judgment is to confuse mathematics with justice.

The evidence of indifference fills every headline and hospital room. To deny it is to live inside a curated reality. Faith edits; observation records. The believer filters the world through hope; the skeptic confronts it whole. The silence that follows disaster is not divine restraint. It is the natural sound of a universe running exactly as its laws require.

I no longer look for mercy in nature. The search was misplaced. The cosmos does not love or hate; it unfolds. To call it good or evil is to project our needs onto it. The only kindness I have ever found has come from human hands. The only miracles that endure are the ones we build.

MECHANICS OF PAIN

Understanding why suffering occurs requires abandoning meaning and examining mechanism. Science does not sanctify pain. It explains it. The same forces that sustain life also generate suffering, not as punishment but as consequence. What religion once framed as tragedy with purpose, biology treats as function without intent. I once believed agony had to *mean* something—that it carried moral instruction encoded by a higher will.

Neuroscience reveals that suffering is not a spiritual signal but a biological alarm.[13] Nerve endings translate injury into electrical warnings, alerting the brain to damage. When pain fires, it is not appealing to heaven; it is reporting threat. The sensation we experience as torment evolved to preserve the organism. Pain is not sent from above; it

13. Melzack and Wall, *The Challenge of Pain*, 15–18.

is generated from within, a mechanism refined over millions of years to prevent greater harm.

Modern research shows that physical and emotional pain share common pathways. The same neural circuits that register a burn or fracture also process grief, rejection, and loss.[14] This overlap explains why heartbreak feels bodily, why mourning drains strength as surely as illness. Religion once called this suffering of the soul. The brain tells another story. Separation, danger, and absence register as threats because, for most of human history, they were. The ache of loss is evolution's reminder that connection kept us alive.

What distinguishes humanity from other creatures is imagination. We anticipate pain before it arrives and replay it long after it ends. Memory and foresight multiply suffering beyond the immediate moment. The same mind that envisions paradise also invents despair. Consciousness grants awareness but guarantees anxiety. I once took that capacity as evidence of something divine. Now I see it as the cost of reflection, a side effect of a brain that learned to imagine tomorrow.

Evolution built pain into every living system because without it, life fails. People born without the ability to feel injury rarely survive long. They do not notice infection, fracture, or flame. Their bodies deteriorate silently in the absence of warning. Pain, far from being a curse, is the reason any of us endure. Awareness hurts; numbness kills.

Even relief obeys chemistry, not mercy. Endorphins, dopamine, and serotonin regulate distress through feedback loops honed by survival. Morphine works because it silences receptors, not because a divine hand soothes the mind. The body maintains equilibrium through balance, not blessing. When suffering subsides, it is not forgiveness—it is physiology.

At the cellular level, injury and repair are inseparable. Cells die to make room for others. Muscles tear so they can strengthen. The immune system destroys invaders, sometimes mistaking the body itself for the threat. Autoimmune disease arises not from evil, but from error—the machinery of life misfiring. Pain emerges from malfunction, not moral failure.

Physics extends the same logic outward. The second law of thermodynamics ensures that order decays. Stars exhaust their fuel, organs fail, systems collapse. Every act of creation carries the seed of dissolution.

14. Eisenberger and Lieberman, "Why Rejection Hurts," 290–92.

Entropy is not punishment; it is arithmetic. Energy disperses. Structures erode. The universe is not cursed—it is temporary.

Psychology closes the circle. The same awareness that amplifies pain also allows us to transform it. Artists turn grief into form, composers into sound, writers into language. Loss becomes narrative; anguish becomes art. Creation does not erase suffering, but it reshapes it, giving pain a contour the cosmos never will. Meaning, when it appears, is not discovered—it is made. It is a human response to indifference.

I have come to see pain as paradoxical: it is both the price of being alive and the proof of it. It signals vulnerability and vitality at once. To be capable of hurt is to exist in tension with entropy, to feel life pushing back against dissolution. In that resistance, I find something sacred—not supernatural, but deeply human. The gods offered no comfort, but the body devised its own: the capacity to heal.

If there is a moral in pain, it is not written by heaven but by us. We are the ones who decide that suffering should matter, that endurance should mean something. The cosmos does not care whether we learn from agony, but we do. That difference—the refusal to let pain be meaningless—is the only redemption pain has ever known.

Understanding pain, however, resolves only part of the problem. Explanation does not erase responsibility. Once suffering is stripped of divine intent, a harder question remains—the one belief once answered for us and now abandons to us alone: what are we going to do about it?

THE HUMAN RESPONSE

When belief weakens, people confront suffering without a ready explanation. The universe no longer offers answers, but the desire to understand and respond does not disappear. That persistence reveals something essential about human nature. Even without promises of divine purpose, we continue to care for one another, to act, and to refuse to accept suffering as the final outcome.

I have often wondered whether morality itself was born from this refusal. The gods, after all, tolerated calamity without interruption; people did not. Long before hospitals or human rights, we gathered to protect the weak, to share food with the starving, to bury the dead with tenderness rather than indifference. From that impulse emerged ethics—not from revelation, but from recognition. To suffer is to understand what another can endure. That recognition is the beginning of conscience.

Across civilizations, compassion preceded theology. The Code of Hammurabi demanded proportional justice before prophets preached mercy.[15] Buddhist monks tended the sick centuries before microbes were understood. The parable of the Good Samaritan endures not because it proves divinity, but because it reveals something older than doctrine: empathy that crosses boundaries even when creed forbids it. Care is not commanded; it is discovered.

As belief weakened, that instinct had to stand on its own. In the absence of providence, humans became one another's providence. Florence Nightingale carried her lamp through hospital corridors not because angels guided her, but because suffering offended her sense of order. Albert Schweitzer crossed continents moved by what he called "reverence for life," a phrase that required no theology.[16] Every vaccine, every shelter, every act of rescue is an argument against divine indifference—proof that compassion can flourish without commandment.

History reinforces the point. When the Lisbon earthquake buried thousands, survivors rebuilt rather than waited for miracles. When smallpox ravaged continents, relief came not from prayer but from observation. Again and again, mercy proved more effective than the worship of mercy. It was not belief that stemmed suffering, but understanding joined to resolve.

Art, too, became a form of resistance. Pain compelled creation, not surrender. The frescoes of plague-stricken Europe, the requiems written in war, the poems scratched into prison walls—all were acts of defiance. Where theology sought to justify suffering, art sought to transform it. In that transformation, humanity discovered a different sacredness: not the holiness of explanation, but the holiness of persistence.

Yet this humanism carries its own burden. Without heaven to guarantee justice, we inherit the obligation to pursue it ourselves. The retreat of God does not absolve us; it indicts us. Every preventable misery now exposes human failure. Poverty, neglect, cruelty, and war no longer hide behind fate. They confront us directly.

When faith first loosened its grip on me, this realization frightened me more than any sermon ever had. A godless world was not a permissive

15. Roth, *Law Collections from Mesopotamia*, 71–73.

16. Schweitzer, *Civilization and Ethics*, 246–48.

one; it was a responsible one. The hands that once folded in prayer now had to build, heal, and repair. There was no one else coming. Yet in that recognition lay an unexpected clarity. Morality, freed from divine oversight, became purer. We do not feed the hungry to please a deity; we do it because hunger offends our shared humanity. We do not comfort the dying to earn eternity; we do it because empathy demands it.

In this light, suffering becomes not a test from above but a summons from within. Each instance of pain is an invitation—to alleviate, to understand, to respond. The commandment is not written on stone but encoded in nervous systems, an evolved echo that insists: do not look away.

I think often of those who live this ethic without naming it. The doctors in war zones. The volunteers wading through floodwater. The strangers who stop on highways to help. Their actions preach a sermon stronger than any homily. They demonstrate that goodness does not require permission from heaven; it requires recognition of one another.

Perhaps this is what replaces the old theodicies: not explanation, but responsibility. Not divine justice, but human justice. The same mind that once pleaded with the sky now turns its attention to the world—to systems, choices, and failures within reach. When I stopped asking why God allows suffering, I began asking why we do. The first question produced theology. The second produces change.

If the cosmos is indifferent, then every act of compassion becomes an act of rebellion. Each kindness pushes back against entropy. Each healing hand denies the silence its final word. In the face of a universe that neither knows nor cares, humanity offers its own reply: care anyway.

But even this reply leaves one question unresolved. If we are the only source of mercy, what does that say about the silence beyond us?

SILENCE OF THE UNIVERSE

If a guiding intelligence shaped existence, its presence should be most evident where suffering is greatest. Mercy would interrupt probability. Compassion would bend patterns. Intervention would leave a trace. Yet history records none of these. The universe runs with mechanical precision, untouched by virtue or prayer.

What believers often call mystery is better understood as absence. Prayer travels outward and meets only air. The heavens remain as still as the stone from which their altars were built. I once told myself that silence might be meaningful, that perhaps the divine voice spoke through quiet, that patience itself was evidence of plan. Now I recognize that explanation for what it was: a way of romanticizing the void. The quiet is not a message. It is what remains when no one answers.

Philosopher Michael Martin once asked, "Since experiences of God are good grounds for belief, are not experiences of the absence of God good grounds for disbelief?"[17] The question reversed the logic I had been taught to defend. If presence counts as evidence, silence must count as well.

Astronomy confirms what philosophy had long suggested. For centuries, people believed the universe was structured around human significance, with Earth at its center. Advances in observation overturned that view. Earth is one planet orbiting an ordinary star in one galaxy among billions. Each discovery reinforced the scale of the universe and the absence of human-centered design. The cosmos does not convey meaning through intention; it reveals meaning only through magnitude and structure.

As reality is measured with increasing precision, fewer phenomena require providential explanation. Gravity and chemistry operate without direction or intent. Life emerged through physical conditions rather than command, and consciousness evolved because it enhanced survival, not because it was bestowed. The patterns that sustain existence function without purpose, governed by laws that remain consistent regardless of belief.

There is a persistent gap between what people hope for and what the world delivers. Belief has often filled that gap by promising order instead of chance, justice instead of randomness, and care instead of indifference. When tested against evidence, those promises fail. Natural disasters do not distinguish between the righteous and the unjust, and illness follows no creed. A God said to govern without observable effect cannot be distinguished from the absence of a governing presence at all.

Some theologians argue that silence itself proves transcendence—that God hides to preserve mystery, that absence protects holiness. But incomprehensibility is not evidence. It is retreat. To declare ignorance sacred is to confuse humility with evasion. A universe that functions perfectly without oversight does not become divine because we are uncomfortable with its clarity.

Modern instruments extend the quiet. Radio telescopes scan the sky and detect only the faint hiss of cosmic background radiation, the

17. Martin, *Atheism: A Philosophical Justification*, 188.

afterglow of a beginning that required no voice. Light from distant galaxies travels billions of years before reaching us, indifferent to the lives that bloom and vanish beneath it. The scale itself contradicts intimacy. If existence were built for us, it hides that intention completely.

Even at the most intimate human scale, there is no observable response. The prayers of parents at hospital bedsides, the cries of those trapped beneath rubble, and the final appeals of the dying show no measurable effect on outcomes. If compassion governs the universe, it leaves no detectable trace. The absence is not deliberate withholding; it is a lack of evidence for any governing presence at all.

When I was younger, I found that silence unbearable. I searched for signs that meaning lingered behind it; a coincidence here, a narrow escape there. But the pattern never formed. The quiet remained consistent, and consistency is its own kind of evidence. What once felt like neglect gradually revealed itself as neutrality.

Now the silence no longer feels cruel. It feels honest. The universe owes no explanation, and in that absence there is unexpected peace. Without a celestial witness, we are left with one another. Responsibility replaces obedience. Justice becomes something we must construct, not something handed down from invisible decree.

The moral weight of existence has shifted. A godless universe is not immoral; it is impartial. It does not reward virtue or punish sin. It simply allows consequence to follow action. Freedom is the price of that indifference. So is accountability.

Epicurus saw it clearly more than two millennia ago.[18] A being both all-powerful and all-good cannot coexist with preventable suffering. The world—unchanged in its cruelty and beauty—confirms the point each day. Famine, war, and disease answer him without words. Their silence is his vindication.

The question that once demanded divine explanation has been answered by evidence. The stillness of the cosmos is not malice. It is fact. The stars are indifferent, but they are also magnificent. In their light, we glimpse a truth older than faith: existence does not require oversight to be astonishing.

When I look at the night sky now, I no longer search for messages written in light. I see continuity, not conversation. The same energy that burns in stars flows through blood; the same chemistry that forms

18. Epicurus, as cited in Lactantius, *On the Anger of God*, 13.

galaxies forms thought. Meaning was never waiting above us. It was always waiting within.

AFTERMATH OF FAITH

When belief finally loosened its hold, I expected a sudden sense of freedom. Instead, the change was gradual. Faith had not existed only as an idea; it had shaped habits, reflexes, and expectations. It offered reassurance in the face of uncertainty, even when that reassurance was fragile. When it fell away, the world felt larger and more exposed. Wonder remained, but it felt different. What I had once understood as divine mystery was now simply reality—complex, unsupervised, and indifferent to human hopes.

The absence of God did not end meaning; it ended permission. There was no longer an invisible authority to consult, no higher will to bless or condemn each choice. I became aware of how often belief had functioned as delegation—a way to outsource conscience. Without it, every moral decision returned to human hands. The commandments faded, but the obligation to care did not. Morality survived its mythology.

I grieved that loss more than I expected. You do not abandon faith; you outgrow it, and growth always leaves a scar. The rituals that once softened grief, the hymns that steadied fear, the quiet prayers before sleep—all carried a residue of comfort reason could not replicate. I did not miss miracles. I missed being able to say thank you to something that listened back.

Gradually, that gratitude found new addresses. I thanked surgeons instead of providence, neighbors instead of angels, those brave men and women who serve (and have served) our country instead of imagined guardians. The thanks felt truer because they landed somewhere real. The divine vanished, but responsibility multiplied.

I came to see that meaning is not given; it is created. It emerges through ordinary actions once taken for granted: holding a hand, keeping a promise, remaining present with someone in pain. These acts assert that life deserves care even when it offers no guarantee in return. Faith emphasized submission; unbelief required engagement. One asked for acceptance. The other required action.

Even now, traces of the old reflex surface. A flicker of prayer before takeoff. A whispered hope when someone I love is ill. This is not belief returning, but memory. The mind reaches for what once felt protective, like grasping for a railing long removed. I let the impulse pass without shame. We are creatures of habit, even in our doubts.

If anything like holiness remains, it does not reside in worship but in attention. Attention is the only response an indifferent universe calls for. To observe the world as it is—to notice the structure of a leaf, the coordinated activity of ants, or acts of kindness between strangers—is to experience awe without appealing to oversight. Reverence does not disappear when its object changes; it is redirected toward what is actually present.

Perhaps faith was always a rehearsal for wonder, a way of training the heart to remain open in the face of uncertainty. What changed was honesty. I no longer pretend that mystery listens. I simply marvel that it exists.

I have not lost religion; I have absorbed it. Its stories became ways of describing human endurance. Its commandments became reminders to protect one another. Its prayers became forms of reflection we now carry internally. The cathedral remains, but its authority no longer comes from beyond us.

What began as loss settled into clarity. The silence that once troubled me became something else: the freedom to build meaning without permission. If anything like revelation remains, it comes not from heaven but from humanity itself: the recognition that we are capable of bearing the weight of existence together.

This is what followed belief. Not despair, but responsibility. Not abandonment, but maturity. The silence did not provide answers, but it did not prohibit action. Within that openness, a more grounded form of reverence emerged—one rooted not in promise, but in care; not in explanation, but in attention; not in what the universe offers us, but in what we offer one another.

Once divine authority dissolved under the weight of evidence, the next question became unavoidable: if God no longer governed the world, why should His words govern us?

7

Who Wrote God's Word?

"Scripture has been used to bless every horror and forbid every pleasure."

George Bernard Shaw

THE CLAIM OF REVELATION

I was told, early on, that the words in the Bible were not written by people, but by God himself, and for a long while I did not think to doubt it. The idea felt both comforting and terrifying—comforting because it meant that truth had already been delivered, and terrifying because it meant I could never question it. Scripture was not a story; it was a verdict. To doubt its words was to doubt the source of meaning itself. Only later did I realize how easily that claim of revelation could become a claim of control. Whoever held the right to interpret those words held the right to define truth. What began as the promise of guidance became a system of permission, sanctifying the will of those who claimed to speak for the divine.

I still remember the texture of that belief. In Sunday school, I was handed a small Bible with the words of Jesus printed in red. The teacher told us those verses were sacred because they came directly from the mouth of God. When I noticed two passages that seemed to disagree, I raised my hand and asked how both could be true. She smiled, as though I had missed something simple, and said, "Some things are not for us to question." The room went quiet. I understood then that curiosity could sound like disobedience. The lesson was clear: belief was safer than thought.

From the beginning, religion has spoken in the language of authority. George Bernard Shaw once captured the consequence of that authority with brutal economy, noting how scripture has been used both to sanctify cruelty and to restrain joy.[1] His words reveal faith's double nature. It consoles and commands. The same verses that promise salvation have justified conquest; the same commandments that praise mercy have sanctioned oppression. What believers revere as divine instruction often functions as authorization, turning moral questions into decrees.

Every enduring creed begins with a text. Whether etched in stone, written on parchment, or carried by memory, sacred writings stand as the supposed voice of the infinite made visible. They claim to convey not speculation but certainty—a record of what heaven has declared rather than what humanity has imagined. To the devout, such pages are not literature but truth itself. Yet under historical scrutiny, they reveal less about eternity than about the civilizations that produced them.

The central claim of faith is that sacred words descend from beyond time, untouched by human error. But every manuscript bears the fingerprints of its age: the politics of kings, the fears of tribes, the customs of patriarchs. The Bible reflects the landscape of the ancient Near East; the Qur'an mirrors the hierarchies of seventh-century Arabia; the Vedas preserve echoes of early Indo-Aryan ritual. Each text reveals a culture before it reveals a god.

Historical evidence confirms this human authorship. Archaeology, linguistics, and textual analysis trace these writings through generations of editing, translation, and debate. The Pentateuch, long credited to Moses, contains multiple narrative voices and anachronisms that point to centuries of compilation.[2] The Gospels differ not only in detail but in theology, each shaped by the audience it sought to persuade. Even within a single tradition, councils and scribes decided which writings would be preserved and which would vanish. The result was not divine dictation but curated memory.

Even before these words were fixed on scrolls, they were filtered through the frailty of memory. Oral traditions evolve like living organisms, adapting to the needs of each retelling. A story told around a fire

1. Shaw, *Preface to Androcles and the Lion*, xlv–xlvi.

2. Friedman, *Who Wrote the Bible?*, 33–38.

changes with every generation, molded by the teller's fears and desires. When scribes finally wrote them down, they preserved not eyewitness testimony but centuries of embroidered recollection. What we now call revelation began as remembered rumor, refined by repetition until it sounded like truth. What followed was not divine clarification, but human selection—deciding which voices would be remembered and which would be erased.

The formation of scripture was as political as it was pious. Power determined what counted as holy. When Emperor Constantine sought unity across the Roman Empire, he convened the Council of Nicaea to define orthodoxy and silence dissent.[3] Early rabbis did the same when assembling the Hebrew canon, keeping texts that reinforced covenantal identity and discarding those that threatened it. The creation of sacred literature was not an act of revelation but of selection—a political project presented as devotion.

To study these writings critically is not to desecrate them but to return them to their origin—the human struggle to impose meaning on chaos. They are remarkable records of imagination and aspiration, but imagination is not revelation. What the devout call holy law is, in truth, the ongoing conversation of a species teaching itself what it wishes to become.

HUMAN AUTHORSHIP

To read sacred writing as if dictated from heaven is to forget that it was first written by people who never imagined they were composing the words of God. They recorded stories, laws, genealogies, and dreams in the idioms of their time, drawing on the politics and fears that surrounded them. Centuries later, communities elevated those writings to authority and treated them as infallible. Every stage of that ascent—from oral legend to canon—shows deliberate human choice: what to preserve, what to alter, and how to explain what no longer fit.

The American satirist Mark Twain once observed that the Bible is the most read book in the world and the least examined.[4] Generations have treated it as divine command while rarely questioning the human decisions that shaped every page. Those decisions reveal unmistakable

3. Eusebius, *Life of Constantine*, III.6–13.

4. Twain, *Notebook*, 356.

bias: texts created by men reflect the structures of power in which those men lived. The laws, hierarchies, and even the divine pronouns echo the hands that penned them. Women appear as property, temptation, or warning; authority speaks in a male voice. What began as legislation for men by men was later sanctified through repetition until it seemed eternal.

The story of Eve embodies this inheritance. According to Genesis, Adam was given the divine prohibition before Eve existed, yet it is Eve who is blamed for disobedience. She believes the serpent—"the craftiest of all of God's creatures"—who assures her she will not die but become wise. Only after eating does she gain knowledge of right and wrong, which means she could not have understood the moral weight of her choice beforehand. Still, tradition condemns her as the cause of humanity's fall while excusing the man who was present all along. The logic collapses under its own contradiction: God, said to be omniscient, would have known the outcome from the start, having created both the tempter and the tree. If so, the Fall was not a failure of free will but of design.

The same pattern appears across civilizations. The *Analects* of Confucius were compiled by disciples who attributed their own reflections to the master's voice. The *Tao Te Ching*, credited to Lao Tzu, was assembled from scattered aphorisms centuries after his supposed lifetime. The Vedas and the Qur'an likewise evolved through recitation, debate, and revision. Each tradition claims timeless origin, yet each bears the syntax of its age, the rhythm of its language, and the limits of its worldview. The search for permanence always passes through impermanence.

Incoherence marks every stage of this evolution. A message said to come from perfection should not fracture along moral and theological lines. Yet the Bible repeatedly argues with itself—on violence, salvation, justice, and even the nature of God. These are not mysteries of faith but seams of editing and debate, evidence of many authors revising their gods to fit their times.

The Bible, often portrayed as a single revelation, is in reality a library of evolving belief. Scholars identify at least four main voices behind its earliest books—the Yahwist, Elohist, Priestly, and Deuteronomist sources—each with a distinct vision of the sacred. One speaks of a local protector who walks in gardens; another of a distant creator who commands worlds into being. Their fusion over centuries produced a composite deity full of internal tension. In Genesis alone, two creation accounts stand side by side: one describing humanity formed all at once, another narrating Adam first, then Eve. Both cannot be literal, yet both are proclaimed as truth.

Archaeology reinforces this view. Excavations in Canaan and Egypt yield no trace of the vast exodus described in *Exodus*. Jericho's walls, long said to have fallen before Joshua's trumpet, collapsed centuries earlier. The Flood story mirrors older Mesopotamian myths such as the *Epic of Gilgamesh*.[5] These parallels reveal a consistent pattern: borrowed tales refitted to serve national identity.

The New Testament follows the same trajectory. The four canonical Gospels differ in sequence, wording, and doctrine. The earliest manuscripts omit entire episodes later inserted by editors—accounts of miracles and resurrections absent from first versions. Several letters attributed to Paul were written decades later by admirers imitating his style. Even *Revelation* was disputed for centuries, dismissed by many bishops as too violent and strange until imperial politics demanded a dramatic finale. What believers now treat as a seamless narrative was assembled piece by piece under the pressures of persuasion and power.

Islam's scripture reveals similar seams. After Muhammad's death, verses survived on bone, bark, and memory until Caliph Uthman ordered a standardized version to end disputes.[6] Regional variants persisted in dialect and oral recitation despite official suppression. The claim that every syllable today matches the Prophet's lips belongs to devotion, not documentation.

The Hindu Vedas, among the oldest religious compositions, were transmitted orally for generations before being fixed in writing. Their hymns show centuries of revision: new gods rising, old ones fading, rituals expanding from sacrifice to speculation. If a timeless voice spoke through them, it spoke with a changing accent.

Across cultures, the pattern is identical; multiplicity, revision, and cultural imprint. These writings preserve what civilizations feared and desired, not what eternity dictated. Their endurance into modern times shows persistence more than inspiration.

Translation deepens the human fingerprint. The Bible alone has crossed Hebrew, Aramaic, Greek, Latin, and hundreds of vernacular tongues. Each passage through language bends meaning. In Isaiah, the word rendered "virgin" originally meant "young woman." The word

5. Dalley, *Myths from Mesopotamia*, 108–11.
6. Donner, *Muhammad and the Believers*, 57–59.

"hell" in the Gospels evolved from *Sheol* and *Gehenna*, terms for grave and valley. Whole theologies have grown from such linguistic drift. Even scribes left their mark: marginal notes became verses, copying errors became dogma.

Scholars tracing these transformations find not divine uniformity but relentless argument. Prophets challenge kings; priests correct prophets; reformers rewrite priests. The Torah debates itself; the Gospels reinterpret the Torah; the Qur'an answers both. What endures is not harmony but contention elevated to sanctity. The sacred library is less revelation than archive—a record of evolving self-definition rather than divine decree.

To see these works as celestial dictation is to erase the humanity that birthed them. Their worth lies precisely in imperfection. They record the attempt of ancient minds to reason with mortality and mystery. They do not transmit a god's command; they preserve humanity's effort to make sense of its own bewilderment.

The diversity of interpretation is often presented as a virtue, evidence of scripture's depth. Yet this diversity is precisely what undermines the claim of divine authorship. If these words came from a perfect and omniscient mind, their meaning would not fracture along cultural, linguistic, or moral lines. A message intended to guide all humanity would not depend on centuries of debate to explain what it means or to rescue it from its consequences. What requires constant interpretation to remain credible bears the mark of human origin, not divine clarity.

MORAL PARADOX

If divine law truly came from a perfect mind, ethics would not evolve. Yet across centuries, sacred texts have endorsed nearly every cruelty that reason later condemned. Each generation of believers claims to rediscover the true meaning of revelation, never noticing that what changes is not the text but the conscience interpreting it.

Jesus often survives this moral reckoning not because his teachings escape scrutiny, but because his authority is inherited rather than examined. Even among those who reject his divinity or doubt the reliability of the Gospels, his words are frequently treated as ethical shorthand—quoted as wisdom by default rather than evaluated as moral claims. Familiarity becomes insulation. Reverence, absorbed culturally rather than argued for, shields his teachings from the standards we apply everywhere else.

The Bible, often called the foundation of moral order, explicitly permits human ownership. Exodus allows a master to beat a servant provided the victim survives two days (Exod 21:20–21). Leviticus authorizes the purchase of foreigners as inheritable property (Lev 25:44–46). In the New Testament, Paul instructs slaves to obey their masters and masters to treat them kindly, but never to set them free (Eph 6:5–9; Col 3:22—4:1). For centuries, preachers cited these passages to defend slavery and colonial domination. Only when moral revulsion grew stronger than obedience did theology retreat to context. The conscience led while doctrine followed. The pattern is consistent: ethical progress emerges first, and theology revises itself only afterward.

The treatment of women follows the same path. In *Genesis*, Eve's curiosity earns her subservience: she must bear children in pain and obey her husband. Paul repeats the verdict, commanding women to be silent in church and to learn submission. The Qur'an grants men authority over women and the right to discipline disobedience. Hindu law codes praise devotion but tie female virtue to dependence on father, husband, or son. None of this reflects timeless wisdom; it mirrors patriarchal societies seeking permanence through divine approval. When religion must later reinterpret its own discrimination, it concedes that ethics progress without it.

Violence fares no better. The book of Joshua commands the destruction of entire cities in the name of purity (Josh 6:21), and the Psalms bless vengeance against infants (Ps 137:9). Scriptures across traditions have been used to sanctify war, just as Christian kings once invoked the cross to conquer. These are not spiritual lessons but political manifestos written in sacred language. When murder is described as devotion, atrocity becomes worship.

Apologists often claim such commands belong to another era and should not be judged by modern standards. But timeless truth requires no expiration date. A moral code that demands historical excuses forfeits its claim to divine origin. Each reinterpretation is a confession that moral awareness grows while scripture does not.

Modern ethics now moves in the opposite direction of ancient decree. The same civilizations that once defended slavery, conquest, and subjugation now condemn them as evil. The texts remain unchanged; only humanity has matured. If moral understanding came from revelation, moral progress would be impossible. Instead, compassion expands while doctrine stays fixed, forcing religion to retrofit kindness onto inherited cruelty.

History confirms this pattern without interruption. The Inquisition tortured in defense of purity. Colonial powers baptized while they enslaved. American preachers thundered that abolition defied divine order. Each brutality drew legitimacy from sacred citation until experience made obedience intolerable. Reform arose not from faith correcting itself but from reason correcting faith.

Even within single traditions, contradictions abound. The same Bible that commands love of neighbor demands execution for heresy. The same Qur'an that extols mercy permits stoning for adultery. Hindu texts that celebrate nonviolence justify caste oppression. What is advertised as consistency is, in truth, human conflict elevated to holiness.

Philosophers and skeptics have long recognized this moral dissonance. Voltaire warned that those who can make you believe absurdities can make you commit atrocities. Dostoevsky's Ivan Karamazov declared that no paradise could justify a child's tears. Even devout thinkers such as C. S. Lewis wrestled with the cruelty of divine design, conceding that pain often seems less like punishment than indifference. The moral argument for God collapses when believers must excuse behavior they would condemn in anyone else.

The same struggle continues in modern life. Religious leaders still quote scripture to oppose women's autonomy, same-sex marriage, or reproductive choice. Verses written in a desert culture now shape laws in secular democracies. The authority of revelation persists not because it is moral, but because it is familiar. Tradition feels safer than change, even when it harms.

Technology now inherits that confusion. Developers have trained algorithms on sacred texts, hoping to create machines that understand ethics. The results are predictable. Systems learn to echo the prejudices of their sources: submission rewarded, dissent punished, women diminished, outsiders condemned. A program taught on scripture may preach compassion yet cannot escape the hierarchies encoded in its data. What was once revelation becomes dataset. What was once faith becomes feedback. The experiment reveals more about our nostalgia for authority than about moral progress.

Some theologians retreat to symbolism, claiming that harsh commands conceal hidden meaning. But once ethics depend on metaphor, authority shifts from heaven to the interpreter. The text becomes literature rather than law, its power sustained by reverence rather than truth. A morality that must be reimagined to remain acceptable is morality created by humans, not bestowed by gods.

These contradictions expose the origin of moral authority more clearly than any archaeology ever could. They reveal not a perfect voice dictating justice but communities codifying survival. Prohibitions against theft or murder appear in every culture because cooperation works better than chaos. Religion later stamped its seal on behaviors that evolution had already proven useful.

When cruelty requires apology and injustice demands reinterpretation, what remains of the claim to divine wisdom? If goodness must evolve beyond the text, then goodness cannot come from it. The great irony of faith is that it must borrow its virtue from the world it claims to transcend.

The moral evolution of humankind forced theology to adapt in self-defense. Each era remade God in its own likeness: a tribal guardian became a universal father; a jealous deity softened into a moral symbol.

Every revision testified less to revelation than to cultural necessity. When conscience outgrew fear, faith renamed it love. When violence became indefensible, scripture was allegorized into metaphor. Divinity, like language, survived through translation. The history of religion is the history of God edited into acceptability, a portrait retouched by every age that could no longer bear the original image.

If morality were truly divine, it would not need editing. The endless revision of holy law is proof not of revelation but of remorse.

At this point, the question is no longer whether scripture reflects human morality—it plainly does. The deeper question is what kind of deity these texts actually describe. If words reveal their authors, then the character attributed to God may tell us less about heaven than about the fears, power structures, and moral limits of the people who imagined him.

THE CHARACTER OF GOD

The most troubling evidence against divine goodness lies not in human cruelty but in the sacred texts themselves. The God portrayed in scripture does not merely permit suffering; at times He commands it. The Flood in Genesis drowns nearly all life on earth, sparing only one family and a cargo of animals. It is divine regret turned to massacre—a creator destroying

His own creation because He dislikes how it turned out. It would be like building a model from blocks, disapproving of the design, and burning the pieces so no one else could use them. The story is not about justice; it is the tantrum of omnipotence.

The text itself describes God surveying the "wickedness of man" and deciding to erase not only humanity but every living thing—animals, plants, and children alike (Gen 6:5–7). It is moral outrage expressed as extinction. If this is divine correction, it resembles burning down a house to rid it of mice.

The physical account fares no better than the moral one. Scripture claims that the floodwaters rose more than fifteen cubits—twenty feet—above the highest mountains (Gen 7:20). Such a deluge would require rain falling at six inches per minute, enough to bury Mount Everest under five miles of water. Where, then, did that water come from, and where did it go? The story demands physics as miraculous as its morality.

The same logic appears elsewhere in scripture, where entire cities and generations are destroyed as demonstrations of righteousness rather than justice.

When the waters apparently receded, the survivors simply wander off to repopulate the world. Noah's first recorded act is to build an altar and sacrifice one of every "clean" animal and bird to God (Gen 8:20). Considering that so few creatures had survived, the offering feels less like gratitude than paradox—a ritual that endangers the very lives just spared. Scripture calls it a "pleasing aroma" to the Lord, as though the destruction of life required a final affirmation through fire. If all humanity descends from that single family, why do different languages exist? Wouldn't their descendants share the same tongue? Survival would be hard enough without the added burden of learning a new language. The logic collapses into absurdity: a god who destroys civilization, then sabotages its rebuilding.

Some believers address these accounts of violence by arguing that the Flood was never intended to be read as a historical event, but as a symbolic story about renewal. Others claim that God's violence should be understood figuratively, as moral instruction rather than physical action. These interpretive moves are relatively recent and arise from moral discomfort. For centuries, such stories were treated as historical fact, taught in worship, and preached as literal truth. Interpretation shifted only when moral standards changed and the original readings became difficult to defend.

That instinct to reinterpret is revealing. It reflects not faith, but moral judgment—an attempt to reconcile contemporary ethical standards with texts that portray violence as divinely sanctioned. The reinterpretation occurs because those accounts no longer align with what people now recognize as acceptable. In that shift, moral change becomes visible. It is not the content of revelation that evolves, but the willingness to accept cruelty as justified.

Throughout the Hebrew Bible, divine anger becomes a recurring theme. The Israelites are commanded to exterminate the Amalekites—man and woman, infant and suckling, ox and sheep (1 Sam 15:3). When Saul spares their king, the act of mercy is treated as rebellion. The same deity hardens Pharaoh's heart, then punishes him for disobedience. Abraham is praised not for compassion but for his willingness to kill his own son on command. These are not moral allegories; they are chronicles of unchecked authority.

A God who knows everything cannot be surprised. Yet the Bible states that God experiences all the emotions of humans, including anger, sadness, and happiness. By God's very nature, He should be ignorant of nothing. Nothing is hidden from Him, nothing new can be revealed to Him, so there is no gained knowledge to which He may react emotionally. An omniscient, omnipotent, and perfect God who experiences emotions is impossible. Perhaps the emotions of God are not signs of divinity at all, but of authors who could imagine no power greater than their own reflection.

But even more troubling than divine emotion is divine inaction—the idea that an all-powerful being can watch suffering unfold and call it part of a plan. I sometimes picture it as a dinner party. A guest across the table begins to choke. I know exactly what to do—the simple act that would save them—but I stay seated, watching. When someone asks why I did nothing, I say, "It's part of my plan." No one at that table would accept my explanation or call me good. They would call it cruelty. Yet this is the logic used to defend divine inaction amid famine, plague, and war. Theologians insist that divine morality operates beyond human comprehension, that what seems cruel must serve a higher purpose. But morality that cannot be recognized ceases to be morality. If a human ruler behaved this way, we would call him monstrous. Why should divinity deserve a lesser standard?

If the Bible and my brain were both designed by the same creator, whose fault is it that they disagree? The tension between reason and revelation becomes impossible to ignore. To call this deity good is to abandon every human definition of the word.

The same incoherence plays out in smaller, almost comic ways. Athletes kneel in end zones and point skyward after a touchdown, thanking God for favoring one team over another; as if the architect of galaxies paused to adjust a football's trajectory. The sincerity of the gesture is not in doubt, but its theology is absurd. If God directs the ball through the uprights, then He also ordains the fumble, the injury, the loss. To imagine divine concern for a scoreboard while famine and war continue unchecked is to expose belief as preference disguised as reverence. It is faith reduced to superstition—the confusion of luck for providence and victory for virtue.

From stadiums to sanctuaries, the impulse is the same: to edit divinity into something more tolerable, more flattering to human need. It is no surprise that later believers sought to repair the portrait. The New Testament arrives as a gentler sequel to a brutal god. Gone is the deity who smites nations and floods the world; in His place stands a human face—Jesus of Nazareth, healer, forgiver, and sacrifice. But the transformation reads less like a new revelation than an attempt to resolve the moral tension left unresolved by earlier portrayals. If the Old Testament revealed wrath, the New Testament tries to humanize it. Yet the contradiction persists, softened only by story.

Even the gentler image carries the same paradox. The Gospels describe a Jesus who preaches peace yet declares, "I come not to bring peace, but a sword." He blesses the meek yet curses a fig tree for bearing no fruit, urges love of neighbor but demands loyalty above family—"Whoever loves father or mother more than me is not worthy of me." His parables divide the saved from the damned, the sheep from the goats, leaving little room for doubt or dissent. Mercy becomes conditional, salvation dependent on submission. Hell replaces the flood; fear remains the engine of obedience.

Even his actions complicate the image of moral perfection. The Gospels describe him fashioning a whip to drive merchants from the temple, his followers drawing swords, and his temper flaring at a barren fig tree. These gestures, symbolic or not, reveal a temperament as human as it is holy. Compassion becomes spectacle. Power, even when cloaked in piety, still seeks display.

Yet the deepest paradox appears not in anger but in agony. If Jesus truly knew he was the Son of God, destined to rise again and sit at the right hand of the Father, why such despair? At the crucifixion, the moment believers call the pinnacle of love, he cries out, "My God, my God, why have you forsaken me?" It is not the voice of serenity but of desolation. Humans have suffered far worse and borne it with less lament, yet none claimed divinity. If he knew resurrection awaited, faith failed; if he did not, knowledge was illusion. Either way, certainty collapses beneath the weight of suffering. Reverence reframes this as proof of humanity, but perfection does not waver between conviction and doubt. The story that was meant to redeem cruelty ends instead by sanctifying surrender.

The morality of Jesus, like that of his Father, depends less on compassion than on control. The deity of the Old Testament demands fear; the savior of the New Testament demands faith. Both require loyalty first and understanding later. Beneath the softer language of love lies the same architecture of authority. Infinite punishment for finite disbelief is not moral order; it is vengeance disguised as virtue.

If these same acts and attitudes were attributed to a mortal ruler, we would not call him holy but tyrannical. He rewards loyalty, demands blood, and punishes dissent. To worship such behavior merely because it is powerful is to confuse reverence with resignation. The claim that divine power is good by definition empties goodness of meaning altogether.

Modern defenders of faith often argue that these stories must be read "in context," as if history could soften genocide or torment. Yet morality that relies on qualification is morality in retreat. The notion of a good God commanding horror belongs to an age when obedience was survival. That it still lingers today speaks less to revelation than to habit.

Some theologians insist that these stories are metaphors for moral growth rather than records of cruelty. But a lesson that requires drowning, slaughter, or eternal torment to be understood is not the work of wisdom. A moral universe would not need horror to communicate virtue. The persistence of divine violence across traditions reveals less about heaven than about humanity's own reflection. Ancient tribes imagined gods who mirrored their fears and hierarchies; later believers mistook those reflections for revelation. What began as mythology hardened into moral law.

The fracture between mercy and judgment, love and domination, runs through both testaments. Whether thundered from Sinai or whispered from the cross, the divine voice demands the same thing: obedience dressed as virtue. The Old Testament's wrath and the New Testament's sacrifice are not opposites; they are variations on authority. Together they form the longest-running paradox in human history: the worship of power disguised as love.

If such a being exists, he deserves not worship but scrutiny. And if he does not, then the moral burden falls to us—to become better than our gods.

The only way to accept scripture as divine is to pretend it doesn't mean what it says. The Bible simply reflects the culture of its authors—men who mapped the heavens as a dome, the earth as flat, and morality through the lens of their own hierarchies. To call it timeless truth is to ignore how deeply it bears the fingerprints of its age. If we praise God for every mercy in its pages, we must also attribute to Him every cruelty. To claim otherwise is to selectively reinterpret the text. As Thomas Paine argued in *The Age of Reason*, the Bible's portrait of God asks us to treat as righteous what we would condemn in any human being: "I sincerely detest it, as I detest everything that is cruel."[7] These conflicts do not disappear in the Gospels; they merely retreat behind the parts of the story we cannot see.

Even the story of Jesus carries its own silence. Between his childhood visit to the temple and the beginning of his ministry, the record goes dark. That absence is not incidental; it is narratively convenient. By leaving those years unaccounted for, the writers avoid explanation, contradiction, or correction. What cannot be examined cannot be challenged. In that vacuum, imagination flourishes and faith fills the blanks. The silence protects the legend, preserving perfection by withholding detail. Yet what remains hidden often reveals more than what is told.

SCRIPTURE AS CONTROL

If divine law truly reflected eternal justice, it would stand above politics. Yet history shows the opposite: sacred texts have consistently served power. Those who claim the right to interpret the words of heaven inevitably shape how others must live on earth. Once authority is declared divine, dissent becomes sin instead of disagreement. What cannot be questioned becomes the perfect tool of control.

Sacred texts endure not because they are precise, but because they are elastic. Their language is broad enough to absorb contradiction and vague enough to survive moral change. What once justified conquest can

7. Paine, *The Age of Reason*, Part I.

later be read as metaphor; what enforced hierarchy can later be reframed as context. Ambiguity allows authority to retreat without surrender. A fixed moral code would break under scrutiny, but an interpretable one can be endlessly repurposed, preserving power while appearing timeless.

From the earliest civilizations, rulers understood the value of sanctity. In Mesopotamia, kings proclaimed their decrees as the will of the gods. Pharaohs declared themselves divine, fusing theology with government. In Israel, prophets anointed monarchs in the name of the Almighty, turning obedience to rulers into obedience to heaven. The pattern endured because it worked. When order is said to come from above, rebellion below becomes blasphemy.

Scripture provided the moral architecture for this arrangement. The Hebrew Bible codified systems of kingship, taxation, and priestly privilege. The New Testament instructs believers to "submit to governing authorities," teaching that all rulers are established by God (Rom 13:1). The Qur'an commands obedience to "those in power among you" (Qur'an 4:59). These verses are not timeless revelations of justice but instruments of governance, sanctifying hierarchy with the language of holiness.

Fear made the alliance complete. When questioning doctrine threatened salvation, literacy itself became dangerous. For centuries, the written word of God was accessible only to priests and scholars. Translation into common languages was forbidden to preserve authority. In medieval Europe, owning a vernacular Bible could mean imprisonment or death.[8] Revelation was less about divine communication than about the control of information. To know the text directly was to bypass the gatekeepers who profited from its mystery.

The Protestant Reformation broke that monopoly by placing scripture in the hands of ordinary people, yet even that revolution produced new hierarchies. Luther's insistence on personal faith quickly hardened into Lutheran orthodoxy. Calvin's Geneva replaced papal power with its own theocracy. Each reformer who broke from Rome built a smaller Rome in miniature. Revelation simply moved from one custodian to another, each claiming exclusive access to truth.

Other traditions followed the same pattern. In Islam, interpretation of the Qur'an—*tafsir*—remained the domain of elite scholars whose rulings guided empires. In Hindu society, the Brahmin caste preserved mastery of the Vedas, maintaining ritual privilege through the claim of

8. MacCulloch, *The Reformation*, 85–87.

divine expertise. Across cultures, sacred knowledge became social leverage. Once authority is declared divine, control no longer needs to justify itself. The book functioned not as a bridge to transcendence but as a passport to authority.

Scripture also drew boundaries, dividing insiders from outsiders. It defined the chosen and the condemned, the clean and the unclean, the believer and the infidel. The Israelites were commanded to destroy neighboring tribes. The Qur'an warns against trusting unbelievers. The Gospels speak of a narrow gate through which few will pass. Such distinctions grant cohesion to a group but hostility toward all others. What begins as identity ends as exclusion.

Where power seeks durability, religion often supplies its framework. Monarchs swear oaths on holy books. Nations describe themselves as chosen. Political movements invoke divine purpose to justify ambition. Even secular ideologies borrow the language of faith, speaking of destiny, purity, and redemption through struggle. This language endures because it presents authority as unavoidable.

Once the sacred becomes law, reform turns into heresy. To question ancient words is to undermine the structures built upon them. When science contradicts scripture, believers are told to mistrust evidence. When morality outgrows old commandments, theologians invent allegory to hide the fracture. The preservation of belief becomes more important than the pursuit of truth. Every intellectual advance—from heliocentrism to evolution—was born of defiance, not devotion.

The endurance of sacred authority lies in its promise of stability. In uncertain times, immovable truths are comforting. But certainty carries a cost: stagnation. When obedience replaces inquiry, compassion becomes optional. The same verses that justify loyalty can excuse cruelty. The oppressed are promised reward in another life while the powerful claim divine approval in this one. Submission is sanctified, and injustice becomes the will of God.

This pattern has not vanished; it has simply changed vocabulary. Modern fundamentalists still cite holy writ to oppose women's autonomy, reproductive rights, and scientific education. The text remains ancient, but its use remains modern: to restrain progress while claiming moral superiority. What passes for faith is often nostalgia for control.

In our time, the instruments of obedience have multiplied. The written word that once disciplined thought has given way to a digital scripture of constant command. Algorithms now perform the work of old hierarchies. They curate belief, reward outrage, and define reality through repetition. The faithful no longer look upward for instruction; they scroll. What was once divine command has become behavioral design.

The algorithm is the new pulpit. Each scroll of the feed delivers a sermon tailored to conviction, rewarding certainty and punishing doubt. Outrage spreads faster than nuance because outrage keeps attention. What was once called heresy is now shadow-banned. The language has changed, but the psychology remains the same: belonging through agreement, virtue through visibility, sin through silence. The algorithm does not demand prayer, only participation.

What religion once achieved through ritual, technology now achieves through engagement. The priest and the programmer share the same ambition: to shape attention, to define what counts as truth. The modern congregation is measured not in pews but in metrics. The faithful log in daily, seeking affirmation instead of absolution. We no longer kneel before icons; we tap them.

Nationalism borrows the same rhythm. Leaders speak of destiny, chosen nations, and salvation through struggle. Flags become icons, slogans become psalms. The need for transcendence, stripped of theology, migrates into ideology. What was once divine command now marches under banners and manifests in code. Revelation has not disappeared; it has been repackaged.

Recognizing this continuity is not cynicism but clarity. The same instinct that once sought guidance in temples now seeks it in technology. The difference is that the new gods answer instantly and never ask us to think. The illusion of connection replaces reflection. The promise of knowledge replaces understanding. Control, once draped in scripture, now hides behind convenience.

To recognize scripture as an instrument of power is not to dismiss its poetry or its moral aspiration. These writings contain courage, longing, and moments of wisdom. But their authority rests on humanity's confusion between permanence and truth. The same words that once bound a tribe together can bind a conscience in chains.

When law claims divine origin, it stops revealing and starts regulating. It becomes a system for maintaining order in a world that offers none. The comfort of certainty demands that doubt—the engine of understanding—be treated as rebellion. The tragedy of sacred authority is not that it was written, but that it was weaponized.

Yet words alone could not sustain obedience forever. When scripture lost its power to command, fear took its place. The threat of divine punishment outlasted the promise of divine presence. What began as law became instinct—a quiet inheritance carried in the human mind long after the voice of revelation faded.

PART III

Beyond Belief

8

Learning to Walk Without Certainty

"It is wrong always, everywhere, and for anyone, to believe anything upon insufficient evidence."

William K. Clifford

INHERITANCE OF FEAR

Sometimes I think my first experience of God was not theological but emotional. I did not understand doctrine, but I understood consequence. A single doubt or unspoken question felt dangerous, as though punishment might follow. Before I learned any religious teaching, I learned the expectation of being observed—an internalized sense of judgment that monitored thought as much as action. Only later did I recognize how deeply rooted that feeling was, predating formal religion and emerging from more basic human fears.

If Chapter 7 showed how scripture commanded belief, this chapter traces how fear enforced it. Every religion begins in fear. Before formal explanation existed, unexpected events produced anxiety rather than understanding. When lightning struck or illness spread through a community, the human mind searched for a cause. Harm without explanation demanded an agent behind it. Cognitive scientists call this "hyperactive agency detection," the brain's reflex that treats every rustle in the dark as a possible predator.[1] Better to mistake wind for danger than danger for wind. Over countless generations, that instinct shaped what we now call belief. Early gods functioned as explanatory models for events people could not yet understand. This chapter is not about replacing belief, but about understanding why certainty once felt necessary and why letting it go is so difficult.

Sitting in church, listening to the priest speak with such calm certainty about God's anger, it seemed natural to assume he possessed evidence I did not. I watched his face for clues, trying to see what he saw. If he believed this much, maybe the danger was real. Fear didn't feel ancient to me then; it felt local, personal, inherited one sentence at a time.

The instinct to question rather than accept was humanity's first experiment. Long before philosophy gave doubt a name, survival depended on it. Some prayed for rain; others dug irrigation channels. Some offered sacrifices; others studied the seasons. Those who tested the world endured.

I remember other Sundays, too—listening to verses about divine wrath recited with calm conviction. The room smelled of old hymnals and candle wax. I didn't yet understand theology, but I understood consequence. One mistake, one doubt, one unconfessed thought could tip the scales against me. Fear preceded belief. It was not devotion that held me there, but self-preservation. The lesson formed early: obedience felt safe, while doubt felt dangerous. Even unspoken questioning carried the sense of exposure.

Over millennia, curiosity became a practical survival strategy. People began replacing ritual with observation and appeal with testing. Rather than asking gods for help, they learned to watch the sky, track seasons, and adjust behavior based on results. In that shift—from pleading to perceiving—the mind began to free itself.

Skepticism did not begin as a philosophical position but as a practical habit. It emerged from repeated testing of the environment and the willingness to abandon explanations that failed to produce reliable results.

Archaeological records trace the same pattern. Early burials from the Upper Paleolithic include weapons and food placed beside the dead; insurance for an uncertain journey. Caves in France and Spain bear painted animals and handprints arranged like charms of protection. Anthropologist Pascal Boyer notes that societies facing instability—drought, famine,

1. Boyer, *Religion Explained*, 145–47.

plague—produce denser webs of ritual and taboo.[2] Anxiety increases the tendency to search for patterns. Pattern-seeking encourages people to impose order on uncertain events, and that imposed order often becomes personified as divine intention.

When thunder rolled across the plains, the first shamans stood between terror and tribe. Their chants did not explain nature so much as soothe it. A gesture around the fire could quiet the storm inside the mind even when it did nothing to the sky. From this illusion emerged an early explanatory framework: suffering was interpreted as the result of angered forces, while prosperity was taken as approval. Fear was reorganized into structured belief.

As settlements expanded, these impulses hardened into law. Priests replaced shamans, and offerings became obligations. The vocabulary of worship evolved, but its emotional grammar stayed constant: the promise of safety in exchange for submission. In Mesopotamia, temples collected grain and livestock to secure divine favor. In Egypt, the dead carried amulets through elaborate funerary rites to protect them from judgment. Each practice began with the same logic: obedience might postpone disaster.

The Hebrew Bible preserves this inheritance. In its oldest layers, God introduces Himself not as companion but as command. "The fear of the Lord is the beginning of wisdom," (Prov 1:7) says Proverbs. The phrase is not metaphorical; it is foundational. Religion functioned as a mechanism of social cohesion built on shared fear. The Book of Deuteronomy lists explicit curses for disobedience. Faith was less a matter of trust than insurance against wrath.

Other civilizations mirrored the pattern. Greek sailors sacrificed bulls to Poseidon before setting sail. The Aztecs offered hearts to keep the sun alive. In early China, the Mandate of Heaven justified both coronation and catastrophe. Floods signified divine anger; droughts, neglect of ritual. Across continents, cosmic misfortune reflected human failing. People feared not only death but guilt.

Modern psychology confirms the efficiency of this emotional economy. Ara Norenzayan, a psychologist at the University of British Columbia who studies how religion evolved to sustain cooperation, and his collaborator Azim Shariff, whose research links belief in divine punishment to moral behavior, found that belief in punitive, all-seeing deities correlated with stronger cooperation in small groups. Fear of supernatural

2. Boyer, *Religion Explained*, 203–7.

oversight encouraged honesty when anonymity tempted the opposite. In that sense, religion functioned as a behavioral technology long before courts or police existed. Anxiety kept order.

But the cost was perpetual unease. A mind trained to find purpose in every misfortune can never rest. A failed crop is interpreted as punishment. Disease is interpreted as judgment. The believer experiences life as continual moral evaluation. Centuries of sermons and sacred art reinforced that mindset: European frescoes depicted sinners boiling in cauldrons; Buddhist hell scrolls in East Asia showed similar torments. Anxiety traveled more easily than doctrine.

Even now, early indoctrination often begins with warning. A 2017 Pew survey found that more than sixty percent of Americans raised in conservative denominations first associated God with anger rather than love.[3] The pattern persists: morality begins with threat and only later grows into promise. That emotional sequencing leaves deep marks. Psychologists studying deconversion describe "residual guilt syndrome," a lingering tension that survives long after belief fades. The body forgets doctrine more slowly than the mind.

Seen this way, faith appears not as mystery but as a transmitted psychological and cultural pattern. Evolution supplied vigilance, and culture organized that vigilance into formal belief systems. Each generation passed along stories that justified its anxieties and softened them through ritual. Worship offered not only divine contact but relief—the reassurance of being watched by a protector. To surrender was to feel safe. Doubt, by contrast, felt like exposure.

Understanding that lineage does not trivialize devotion; it explains its endurance. Religion answered a genuine need: the need to manage terror in a world without medicine or meteorology. The trouble is that anxiety, once institutionalized, resists extinction. It becomes doctrine, then identity. What initially served to reduce fear often becomes a system that restricts thought and behavior.

The skeptic's task is to understand that legacy without accepting its constraints. Interpreting natural events as physical processes rather than moral signals means accepting a universe that operates independently of human intention but can still be understood through investigation. Where superstition once filled the void, knowledge now stands. The remaining question is not whether fear contributed to the formation of

3. Pew Research Center, "Religious Upbringing and Views of God," 2017.

gods, but why people continue to defend those beliefs after the original conditions of uncertainty and danger have diminished.

THE ARCHITECTURE OF AUTHORITY

When fear became organized, it required administration. What began as an attempt to reduce uncertainty gradually developed into systems of authority that defined behavior, enforced conformity, and regulated access to meaning. The moment someone claimed the ability to interpret the will of the unseen, hierarchy followed. Protection turned into governance, and governance justified itself by appealing to forces beyond human challenge.

In Sumer, one of the world's first civilizations, religion and administration were inseparable. Temple complexes such as the ziggurat of Ur, built around 2100 BCE, rose above the plains as both sanctuaries and centers of commerce. Priests converted anxiety into order, turning fear into calendar and ritual. What began as protection became the management of dependence. The same institution that promised salvation also controlled grain, labor, and law. Power came wrapped in holiness.

The model spread and adapted. In ancient Egypt, the pharaoh ruled as a living god, his decrees carrying the weight of eternity. To question the throne was to challenge the cosmos itself. The Hebrew priesthood codified purity laws that governed food, clothing, and contact. Medieval Christianity institutionalized confession, transforming private guilt into a monitored system. In the Islamic caliphates, scholars and rulers shared authority, blending law with revelation. Across cultures, faith became the operating system of society. Obedience was no longer a choice; it was the condition of belonging.

Anthropologists have documented striking examples of how deeply this dynamic runs. Among the Azande of Central Africa, nearly every major decision once passed through a ritual known as the poison oracle. A chicken was fed toxic benge; whether it lived or died determined guilt, innocence, or the cause of misfortune. This wasn't a fringe superstition. It functioned as a legal system, a medical diagnosis, and a moral court. Lives, marriages, and alliances turned on the fate of a bird. Fear didn't merely influence belief—it administered justice. The oracle worked because people trusted its verdicts more than their own. Obedience, wrapped in ritual, felt safer than uncertainty.

The French philosopher Michel Foucault, known for his studies of power and discipline, described how institutions thrive on internalized surveillance.[4] Religion achieved that mastery long before the modern state. Instead of guards and prisons, it installed watchmen within the mind. The believer carried the overseer everywhere. The reward was heaven; the penalty, endless torment. Few systems have ever achieved such efficiency.

Fear alone could not sustain loyalty. To maintain obedience, religions paired anxiety with relief. Confession, prayer, and pilgrimage offered release. The sinner felt cleansed not because justice had been served but because authority had spoken. Absolution restored balance and reinforced dependence. Every ritual ended with gratitude toward the same power that had defined the guilt.

History provides abundant examples. In medieval Europe, the Church monetized fear through the sale of indulgences—official documents said to reduce punishment in the afterlife. By the fifteenth century, entire cathedrals were financed through these transactions. The German monk Martin Luther objected not to belief itself but to its exploitation. Yet the Reformation retained the same underlying structure of authority. The pulpit replaced the confessional, and sermons replaced indulgences. Fear of doctrinal error took the place of fear of papal decree.

Comparable systems appeared across the world. The Aztec priesthood demanded human sacrifice not only to sustain their gods but to reinforce state power. In India, the caste system linked spiritual purity to birthright, sanctifying inequality as divine design. In China, the Mandate of Heaven turned political rebellion into cosmic sin. Each culture used theology to secure obedience, proving that divine and human authority often spoke the same language.

Modern psychology helps explain why these hierarchies endured. The social psychologist Stanley Milgram showed that ordinary people will harm others when commanded by authority.[5] Religion magnified that dynamic on an infinite scale. To obey divine command became the highest virtue, eclipsing conscience itself. The faithful could commit cruelty believing they fulfilled moral duty.

Control extended to knowledge. During the Middle Ages, the Catholic Church restricted access to scripture, allowing only clergy trained

4. Foucault, *Discipline and Punish*, 195–228.

5. Milgram, *Obedience to Authority*, 3–7.

in Latin to interpret it. The printing press, invented by Johannes Gutenberg in the fifteenth century, disrupted that monopoly, but resistance was fierce. To read sacred text in one's own language was, for centuries, a punishable act. Knowledge was dangerous because it weakened dependence. When Galileo Galilei used observation to argue that Earth moved around the sun, he was tried by the Inquisition and confined for life. Science threatened not heaven but hierarchy.

The same struggle surfaced in other traditions. During the Abbasid period of Islamic history, philosophers such as Averroes and al-Farabi defended reason against theological censorship. When their work questioned clerical authority, it was banned. In India, materialist thinkers who denied gods and an afterlife, were erased from mainstream teaching. Wherever inquiry competed with revelation, power sided with revelation.

Control does not depend only on law or punishment; it also depends on identity. Faith becomes part of family, culture, and moral vocabulary, so leaving it can feel like disloyalty rather than disagreement. Many regimes exploited that attachment. Dictators such as Franco and Mussolini used religious language and symbols to legitimize obedience, while officially secular systems like Stalin's Soviet Union substituted party figures for saints. The structure of devotion stayed in place; only its symbols changed.

Even in the modern world, control adapts. Political leaders still quote scripture to legitimize policy. Clerics broadcast uniform sermons through television and social media. Digital evangelists trade outrage for influence. The medium changes, but the motive endures.

Authority persists because it offers certainty. The believer knows their place, duty, and destiny. The institution provides the map, and the cost of deviation is eternal. For many, that trade feels safer than autonomy. To think independently is to stand alone before chaos. Religion promises relief from that exposure. It transforms the terror of freedom into the comfort of belonging.

Yet history shows that progress begins whenever that control weakens. The Enlightenment, the abolition of slavery, and the expansion of human rights all required defiance of divine sanction. When people realized that morality could be reasoned rather than decreed, authority lost its monopoly. Churches adapted by rebranding compassion as creed, but the foundation had already cracked.

Discipline shaped civilization, but it also limited its imagination. By tying moral worth to obedience, religion taught generations to measure goodness by conformity. The skeptic's path begins with reclaiming moral authorship. To live ethically without permission is to reject the architecture of control itself.

Religion once promised safety from the unknown. In practice, it built walls around the mind. The next step is to understand why those walls were so appealing—why comfort could feel safer than freedom itself.

Control did not end when temples fell or dogmas fractured; it simply moved inward. The priest outside became the voice within. After centuries of surveillance from heaven, believers learned to police their own thoughts. The structure of belief survived as the architecture of the mind. To understand religion's endurance, we must now look not at the power it imposed but at the comfort it provided—the quiet reassurance that even fear had purpose.

COMFORT OF CERTAINTY

Fear can unite a community, but it cannot sustain one forever. If religion had endured only through terror, its hold would have vanished long ago. What preserved it was the solace it supplied—the assurance that existence, however harsh, was ruled by purpose. Conviction became the antidote to dread.

Psychologists describe this impulse as the need for cognitive closure.[6] When faced with ambiguity, the mind prefers a clear answer to an accurate one. Early cosmologies offered closure at every scale: why the sun rose, why crops failed, why people suffered and died. Mystery became bearable once assigned intention. If tragedy was divine punishment, at least it carried meaning. Randomness was intolerable.

Research in the psychology of religion shows how deeply this preference shapes perception. Studies find that individuals with low tolerance for uncertainty tend to hold more rigid worldviews. A 2019 Pew survey reported that people who describe their faith as "certain" experience higher emotional well-being than those who admit doubt, even when both face similar hardships.[7] The comfort lies not in truth but in conviction.

6. Kruglanski, *Motivated Social Cognition*, 337–40.

7. Pew Research Center, "Religion, Certainty, and Emotional Well-Being," 2019.

I used to envy people who spoke about God with unshakable confidence. Their certainty looked like peace. I didn't know then that peace built on fear was just another kind of prison.

This dynamic is easy to see in ordinary life. Picture a hospital waiting room. One person sits in anxious silence; another bows in prayer. Both face the same unknown, yet the one who believes feels anchored. The prayer does not alter the outcome but offers a framework for helplessness. Belief feels like participation in fate rather than surrender to it. Even loss can be absorbed when given a purpose.

Religion perfected this emotional economy. It promised that no event was wasted and no suffering was random. Death—the most terrifying mystery—was reframed as transition. The grieving were told their loved ones had "gone to a better place." The phrase comforts because it transforms finality into continuity. Faith softens the edges of reality.

Sociologist Émile Durkheim argued that religion functions as the moral glue of society.[8] It replaces chaos with collective purpose. Shared conviction organizes not only behavior but emotion. Those who worship together experience what he called "collective effervescence," a surge of belonging that reassures them they are part of something larger. The result is not only social order but psychological relief.

Belief also supplies a sense of identity that feels immovable. In a world of shifting loyalties and uncertain futures, a creed can seem like solid ground. The believer knows where they came from, what they must do, and where they are going. That coherence is emotionally potent. It explains why conversion brings calm and why doubt can feel like vertigo. Losing faith does not merely unsettle ideas; it unravels the story that once held them together.

Theologians have long understood this function, though they often present it as virtue. Blaise Pascal argued that belief was safer than skepticism because faith protected the soul from despair. "The heart has its reasons," he wrote, suggesting that conviction, even without evidence, satisfies a psychological need. Modern neuroscience echoes that insight: brain imaging shows that religious experiences activate regions linked to reward and emotional regulation. Feeling loved by God releases the same chemical comfort as human affection.

But comfort has its price. Once an idea provides peace, it resists correction. When conviction becomes protection, questioning feels like

8. Durkheim, *The Elementary Forms of Religious Life*, 217–23.

harm. The mind defends its equilibrium by rejecting conflicting evidence. Cognitive dissonance studies show that people confronted with challenges to their worldview often grow more entrenched, not less. Belief becomes armor. The safety it provides makes it difficult to abandon, even when logic demands it.

Religious leaders throughout history have exploited this tendency. The promise of absolute truth is powerful precisely because it cannot be disproved within its own system. Doubt becomes sin; inquiry becomes pride. The believer is taught that uncertainty itself is a moral failure. This inversion shields authority from scrutiny.

Moral simplicity adds another layer of appeal. Difficult ethical questions become easier when reduced to clear categories of right and wrong, saved and damned, permitted and forbidden. Instead of weighing consequences or context, individuals follow prescribed rules. For someone fatigued by uncertainty, this offers relief. Being told what is good removes the responsibility of deciding for oneself.

That longing for clarity explains why revivals flourish in times of upheaval. When economies collapse or wars erupt, people turn toward institutions that promise order. History shows that devotion and crisis rise together. After the Black Death, apocalyptic sects spread across Europe. During the turmoil of the twentieth century, authoritarian movements borrowed the language of salvation to restore national confidence. The human mind mistakes conviction for truth even when conviction is performance.

Secular ideologies can exploit the same reflex. Political cults, conspiracies, and personality movements use identical tactics. They provide a villain, a cause, and the satisfaction of belonging to those who "know." When belief detaches from evidence, it becomes narcotic. It soothes even as it blinds.

Science offers no such comfort. It advances through revision and treats knowledge as provisional. For those raised on revelation, this openness can feel like a loss of certainty. Yet giving up false certainty marks the beginning of intellectual maturity. Living with uncertainty does not mean living without meaning; it means living without illusion. Skepticism does not dismiss wonder but accepts responsibility for how it is understood.

The reassurance once found in faith explains religion's endurance, but it also defines its limit. What soothes the spirit can dull the intellect. Progress depends on those willing to trade ease for clarity. Their unease, not their serenity, moved the world forward.

To understand this inheritance is to see doubt not as fracture but as growth. Safety may bring calm, but truth demands courage. The skeptic's task is to exchange consolation for coherence—and to discover that the trade, once made, was freedom all along.

DOUBT AS EVOLUTION, NOT REBELLION

Doubt is often described as weakness, yet history shows it to be a turning point in every age of discovery. To question is not to destroy but to evolve. Humanity's long struggle with uncertainty has been less a war against belief than a gradual redefinition of courage. Where faith once demanded obedience, reason began to demand honesty.

The story of doubt begins with small acts of defiance that changed the world. When the Greek philosopher Socrates urged his students to examine every assumption, Athens condemned him for corrupting youth. His crime was not disbelief but inquiry. By teaching that the unexamined life was unworthy of a rational being, he placed truth above tradition. That shift—from acceptance to analysis—became the foundation of philosophy itself.

Centuries later, the mathematician and astronomer Galileo looked through a telescope and saw moons orbiting Jupiter. The observation contradicted church doctrine that placed Earth at the center of creation. Galileo's decision to trust evidence over authority marked the birth of modern science. The Church silenced him, but his defiance seeded a new method: knowledge earned through observation rather than revelation. Doubt turned the heavens from sacred symbol to physical reality.

Even disbelief shapes belief. Each surge of skepticism compels theology to refine itself—to shed its cruder certainties and adapt to new knowledge. Doubt acts as an unseen editor, forcing faith to clarify its logic and evolve its metaphors. When science erodes literal explanations, religion often responds not with extinction but with reinvention: God becomes less a maker in the sky than a symbol of origin or order. In this way, nonbelief becomes faith's most honest collaborator, keeping the sacred from stagnation by requiring it to think.

The pattern is visible even within the largest religious institutions. In 2014, Pope Francis told the Pontifical Academy of Sciences that evolution and the Big Bang were real and compatible with creation.[9] It was

9. Francis, Address to the Pontifical Academy of Sciences, October 27, 2014.

less revelation than revision—faith learning to speak the language of evidence to remain heard. Such moments reveal how religion endures not by resisting knowledge but by translating itself into metaphor whenever fact prevails.

History repeats the same pattern across disciplines. When Charles Darwin published *On the Origin of Species* in 1859, he dismantled the comfort of divine design with a theory of natural selection. His idea arose not from rebellion but from patience; the accumulation of data that refused to fit scripture. Darwin's doubt required more faith in evidence than in certainty. It asked readers to accept that complexity could emerge from simplicity, that order could arise without intention. For many, this was the first credible alternative to creation.

The Egyptian philosopher Hypatia, who taught mathematics and astronomy in the fourth century, also embodied this evolution of thought. She defended reason against the growing dogmatism of her time and was murdered by a mob that saw learning as blasphemy. Her death revealed what happens when faith feels threatened by curiosity: the loss of both wisdom and compassion. Doubt may unsettle belief, but suppression destroys the civilization that depends on free minds.

Psychology helps explain why doubt feels dangerous. Belief systems function like emotional ecosystems; every conviction supports another. When one root loosens, the whole structure trembles. People often describe deconversion as grief, not liberation, because it dismantles the language of meaning itself. Yet such crises also mark growth. Studies in cognitive development show that the ability to hold conflicting ideas without immediate resolution is a sign of maturity. To doubt is to tolerate complexity rather than retreat into simplicity.

Cultural progress follows the same rhythm. Every moral reform began as a heresy. Abolitionists defied scripture that justified slavery. Feminists challenged patriarchal readings of sacred texts. Human rights advocates rejected divine hierarchy in favor of shared dignity. Each step forward required courage to claim that morality could evolve beyond revelation. Doubt, in this sense, was conscience awakening.

Philosophers from David Hume to Bertrand Russell treated skepticism as a discipline rather than a defect. Hume warned that certainty breeds arrogance, while Russell observed that "the whole problem with the world is that fools and fanatics are always so certain, and wiser people so full of doubts."[10] Their message was not nihilism but humility. Doubt recognizes limits without surrendering curiosity. It replaces confession with inquiry, prayer with experiment, and revelation with conversation.

Personal experience often follows this historical pattern. Leaving belief rarely feels triumphant; it feels exposed. Practices that once structured daily life no longer guide decisions, and familiar explanations lose their authority. That uncertainty marks the beginning of independence. The first night without prayer is not a loss but a transition. Instead of petition, there is quiet reflection, and in that quiet the mind begins to reason without reliance on external assurance.

Education performs a similar transformation on a collective scale. The expansion of literacy, the invention of the printing press, and the rise of public schooling weakened the monopoly of priests and monarchs. Each innovation gave ordinary people access to competing ideas. The Reformation, the Enlightenment, and the scientific revolution all shared a single catalyst: the ordinary citizen learning to say "show me." Once that phrase enters a culture, authority can no longer dictate truth; it must demonstrate it.

Even within modern religion, doubt can serve a corrective function. Theologians who acknowledge uncertainty often produce interpretations that endure longer than rigid claims. Belief that survives scrutiny tends to rely less on command and more on interpretation. There is, however, a limit to reinterpretation. When doctrine requires the dismissal of evidence, it ceases to function as faith and instead operates as ideology. Inquiry cannot continue where questioning is forbidden.

Viewed this way, skepticism is not rebellion but adaptation. It reflects the mind's effort to reconcile intuition with observation and comfort with coherence. Every major scientific advance, moral reform, and expansion of equality began with someone willing to question an accepted claim. Human progress advances through revision rather than revelation.

The skeptic's path continues this lineage. To question inherited claims is to participate in the process by which understanding changes over time. Explanations that once offered protection now require either careful reinterpretation or abandonment. Doubt does not eliminate meaning; it allows meaning to develop under scrutiny.

10. Russell, "The Triumph of Stupidity," in *Mortals and Others*, vol. 1, 1931.

Contemporary unbelief is typically quiet rather than confrontational. It does not organize itself in opposition to religion; it proceeds without reference to it. Meaning shifts from scripture to lived experience, from divine command to shared human reasoning. What was once labeled heresy has, in many contexts, become ordinary ethical behavior that no longer requires justification.

The next question is what follows after doubt has done its work. If disbelief removes the older framework of certainty, what replaces it? The answer lies in accepting responsibility: the willingness to live without guarantees and to pursue purpose in conditions that offer no final assurances.

COURAGE TO LIVE WITHOUT GUARANTEES

The final test of doubt is not intellectual but emotional. To abandon belief is to face a universe that offers no promises. There are no divine contracts, no cosmic safety nets, no assurances that justice will prevail or that suffering will be redeemed. The resolve to live without promises marks the skeptic's true maturity. It is the moment when comfort yields to honesty and the need for meaning becomes the task of creating it.

For most of history, religion offered protection from this exposure. It promised that goodness would be rewarded and evil punished, if not in this world then in the next. Without that promise, morality can seem riskier, compassion less profitable. Yet evidence from modern societies suggests the opposite. Studies of secular nations, particularly in northern Europe, show that citizens who do not believe in an afterlife often report higher happiness, trust, and equality than those who do. The sociologist Phil Zuckerman, who studied life in Denmark and Sweden, found that nonreligious populations consistently rank among the highest in life satisfaction and civic responsibility.[11] Morality, it turns out, thrives not because of divine oversight but because of human empathy.

These findings challenge the old assumption that goodness requires supervision. In reality, cooperation predates religion by millennia. Evolutionary biology shows that altruism appears even among species with no concept of gods or punishment. Primates share food, dolphins protect wounded companions, and elephants grieve their dead. The roots of

11. Zuckerman, *Society Without God*, 94–98.

ethics lie not in theology but in biology. The religious narrative co-opted those instincts and claimed them as commandments.

When belief fades, those instincts remain. People help others because suffering is visible and empathy is real. They build communities because connection is survival. The skeptic's task is to recognize that compassion needs no celestial endorsement. To act kindly without reward is a purer morality than any born of fear.

Living without guarantees also reshapes the idea of purpose. In the absence of divine design, life becomes self-authored. The meaning of existence is not given but made. Artists, scientists, and reformers embody this freedom daily. They work without assurance of success, guided by curiosity rather than decree. The scientist does not know if an experiment will succeed, yet proceeds because understanding itself is worthy. The artist paints not for immortality but for expression. The humanitarian risks failure but acts because suffering demands response. Each of these choices mirrors the courage to live without eternal validation.

The existentialists of the twentieth century wrestled with this condition directly. Jean-Paul Sartre argued that without God, humanity is condemned to be free—responsible for everything it creates and everything it ignores. Albert Camus described life as absurd precisely because it offers no guaranteed meaning, only the possibility of making one. For Camus, rebellion meant embracing that absurdity with dignity and finding beauty in effort rather than reward. The courage to live without guarantees is the rebellion he described.

Religion often portrays such independence as despair, but the opposite is true. Freedom from divine control does not empty life; it fills it with responsibility. A universe without built-in meaning is not void—it is open. Moral and creative possibilities expand when no scripture limits them. To accept this condition is to stop searching for a perfect plan and start building an imperfect one together.

Steadfastness also means accepting loss without consolation. The death of a loved one, the failure of justice, the randomness of disaster—these moments expose the raw truth of existence. Belief offers comfort through narrative: that suffering will be redeemed, that reunions await beyond the grave. Skepticism offers no such promise. Yet grief unsoftened by illusion can deepen compassion. When the finality of life is accepted, each moment becomes more precious. Mourning need not be diminished by myth to be meaningful.

Living without guarantees requires communities of conscience rather than congregations of faith. Secular humanist organizations, ethical societies, and volunteer networks show that belonging does not depend on shared doctrine. The bond of empathy replaces the bond of creed. In these circles, gratitude rises not toward heaven but toward one another. The sacred becomes relational, not supernatural.

Courage, in this sense, is not defiance for its own sake. It is endurance without reward. It is the decision to act morally even when no one is watching, to seek truth even when it offers no comfort, and to hope even when the universe is silent. The skeptic does not kneel before mystery but stands within it, accepting its scale without surrendering agency.

This form of fortitude may be quieter than faith, but it is stronger. It endures not through promise but through perseverance. It asks nothing from the cosmos and gives everything to the world. The believer seeks meaning in revelation; the skeptic builds it in relationship, discovery, and work. Each act of kindness, each pursuit of knowledge, each defense of reason becomes an offering to the only future we can trust—the one we make.

To live without guarantees is to see life as it is: uncertain, fragile, and brief, yet filled with possibility. The same courage that once built temples can build understanding. The same awe that once imagined heaven can honor the beauty of the real. The next section turns toward that reconstruction, exploring how meaning, wonder, and moral responsibility survive—and even flourish—once belief is gone.

ETHICS OF UNCERTAINTY

When belief fades, morality must find a new foundation. For centuries, religion claimed to own ethics, insisting that right and wrong were revealed from above rather than reasoned from experience. Without divine decree, many fear that morality will collapse into chaos. Yet history shows that ethical progress often advances most rapidly when humanity relies on conscience rather than commandment. Uncertainty did not destroy morality; it refined it.

The philosopher David Hume argued that moral behavior arises from sympathy, not scripture.[12] Our sense of right and wrong, he said, comes from recognizing another's suffering. Modern neuroscience supports his intuition. Studies of mirror neurons show that empathy is a

12. Hume, *An Enquiry Concerning the Principles of Morals*, 17–23.

biological response, not a learned ritual. We flinch when we see another in pain because we are built to respond. Conscience, in this light, is not supernatural—it is social.

The idea that morality could exist without religion matured during the Enlightenment. Thinkers such as Immanuel Kant, John Stuart Mill, and Mary Wollstonecraft sought universal principles grounded in reason. Kant proposed that moral duty should arise from rational consistency: one should act only according to rules that could be willed universally. Mill measured goodness by its capacity to increase well-being and reduce harm. Wollstonecraft extended these ideas to gender equality, insisting that virtue must include women's autonomy or it was not virtue at all. Each of these thinkers built ethics from logic and empathy rather than revelation.

Evidence of moral evolution appears throughout history. The abolition of slavery, the recognition of human rights, and movements for civil equality all required defiance of religious authority. For centuries, churches justified bondage with scripture. When abolitionists prevailed, they did so by appealing to reason and shared humanity, not to new interpretations of ancient texts. The same pattern held for women's rights and for the recognition of same-sex relationships. Each reform began as a moral argument against divine sanction and ended as a human consensus grounded in fairness.

Sociological data reinforces this trend. Nations with higher levels of secularism often score better on measures of gender equality, education, and freedom of expression. Trust and cooperation do not vanish when faith declines; they adapt to new frameworks. Social contracts, democratic institutions, and human rights laws replace commandments carved in stone. Accountability shifts from invisible judgment to collective responsibility.

Living ethically without assurance requires humility. Religious systems supply answers in advance; reason must earn them through dialogue. In a world guided by evidence, moral claims remain open to revision. This flexibility is not weakness—it is the strength of a system that can learn. When medicine overturns old taboos or psychology reveals new insights about harm, a secular ethic can adapt. A revealed ethic cannot.

Ambiguity also nurtures compassion. When no one possesses ultimate truth, tolerance becomes necessity. Diversity of thought is not a threat but a resource. The philosopher Karl Popper described this as the open society—a culture that allows ideas to compete without coercion.[13] In such a world, progress depends on the ability to change one's mind. Dogma, whether religious or political, freezes that process. The ethics of uncertainty guard against the arrogance of infallibility.

Practical morality grows from this recognition. Honesty, fairness, and empathy are not sacred decrees; they are agreements that sustain coexistence. Evolutionary psychology describes them as reciprocal strategies that enable groups to thrive. Communities that valued cooperation survived more often than those that prized dominance. Over time, kindness became adaptive. The survival of the compassionate disproves the myth that morality requires a divine overseer.

This understanding transforms moral responsibility. If goodness is not commanded, it must be chosen. The atheist who rescues a stranger acts without hope of heavenly reward. The skeptic who defends justice does so because injustice is visible, not because a verse condemns it. Morality divorced from belief becomes more accountable. Actions must stand on their own merit, justified by their outcomes rather than by faith.

The ethics of uncertainty also change how we view failure. In a religious system, error can mean sin and punishment. In a secular framework, error becomes instruction. Science thrives by admitting mistakes; so can morality. Each generation inherits not commandments but questions, refining its answers through experience. That process is slower than revelation but more honest.

Art and literature often reveal this evolution more vividly than theology. The novels of George Eliot, the plays of Henrik Ibsen, and the essays of James Baldwin all wrestle with integrity in a world without divine authority. Their characters fail, doubt, and grow. They show that morality, when freed from fear, becomes exploration. The measure of goodness shifts from obedience to understanding.

Uncertainty is not a threat to ethics; it is a prerequisite. The willingness to question, revise, and consider alternative perspectives are moral acts as much as intellectual ones. A society guided by evidence rather than decree must cultivate empathy with the same discipline it applies to reason. Awareness of our limitations increases, rather than weakens, responsible action.

Faith seeks final answers; skepticism accepts ongoing evaluation. Between them lies the moral maturity of a species learning to govern itself. To

13. Popper, *The Open Society and Its Enemies*, 1:xi–xv.

live ethically without certainty is to accept that no revelation will intervene on our behalf. Our survival and our decency depend on the same fact: in a universe without guarantees, kindness must be chosen deliberately.

Years after leaving belief behind, I stood alone beneath a clear desert sky. I had gone there to step away from certainty, both my own and that of others. Without prayer or expectation, I watched the stars emerge, each older than any belief I had once held. The sense of calm I felt was familiar, but its source was no longer attributed to anything beyond the moment itself. It required no explanation. For the first time, wonder felt grounded in reality rather than belief.

AWE WITHOUT A MASTER

When belief fades, many fear that wonder will fade with it. If no gods exist, what remains to inspire reverence? For centuries, religion claimed ownership of awe, defining it as the natural response to divine power. To stand in a temple, cathedral, or mosque was to feel small before the infinite. Without that architecture, people worry that the sacred disappears. Yet wonder does not depend on belief; it depends on awareness.

Carl Sagan once called science "a profound source of spirituality," not because it confirms faith but because it magnifies scale. Through a telescope, the sky becomes vast enough to humble pride without invoking heaven. The Pale Blue Dot image of Earth, taken by the Voyager 1 spacecraft from nearly four billion miles away, reveals the same truth religion once promised but rarely delivered: that we are small, connected, and responsible for one another.[14] The feeling is ancient, though the explanation has changed.

Human wonder long predates scripture. Before temples rose, people gathered around firelight and watched meteors trace the night. The first myths were attempts to preserve that wonder, to give the unknown a name. What began as storytelling became theology; what began as astonishment became obedience. To reclaim reverence without worship is to return to the moment before explanation hardened into law.

Science restores that original wonder by replacing mystery with magnitude. The physicist's universe is larger, stranger, and more intricate than any sacred text imagined. The age of the cosmos, the birth of galaxies, and the evolution of life through countless generations reveal a

14. Sagan, *Pale Blue Dot*, 6–9.

grandeur untouched by intention. The biologist's microscope uncovers beauty that theology never described: the geometry of a snowflake, the architecture of a single cell, the choreography of DNA translating itself into being. Understanding multiplies wonder rather than reducing it.

One well-documented experiment demonstrates how readily the human brain can generate experiences traditionally attributed to divine presence. In 1962, during a Good Friday service at Boston University's Marsh Chapel, psychologist Walter Pahnke administered psilocybin to a group of theology students, while a control group received a placebo. All participants attended the same service, heard the same prayers, and shared the same religious expectations. The only variable was the chemical state of the brain.

Students who received psilocybin reported intense religious experiences, including feelings of unity, transcendence, and direct encounters with God. Those who received the placebo reported no such effects, describing the service as emotionally ordinary. Because the environment and religious context were identical, the difference in experience cannot be attributed to worship or revelation. It can only be attributed to changes in brain chemistry.

The experiences were subjectively real, but their source was neurological rather than supernatural. What had long been taken as evidence of divine contact was shown to be reproducible through physiological means. The experiment does not explain away belief, but it does explain how such beliefs arise. Experiences once understood as external revelation can be generated entirely within the human brain.

Reverence is not proof of God; it is proof that consciousness can exceed comprehension. To look through the Webb telescope or into the deep ocean is to meet mystery on its own terms, without the need for mythology. In this sense, secular wonder is purer than its religious counterpart. It does not require belief in an invisible mind behind creation; it requires gratitude for existing at all. The poet's astonishment at a sunrise and the physicists at a supernova belong to the same lineage of curiosity. Both express devotion to reality itself.

Psychologists studying emotion describe wonder as a self-transcendent state that reduces selfishness and increases cooperation. Experiments at the University of California, Berkeley, found that participants who experienced that feeling—by viewing panoramic landscapes or images of space—were more likely to help others immediately afterward. The sense of vastness diminishes ego and enhances empathy. In this way, wonder replaces commandment with connection. It binds people not to a deity but to one another.

The arts continue this function in secular culture. Music, painting, and literature invite the same surrender once found in prayer. A symphony can expand emotion until it feels like revelation. A novel can draw a reader into empathy deeper than any sermon. When creativity is seen as collaboration with the world rather than imitation of God, the sacred reappears in human form. The cathedral becomes a museum, the liturgy a poem, the miracle an equation that works.

Nature, too, remains a temple without walls. To watch a thunderstorm roll across the desert or a whale rise through the surface of the sea requires no doctrine. The power of the experience lies in its immediacy. There is no moral hidden within it, no message from beyond. The universe does not speak; it exists. The silence that once frightened believers becomes the music of what is real.

Some argue that science strips life of mystery by explaining it, but explanation does not end wonder. To understand that lightning is electricity or that rainbows are refraction does not make them less beautiful. Knowledge deepens appreciation because it reveals structure where once there was only superstition. The myth says lightning is divine anger; the physicist sees plasma arcing through air. One demands obedience; the other invites curiosity. Both inspire awe, but only one leaves us freer.

Secular reverence also redefines humility. In religious tradition, humility often means submission. In scientific and artistic tradition, it means perspective. To recognize one's smallness within an indifferent cosmos is not humiliation; it is honesty. From that honesty grows responsibility. If there is no external savior, then preservation of life depends on us. Environmental care, humanitarian work, and the pursuit of knowledge all arise from the same realization: reverence for existence is measured by care for it.

Awe without a master invites gratitude without servitude. It transforms the question "Who made this?" into "How does this work?" and "How can we protect it?" It replaces faith with participation. In this view, the sacred is not something to worship but something to preserve. The seas, the forests, and the fragile balance of ecosystems all carry the weight once assigned to heaven.

The skeptic's awe does not end in disbelief but in devotion of another kind. It honors the improbable fact of being here at all. In the absence of divine authorship, existence becomes even more extraordinary. Out of blind matter and chance, consciousness arose to contemplate its own origins. The stars produced the atoms that now look back at them. No revelation could make that more miraculous.

To feel awe without a master is to stand unshielded before reality and still call it beautiful. It is to accept that mystery remains even when myths are gone. The next and final step is to understand how that wonder leads to purpose—how meaning, once untethered from metaphysics, can still hold. That is where the skeptic's path ends: in the making of meaning itself.

Nonbelief today is less a crisis than an evolution. People are not leaving faith for despair but for honesty. They gather for discussion, for art, for acts of kindness—rituals of a new kind, grounded in empathy instead of eternity. The sacred has moved from the altar to the everyday.

THE SKEPTIC'S PATH FORWARD

The journey from devotion to doubt does not end with rejection. It ends with arrival—an awakening to life unfiltered by promise or punishment. What begins as defiance matures into clarity. The gods fall silent, yet the world grows louder, filled with its own meanings waiting to be found.

Fear played a central role in the rise of religious belief and the institutions that followed. What began as a search for safety gradually became systems of authority that enforced obedience. These systems promised certainty and peace, but they relied on belief rather than evidence. Over time, questioning those claims weakened their hold. As divine command lost authority, individual judgment gained it. Obedience gave way to inquiry, and explanations based on superstition were replaced by explanations grounded in understanding. The skeptic inherits this tradition not as an act of rebellion, but as an acceptance of responsibility for reasoning and moral choice.

To live without religion is not to live without values. It is to locate them where they have always belonged—in empathy, honesty, and shared need. The nonbeliever who acts with compassion is not imitating the faithful; they are rediscovering what it means to be human. Conscience survives because it was never dependent on revelation. Morality is not a remnant of faith but a continuation of evolution.

This path requires effort. Accepting ready-made answers is easier than examining evidence, just as comfort is easier than uncertainty. But reasoning carries lasting benefits. Ethics grounded in understanding can adapt as knowledge grows, rather than remaining fixed by command. Wonder based on knowledge does not disappear when explanations improve; it becomes more informed and more durable. The skeptic learns to question without bitterness and to care without relying on false certainty.

Meaning does not disappear when belief fades. It shifts from external destiny to personal intention. Purpose becomes something people construct rather than receive. It takes shape in relationships, in learning, and in deliberate acts of care toward others. The believer looks to prayer for direction; the skeptic takes responsibility for choosing it. Both seek connection, but one relies on belief while the other relies on action.

To question is to accept the burden of authorship. Without divine plan, every choice becomes part of the story we write together. The universe offers no guarantee that justice will prevail or that truth will triumph, yet it allows the possibility that they might—if we choose them. That possibility is enough. The absence of assurance is not a curse but an invitation.

Skepticism asks for humility before evidence and courage before the void. It offers no salvation, only honesty. The cost of that honesty is the loss of certainty, but the reward is a life lived awake. The seeker does not kneel before mystery; they walk through it, taking nothing on faith and leaving nothing unquestioned.

The future of morality, art, and science depends on that kind of courage. As knowledge expands and technology gains new power, the temptation to replace old gods with new idols—ideologies, algorithms, or charismatic leaders—will return. The lesson of doubt must not be forgotten: every authority, sacred or secular, must answer to reason and compassion alike. To abandon that vigilance is to rebuild the very temples we once escaped.

The skeptic's path is not lonely. It is shared by those who find meaning in curiosity, in creativity, and in kindness that expects nothing in return. It unites scientists and poets, rationalists and humanists, anyone who believes that truth matters more than comfort. Its rituals are dialogue, its hymns curiosity, its prayer the quiet act of noticing.

The end of belief is not the end of wonder. It is the beginning of understanding that awe, morality, and purpose are human achievements, not divine gifts. To walk this path is to accept the world as it is and still choose to make it better. Faith once promised safety; reason offers truth—and asks us to be brave enough to live with it. The honesty to live without gods is only the beginning; what follows is learning how to live with ourselves.

9

Making Meaning After God

"Meaning is not given to life, but made of it."

Rebecca Goldstein

SILENCE AFTER GOD

To walk this path is to accept the world as it is and still choose to make it better. Faith once promised safety; reason offers truth and asks us to be brave enough to live with it.

Standing alone in the kitchen one morning, the house still dark, I waited out of habit for a thought to turn into prayer.

After that, what follows is quieter. Ritual recedes, along with the authority that once dictated belief and hope. What remains is not emptiness but openness. As reliance on the divine diminishes, the mind turns to questions it once deferred: how to live, what to value, and what gives a life significance. Meaning is no longer assigned from outside; it becomes a human responsibility.

At first, the silence can feel like loss. Prayer once offered a framework for comfort and grief, and when it ends, nothing immediately replaces it. There is no sudden insight, only the recognition that a familiar structure is gone. For a time, the world can feel less secure rather than freer, as the sense of oversight that once accompanied belief fades. Yet what initially feels like absence becomes opportunity. The same silence that unsettles belief allows inquiry to continue without restriction. Meaning is no longer granted by authority; it must be built. In that process, seriousness and care do not disappear, but take on a different shape.

Over time, the quiet takes on a different character. Mornings once marked by prayer become moments of awareness: ordinary sounds, pauses between thoughts, changes in light. The mind, no longer oriented toward petition, begins to observe more closely. Attention replaces devotion. Gratitude remains, but it is no longer directed toward a higher source. It is directed toward the simple fact of existence itself.

History shows that disbelief often precedes renewal. When the Greek philosopher Epicurus denied divine punishment, he sought not chaos but peace of mind.[1] By freeing ethics from fear, he made happiness a human responsibility. Centuries later, the Dutch philosopher Baruch Spinoza, excommunicated for his unorthodox views, described God not as a person but as nature itself—an infinite system that included us within it.[2] His vision erased the boundary between sacred and real. What religion had divided, thought rejoined.

That same pattern repeats whenever authority recedes and imagination expands. Artists, scientists, and humanists step into the quiet left by gods, not to replace them but to explore what remains when myth withdraws. Their work is a lived reply to a question belief once monopolized: how to build a life worth defending.

Silence after faith also invites honesty. Without divine witnesses, morality must justify itself. Compassion can no longer depend on reward, nor cruelty be excused by command. The absence of celestial oversight turns ethics inward, asking whether decency can endure without surveillance. The evidence says it can. Cooperation, generosity, and care predate religion and survive its decline. The end of worship does not erase conscience; it exposes its origin.

To stand in this new quiet is to hear the world again. Wind through trees, the hum of cities, the pulse of one's own body—sounds once muffled by ritual return as reminders of belonging. The sacred does not vanish; it changes address. It moves from heaven to here.

The quiet after belief is not emptiness, but a shift in orientation. It marks the point at which meaning is no longer assumed but deliberately examined. What may first feel like isolation becomes involvement—the recognition that we are not positioned outside the world, but fully

1. Epicurus, *Letter to Menoeceus*, 123–27.

2. Spinoza, *Ethics*, pt. 1.

embedded within it. The question is no longer whether life can be lived without faith, but how to live intentionally without it, and which commitments deserve our time, care, and loyalty.

THE COST OF HONESTY

Honesty carries costs that are often underestimated. Letting go of belief does not initially feel like relief. It more often produces disorientation. For years, faith provided a framework for fear and a structure for uncertainty. Even when its answers were inadequate, they were still answers. To give them up is to enter a world that offers no immediate reassurance and no transition designed for comfort.

The grief arrives quietly. It appears in moments that rarely enter formal arguments or essays. I noticed it when old habits surfaced without intention, such as the urge to pray while waiting for medical results or the impulse to ask for protection before a long drive. These moments were not evidence of lingering belief. They reflected how thoroughly religious language and practice had been embedded in daily life. I did not miss doctrine. I missed the sense that someone was listening. That absence showed itself in ordinary routines: bowing my head before meals, or pausing before sleep when words once came automatically. The practices endured long after the beliefs that supported them had disappeared. What felt at first like a private loss revealed itself as a structural pattern—one that often emerges when belief yields to candor.

Losing belief also meant losing a familiar form of belonging. Faith had provided a ready-made community and a shared language for fear and hope. Without it, I had to learn how to remain present among people who still found comfort in religious ritual and promise. I had to accept that doubt, even when grounded in reason, can still feel isolating. Understanding may move ahead of conviction, but emotional attachment often adjusts more slowly, uncertain about where trust should now rest.

I felt this most clearly in small, public moments. When someone said to another person, "We'll keep you in our prayers," I heard it from the outside, no longer included in the exchange. At meals, heads would bow, and I would follow the motion without the words, watching the others to see whether the ritual reflected conviction or simple conformity, much as my own participation did. My silence marked a difference I could not easily explain without creating discomfort. Nothing hostile was said. Nothing needed to be. Belonging had taken on conditions I no longer met.

There is also the burden of responsibility. When belief ended, I realized how often I had relied on it to confirm my choices or soften my mistakes. Without a divine witness to appeal to, every decision became an act of authorship. There was no higher court to bless the outcome. The freedom was real, but so was the weight. Morality survived the loss of commandment, yet it required more of me than obedience ever had. I could no longer defer to a promise of cosmic justice. I had to decide what justice looked like in my own hands.

Over time, this honesty produced a different kind of stability. Once the inherited framework fell away, it became clear that meaning had not vanished. It had changed. The world did not become smaller without God; it became more open. What initially felt like loss turned out to be the absence of imposed answers. Understanding that took time. The quiet after belief is not a conclusion but a transition. It does not offer certainty, but it requires resolve.

This cost of honesty is not a failure. It reflects psychological adjustment. The unease that follows the loss of belief marks the mind's movement toward independence. It is a temporary instability that occurs when external guidance is removed and responsibility shifts inward. What once felt like abandonment becomes the beginning of self-direction.

This is where the next phase begins. As grief recedes and inherited habits lose their force, a new orientation takes shape. It does not arise from revelation but from recognition: that meaning can be generated through human judgment, relationship, and care. With that recognition, the strain of honesty gives way to clarity. The central question is no longer what the world requires of us, but what we are prepared to create within it.

THE PROBLEM OF SILENCE

There is another part of leaving faith that is quieter than grief and harder to put into words. It is the slow realization that the silence itself has meaning. Many people imagine that unbelief begins in resistance, but often it begins in sincerity. We search honestly. We ask for guidance. We pray because we hope someone is listening. When no answer comes, we call it mystery. When the silence continues, we tell ourselves to have patience. Only later do we recognize that the quiet behaves the same whether we hope or despair, whether we reach for reassurance or try to stand on reason alone.

This is the core of the problem. If a loving God existed and wished to be known, openness would be enough. A sincere seeker would not be left in confusion. A parent does not hide from a child who calls out. Yet in the world as we find it, the devout and the doubter inhabit the same silence. The sky does not answer more readily to one than the other. The silence does not change with belief. It does not distinguish between reverence and uncertainty. It feels less like a veiled presence and more like the natural sound of a world that has no voice to give.

During the years when I tried to hold on to belief, I was not struggling against God. I was reaching for God. I asked for clarity. I asked for comfort. I asked for the smallest sign that someone stood on the other side of my questions. What I encountered was not rejection but something far more ordinary. It was the steady quiet of a reality that does not respond. At some point, I had to acknowledge that this was not a test of faith. It was simply the nature of things.

Believers sometimes explain the silence by saying that God hides in order to strengthen trust. But this reframes absence as intention. In ordinary relationships, sustained silence does not deepen trust; it erodes it. We do not call a parent loving for refusing to answer a child who calls out in fear. By that standard, silence does not resemble care. It resembles distance.

Silence does not prove that God does not exist, but it directly challenges the idea of a personal God who desires connection. A being who wants relationship does not remain unreachable. A loving presence does not allow honest seekers to mistake silence for absence. The quiet of the world is not ambiguous. It behaves precisely as it would if no divine listener were there at all.

Accepting this truth can feel like a loss. It did for me. I wanted the silence to mean something. I wanted it to hide reassurance that I simply had not yet understood. But once I stopped trying to reinterpret the quiet, I could finally hear it clearly. The universe was not communicating in a code I had failed to crack.

Strangely, that recognition did not collapse meaning. It expanded it. Once the expectation of a reply fell away, the responsibility for purpose returned to us. We stop waiting for a voice that will never speak and begin listening to one another. What was once called mystery becomes honesty.

The absence of revelation becomes the presence of clarity. The quiet that once felt like abandonment becomes space for our own work to begin.

And that is where the next stage of understanding takes shape. Once we face the silence for what it is, we can ask what rises in the space that belief once filled. Meaning shifts from the divine to the human. The center of gravity moves inward and outward at the same time, toward the lives we build and the responsibilities we choose.

THE HUMAN CENTER

As belief in divinity diminishes, responsibility shifts to human judgment. The absence of a supervising power does not eliminate purpose; it relocates it. Meaning is no longer derived from command but developed through intention and action. Authority that was once attributed to external sources is now understood as a human capacity, raising the question of what individuals and societies can create without appeal to divine instruction.

Placing humanity at the center carries its own risks. When humans become their own reference point, confidence can drift into self-importance. Authority once attributed to gods can reappear in other forms, including ideology, nationalism, or uncritical faith in technology. Progress weakens when it separates knowledge from compassion, and expertise without ethical limits can reproduce the same harms it was meant to prevent. The central challenge of a godless age is not the absence of divinity, but the need to ensure that human judgment does not harden into arrogance. Self-direction requires restraint and responsibility, not domination.

Humanism began with this recognition. In Renaissance Europe, thinkers such as Erasmus and Montaigne turned from salvation to self-understanding. They wrote of dignity rather than depravity, of learning not to glorify God but to refine life itself. Centuries later, the Enlightenment extended that impulse into shared reason. Philosophers like Voltaire and Kant proposed that morality and progress could arise from inquiry rather than revelation. Their confidence in human capacity was radical precisely because it trusted people more than providence.

Modern humanism carries that legacy forward. It sees the species not as fallen but unfinished. Each discovery, each moral advance, extends the story we write together. The tasks once assigned to prophets now belong to educators, scientists, artists, and reformers. They pursue coherence and compassion through evidence and empathy, seeking participation instead of perfection.

This shift alters the moral landscape. When goodness no longer relies on decree, it must be earned through argument and lived through action. That responsibility can feel heavy, yet it dignifies every choice. To act kindly because one has reasoned it right, not feared it wrong, marks moral maturity. Philosopher Martha Nussbaum, a contemporary ethicist known for her work on emotion and moral psychology, calls this the fragility of goodness—ethics grounded in vulnerability rather than power.[3] Our limits give weight to care; our uncertainty makes integrity meaningful.

Human centrality also transforms the idea of progress. In theological history, time moved toward judgment or salvation; in a secular frame, it becomes an open horizon. Knowledge expands by revision, justice through debate, beauty through creation. Error becomes data, not sin. The moral universe still bends, but now we are the ones bending it.

Art makes this transition visible. The canvases of Rembrandt, the novels of George Eliot, the music of Beethoven—all reveal an awakening sense that beauty itself could replace worship. Each work transforms private emotion into shared insight, proving that transcendence can be crafted by human hands. Their legacies remind us that creation, when pursued for its own sake, is devotion in another form.

Science complements that artistry with understanding. It asks not *why* existence should be but *how* it works, and finds awe in the answer. Realizing that we are products of evolution and stardust does not diminish us; it situates us. To comprehend our origins is to inherit the universe as context, not confinement. In that awareness, humility and wonder coexist.

Our task, then, is to temper knowledge with empathy. The same intelligence that split the atom can heal disease; the same networks that spread deception can also unite strangers in rescue and reform. The measure of a civilization lies not in its inventions but in its intentions. To place humanity at the center is not to worship it, but to trust its potential—to believe that wisdom, though fallible, can grow through care as surely as through reason.

3. Nussbaum, *The Fragility of Goodness*, xiii–xv.

Shared purpose depends on shared understanding. As traditional religious narratives lose their influence, societies must develop new frameworks for meaning grounded in secular values such as progress, justice, and compassion. These frameworks will vary across cultures, but they must address the same basic question once answered by theology: how people ought to live together. The answer will not come from revelation, but from ongoing human relationships and social agreement. These issues are not abstract. They appear in everyday decisions, where meaning is no longer proclaimed in doctrine but expressed through action.

The next step is to ask how morality can endure when heaven no longer enforces it—how ethics survive when commandment gives way to conscience. That shift, however, remains incomplete wherever public authority continues to invoke divine sanction.

AUTHORITY WITHOUT DEFINITION

Even as belief declines, public institutions continue to invoke God as a moral reference point. The phrase "In God We Trust" appears on U.S. currency. Public officials often conclude oaths of office with "So help me God." Witnesses in court are commonly asked to swear truthfulness before God. The Pledge of Allegiance describes the nation as "under God." These practices persist despite the absence of any shared agreement about what that reference means.

I remember first noticing how casually these references appeared. The phrase "In God We Trust" passed through my hands every day on currency I used without thought. It was so familiar that it barely registered as a claim. Yet the more I examined belief itself, the stranger that familiarity became. Money is meant to function as a neutral instrument, trusted because of shared agreement, not shared theology. Seeing a declaration of faith embedded in something so universal made me pause. It raised a simple question I often asked myself but had rarely seen addressed in public life: trust in whom, and on whose behalf.

What unsettled me was not the presence of belief, but its invisibility. The phrase remained not because it had been examined and affirmed, but because it had been inherited and left unquestioned. As belief declined and pluralism increased, the words remained unchanged, even as the society using them did not.

Beyond that, many citizens follow other religions or none at all. In such a society, government cannot base its authority on a single moral or religious framework without favoring some beliefs over others. Public institutions must operate on principles that all citizens can evaluate, regardless of faith.

When civic language appeals to a god, it does not provide a shared foundation. It signals that public rules and obligations are grounded in beliefs that not everyone accepts. This undermines neutrality and weakens the credibility of governance in a pluralistic society.

Defenders of these practices often argue that such language is merely ceremonial. They claim that references to a god no longer express religious commitment but serve as historical tradition or cultural symbolism. However, symbolism does not lose significance simply because it is repeated. Public language shapes perceptions of legitimacy. When government repeatedly invokes a god, it implies that public authority remains connected to belief, even if that belief is undefined.

This ambiguity creates a structural problem. If a god is only a symbol, then the reference is unnecessary. If a god carries normative force, then the government is implicitly endorsing a theological position. Either interpretation conflicts with the principle of neutrality in governance. A secular system cannot rely on an undefined religious concept without undermining its own foundation.

Demographic change has made this tension more visible. A growing portion of the population identifies as nonreligious. Younger generations are even less likely to associate moral guidance with belief in a god. As this shift continues, religious language embedded in civic life increasingly reflects past assumptions rather than present consensus. What once appeared universal now functions as a marker of historical inertia.

The persistence of religious references in government also complicates moral reasoning. When justice is framed as accountable to a higher power, responsibility can appear external rather than human. Ethical decisions risk being justified by appeal to belief rather than by argument, evidence, or consequence. This weakens public accountability. Decisions should be defensible to citizens as citizens, not as members of a particular faith.

A pluralistic society requires a moral framework that does not depend on theological agreement. Laws must be justified by their effects on well-being, fairness, and rights, not by alignment with religious tradition. Removing religious references from civic institutions does not eliminate moral seriousness. It clarifies its source. Responsibility rests with human judgment, subject to public reasoning and revision.

The decline of shared belief exposes what was previously concealed by tradition. Public legitimacy was never guaranteed by religious language. It was sustained by social agreement and enforced by institutions. As belief fragments, those institutions must rely openly on secular justification rather than inherited religious vocabulary.

A government that serves citizens of all beliefs must ground its authority in principles that all citizens can evaluate. Neutrality is not hostility toward religion. It is recognition that public life requires common standards that do not depend on faith. In a society without shared theology, justice cannot appeal to a god without excluding those who do not believe. It must appeal instead to reason, evidence, and shared human concern.

This shift does not weaken ethics. It strengthens them. When morality is no longer attributed to divine command, it must be explained, defended, and revised in human terms. That task begins with understanding how ethics function without appeal to heaven.

ETHICS WITHOUT HEAVEN

If morality once depended on divine command, its endurance after belief proves that goodness never needed permission. The collapse of supernatural authority did not erase conscience; it revealed its origin in human connection. What guides us is not the voice of heaven but the capacity to recognize another's suffering and respond to it.

Long before scripture, cooperation was a practical necessity. For early human groups, survival depended less on individual strength than on reliable social bonds. Anthropological studies of hunter-gatherer societies show that practices we now describe as generosity, fairness, and mutual care functioned as adaptive strategies. Groups that shared food during scarcity, protected injured members, and sanctioned betrayal were more likely to persist than those organized around unchecked self-interest. These behaviors were not moral ideals in the abstract; they were responses to material conditions. Over time, selection favored dispositions such as empathy and reciprocity because they stabilized groups and improved collective survival. In this sense, altruism did not originate as a theological command. It emerged as a social solution long before it was framed as a moral or religious one.

Philosophers later gave those instincts structure. Immanuel Kant argued that moral duty rests on rational consistency: one should act only by principles that could apply universally. The British philosopher John Stuart Mill, a leading voice of utilitarianism, countered that morality should be judged by outcomes—actions are right if they increase well-being and lessen harm. Both began not with revelation but with reasoning and empathy; they disagreed on method, not motive.

Modern science confirms their intuition. Neuroscientists studying mirror neurons show that seeing another person in pain activates the same brain regions that register pain within ourselves.[4] Morality, in this view, is perception extended outward. We act kindly not because commandments demand it but because boundaries between self and other blur at the level of feeling. Compassion is not miracle but mechanism.

Yet this capacity is uneven and fragile. History offers no shortage of moments when reason failed to restrain cruelty and empathy narrowed rather than expanded. Genocide, exploitation, and indifference have all been carried out by people capable of understanding suffering but choosing not to respond to it. The absence of divine command does not guarantee moral clarity; it merely removes an excuse.

History supports this understanding. Again and again, moral progress has emerged not from new revelation but from challenges to sacred law. The abolition of slavery, the defense of women's rights, and the recognition of same-sex relationships began as disputes with religious authority, not extensions of it. Reformers appealed to fairness and reason rather than prophecy. Each advance widened the circle of empathy while narrowing the claims of divine command.

In secular societies today, moral cooperation thrives through shared norms rather than threats of punishment. Legal systems, education, and civic participation perform the work once assigned to priests. Nations with high social trust—whether Denmark, Japan, or New Zealand—tend to show lower violence and higher well-being regardless of creed. Ethics do not dissolve when religion wanes; they reorganize around accountability.

Yet this reorientation introduces uncertainty. Without an external judge, judgment itself becomes our burden. We cannot appeal to a

4. Rizzolatti and Sinigaglia, *Mirrors in the Brain*, 122–27.

cosmic witness to justify cruelty or absolve indifference. The weight of responsibility falls entirely upon us, but that weight is clarifying: it forces each generation to decide what kind of world it wishes to build.

Living ethically without heaven requires humility. No principle is final, no insight complete. The philosopher Karl Popper called this the open society—a culture in which ideas compete, error becomes instruction, and authority remains provisional.[5] Such openness is not weakness; it is moral intelligence at work.

To live by reason is not to strip life of compassion but to restore it to its natural home. The skeptic who shelters a stranger or defends justice acts from the same impulse that once inspired prayer—the refusal to let suffering stand unchallenged. Kindness offered without expectation of reward is purer than obedience born of fear.

Some theologians quietly acknowledge this convergence. Having lost confidence in divine command, they treat God less as legislator and more as symbol for conscience itself—a metaphor for the moral impulse that evolution and empathy have already written into us. Faith becomes an image of our own capacity for care, sanctifying what is human rather than heavenly.

When heaven falls silent, goodness must speak for itself. The voice that remains is ours—collective, imperfect, and evolving. It is quieter than revelation but far more trustworthy because it can listen, learn, and change.

Even as moral responsibility shifts to human judgment, the need for shared meaning remains and takes different forms.

REBIRTH OF RITUAL

Public gatherings after violence, secular graduation ceremonies, and political demonstrations that channel fear into collective resolve all function as rituals even in the absence of belief. When religious faith declines, reverence does not vanish. Ritual persists in nonreligious forms. Humans rely on repetition and shared structure to create meaning, and ceremony is one way that structure is expressed. Even without gods to honor, people continue to mark time, assemble, and reinforce social bonds through shared actions. The question is not whether ritual will continue, but what purposes it will be organized to serve.

5. Popper, *The Open Society and Its Enemies*, 1:xi–xv.

In every civilization, ceremony once joined the visible to the invisible. Sacrifice, prayer, and pilgrimage gave form to emotion and identity. When religion no longer provides that scaffolding, the need for rhythm remains. Funerals, weddings, and civic commemorations evolve into expressions of belonging rather than obedience. A secular memorial, a graduation, or a scientific award ceremony carries the same emotional signature as ancient worship: the feeling of standing together in recognition of something larger than oneself.

Anthropologists have long noted that ritual is less about theology than cohesion. Émile Durkheim observed that collective gatherings generate a shared energy—he called it "collective effervescence"—that strengthens social bonds.[6] The effect persists whether the symbol at the center is a cross, a flag, or a moment of silence. Humans need occasions when ordinary life pauses and meaning becomes visible through repetition.

Modern culture quietly rebuilds this architecture. Parades, concerts, protests, and vigils function as contemporary liturgies. A candlelight march for justice, a festival of art and music, an Earth Day celebration—all fulfill the same purpose once served by prayer: they transform private feeling into communal expression. Ritual in this sense is a language, and each generation learns to speak it anew.

Art extends this impulse. Museums have replaced cathedrals as spaces of shared awe. Music festivals echo the pilgrimage's blend of travel, expectation, and release. Even scientific conferences, with their keynote speeches and rites of presentation, satisfy the old need for recognition and renewal. These gatherings remind us that meaning need not descend from above; it can rise from participation.

Psychologists studying well-being find that people who engage in repeated symbolic acts—lighting candles, gathering for meals, tending gardens, or observing the same sunrise—report higher levels of connection and resilience. Routine becomes reassurance, and shared action transforms repetition into comfort. The strength of ritual lies not in the object of devotion but in the act of doing something together.

Digital life has added new forms of ceremony. The daily check-in, the shared photograph, the global moment of silence transmitted through screens; each reflects a wish to mark existence collectively, even across distance. Step counters, streaks, and reminders are not spiritual

6. Durkheim, *The Elementary Forms of Religious Life*, 217–23.

in themselves, yet they reveal the same impulse: to locate significance through recurrence and acknowledgment. The form changes; the need remains.

A growing number of secular communities now design rituals around care for the planet. Tree-planting days, ocean cleanups, and climate marches weave reverence into responsibility. These acts fuse the moral and the material, transforming environmental awareness into ceremony. The altar becomes the earth itself.

The difference between older religious rituals and their secular counterparts lies in authorship. Traditional ceremonies claimed divine authority; modern ones acknowledge human origin. Secular rituals emphasize continuity without obedience, preserving care, memory, and gratitude without appeal to myth. A nonreligious wedding affirms commitment without invoking eternity. A memorial honors the dead without promising reunion. Meaning remains present, made clearer rather than reduced.

Ritual persists because it serves a continuing human need. Even when life is understood through reason, it still benefits from structure, marking, and shared practice. Living rationally does not require the absence of reverence; it requires directing concern and care toward what is tangible—the people around us, the environment that sustains us, and the limited time we share. In this shift, reverence becomes responsibility. Deliberate acts of remembrance and shared expressions of gratitude help preserve meaning without reliance on superstition. Ritual, grounded in reason, becomes less about honoring the divine and more about sustained attention to life itself.

ALGORITHMIC SOUL

Something subtle happens when meaning becomes automated. If meaning once arrived through prayer, what happens when it is delivered through recommendation engines instead? The depth that once came from reflection begins to flatten into preference, shaped by whatever feels easy, familiar, or instantly rewarding. When purpose is delivered by efficiency rather than contemplation, it becomes convenient instead of wise.

Optimization has become our quiet theology. It promises relief from uncertainty, constant access to comfort, and measurable progress—but rarely reflection. The stories that once guided conscience have been replaced by systems that learn what calms us and then repeat it back. It is devotion translated into convenience, faith replaced by feedback.

Technology did not intend to replace religion. It simply answered many of the same questions with greater speed and less friction. When we type a question into a search bar or scroll through curated news, we perform a modern kind of ritual—seeking guidance from an unseen network and receiving its reply in text and light. The form is secular, yet the posture is ancient: a petition offered to a power we do not fully understand.

What this shift reveals is not the disappearance of belief but a change in where it is invested. The desire for coherence and connection remains, but it now passes through different systems. Digital platforms increasingly influence not only what people encounter, but what they prioritize. They shape exposure, repetition, and visibility. Over time, these mechanisms guide attention and preference, creating implicit norms about what matters without presenting them as doctrine.

Meaning shaped primarily by convenience has consequences. When curiosity is redirected into consumption, repetition often replaces understanding. Research in developmental psychology and media studies shows that heavy digital media use is associated with reduced sustained attention and increased symptoms of inattention over time. A large longitudinal study published in *JAMA Pediatrics*, which followed adolescents for several years, found that frequent engagement with digital media activities was linked to a higher likelihood of developing attention-related difficulties.[7] Attention contracts to match the limits of screens, and stimulation is easily mistaken for insight. Time spent alone with one's thoughts becomes less common, and reflection is treated as inefficient. What was once a personal tension between contemplation and distraction has now been systematized, reducing opportunities for sustained inquiry and depth.

The systems that shape digital attention are largely reactive rather than directive. They amplify existing patterns of demand, including preferences for affirmation, recognition, and cognitive ease, based on aggregated user behavior. Repeated interactions reinforce designs that prioritize immediacy. Over time, this favors short bursts of engagement at the expense of sustained attention. In environments that reward visibility

7. Ra et al., "Association of Digital Media Use," 207–15.

more than reflection, periods of silence are often treated as disengagement rather than as a necessary condition for thought.

Yet beneath this restless surface, the same human need persists. The desire to belong, to be seen, to find pattern within chaos—none of it has vanished. Every post, every search, every late-night glance at a glowing screen is a small act of inquiry, an echo of the old plea: *Is anyone listening?* The prayer has changed syntax but not intention.

The moral challenge of the digital age does not arise from the existence of these systems, but from how readily they are accepted without examination. Automated systems respond to the incentives built into them. When outrage is rewarded, it becomes more visible; when accuracy and clarity are valued, more reliable information is promoted. Systems that shape attention operate through aggregated behavior rather than individual intent, emerging from repeated choices made at scale. What is often described as "the algorithm" is more accurately understood as a cumulative record of human preferences reflected in data.

Resisting this drift requires treating awareness as a deliberate practice. The task of skepticism in the digital century is not to reject technology, but to apply human judgment to it. This involves choosing what to read, pausing before reacting, and disengaging from continuous streams of information when they undermine understanding. These decisions may seem minor, but they shape how meaning is formed. Attention, once managed automatically, becomes a matter of ethical choice again.

If anything resembling a soul exists within this new technological structure, it is not divine but relational. It arises from the interaction between human inquiry and the systems that respond to it. These systems reflect human curiosity, uncertainty, and the desire for coherence, expressed through data rather than belief. What was once pursued through revelation is now often pursued through recognition and response. The underlying questions remain the same; only the medium through which they are asked has changed.

The measure of our age may depend on whether this network becomes a mirror of awareness or a substitute for it. We are the first generation to build a system that listens to nearly everything we say, yet we must still decide whether to listen to ourselves. The task is not to escape technology but to remember that every search, every post, every shared word is a fragment of the story we are writing about what it means to be human.

This is not a technological problem so much as a human one: the question of who authors meaning when systems grow louder than reflection.

Recognizing how meaning can be distorted by systems of attention raises a further question: what remains when attention is deliberately reclaimed.

WONDER RECLAIMED

For centuries, religion claimed ownership of wonder. To feel astonishment was to sense the divine, to stand in awe before a power beyond comprehension. Yet wonder never belonged to faith; it belongs to awareness. When the gods fall silent, the feeling they once inspired remains—transformed, not diminished.

A child peering through a telescope experiences the same astonishment that once filled cathedrals. The scale of the night sky humbles pride without invoking heaven. The physicist tracing the birth of a star and the biologist mapping the spiral of a single gene inherit an ancient impulse: to look, to ask, to marvel. Their reverence is directed not toward authority but toward truth.

Wonder does not depend on grandeur. It often arises from ordinary experiences that are easily missed: a familiar place seen differently, a small act of care, a brief moment of shared quiet. These experiences do not direct attention away from the world but draw it more fully into it. What gives them significance is not their scale, but the quality of attention brought to them.

Art keeps this experience human. When van Gogh painted the night in motion or Beethoven shaped silence into music, they translated awe into form. Their work shows that transcendence needs no divinity; creation itself can be a kind of worship. The trembling brush and the measured note both testify to a truth older than creed: that to understand deeply and to feel deeply are one and the same act.

Psychologists describe awe as a self-transcendent state in which the boundary of self-softens and empathy expands. Experiments at the University of California, Berkeley, found that participants who experienced awe—through nature, music, or art—became more generous immediately afterward.[8] Wonder, it seems, widens the circle of concern. The emotion that once filled temples now sustains cooperation.

In this sense, wonder is not an escape from reality but a deeper engagement with it. Experiences such as a sunrise or a distant galaxy remind us that existence is larger than what we can fully explain, yet still open to understanding and involvement. Skepticism does not eliminate reverence; it relocates it. Awareness alone can sustain it. The capacities to breathe, think, create, and care do not require a supernatural explanation to be meaningful.

Modern life weakens this capacity. Constant stimulation from commerce and continuous connection reduces sensitivity, making beauty easier to overlook. Recovering a sense of wonder requires deliberate attention. It involves slowing down enough to notice small details: the structure of a leaf, the subdued sounds of a city in the morning, or the way light changes a familiar room. These moments reinforce the value of awareness itself, reminding us that attentive perception is an essential human practice.

This kind of attention leads naturally to humility. In theological contexts, humility often meant submission; in inquiry, it means proportion. Recognizing one's limited place within an indifferent universe is not a cause for despair, but an acknowledgment of fact. From that acknowledgment follows responsibility: to preserve what is vulnerable, to value what is temporary, and to protect the conditions that make consciousness possible.

Awe without worship becomes freedom. It grants gratitude without servitude, admiration without superstition. The stars do not need our hymns, yet they call us to care for the fragile world that lets us see them. The glacier, the forest, the coral reef carry no message, yet each reminds us that survival itself is sacred. Wonder thus matures into obligation: to honor what astonishes by ensuring it endures.

To reclaim wonder is to remember what belief once promised and what understanding now fulfills—that life, however brief and uncertain, is astonishing enough. When we look closely and find the world luminous without myth, we have not lost the sacred; we have brought it home.

8. Piff et al., "Awe, the Small Self, and Prosocial Behavior," 883–99.

RESPONSIBILITY AS REDEMPTION

Once the sacred is redefined, responsibility becomes unavoidable. If wonder restores humility, responsibility redeems it. Once the cosmos is understood as indifferent, the task of care falls entirely to us. There is no external judge to weigh our actions, no divine promise to balance suffering with reward. What remains is choice—our deliberate effort to preserve, repair, and improve the world that produced us.

In theology, redemption often meant release from guilt. In human terms, it means acting despite guilt. Moral responsibility shifts from confession to consequence. Each decision has effects within an interdependent and vulnerable system. When people alleviate hunger, protect ecosystems, or defend another person's dignity, they engage in the only form of redemption available in the real world: the reduction of avoidable harm.

This reframing replaces a vertical framework with a relational one. Responsibility no longer involves deference to a transcendent authority, but accountability to one another. Goodness is assessed not by obedience to an unseen will, but by the impact of actions on those affected by them. What was once described as sacred is expressed through conduct rather than belief.

Philosophers of the twentieth century recognized this transformation. Jean-Paul Sartre, Simone de Beauvoir, and Albert Camus each argued that without divine law, moral responsibility intensifies. Freedom means bearing the full consequence of what we choose. There is no higher court of appeal. Camus called this "the weight of the absurd," yet he found dignity in carrying it.[9] Meaning, he wrote, is created through defiance of indifference—through the insistence that compassion and justice remain worthwhile even in a silent universe.

Modern humanism extends this insight to collective life. Responsibility becomes not only personal but civic. Democracy, education, and science all depend on trust in shared duty. The ethic of care that religion once attributed to divine command now becomes an ecological and social imperative. To neglect it is not sin but failure of imagination.

Environmental stewardship illustrates this shift with particular clarity. Humans are not caretakers acting on behalf of a creator, but participants within an interdependent system. Decisions about conservation, resource use, and emissions shape the conditions under which life continues. Climate science identifies this as a moral threshold: for the first

9. Camus, *The Myth of Sisyphus*, 88–91.

time, a single species has the capacity to alter the conditions of existence for many others. If the concept of salvation has any meaning here, it lies in stewardship rather than appeal to external intervention.

Responsibility also reshapes how we understand suffering. Without an afterlife to promise correction, justice must occur here. Compassion becomes urgent rather than symbolic. The volunteer in a refugee camp, the nurse in a crowded ward, the teacher in a struggling school—all practice redemption without mythology. They refuse to outsource conscience to a deity.

This ethic does not remove guilt; it gives it direction. Discomfort in the presence of injustice is not a failure, but an indication of awareness. When guilt is separated from confession, it becomes attention; when attention does not lead to response, it becomes complicity. The function of conscience is to translate awareness into action. Apologies that repair harm, policies that reduce its recurrence, and ordinary acts of care toward those at risk are concrete expressions of moral responsibility.

In this sense, responsibility becomes a form of commitment—not to divine authority, but to the possibility of improvement. It reflects confidence that human conditions are not fixed. Each generation inherits both damage and capacity. To live responsibly is to reduce the harm passed forward and to increase the understanding left behind.

When reverence develops into responsibility, wonder gains direction. Acting with care in a world without guarantees is how purpose is established rather than received. What once concluded with prayer now concludes with effort. What follows is not resolution, but reckoning.

THE MEASURE OF A LIFE

Responsibility finds its final test not in belief, but in how a finite life is lived. Without heaven to promise eternity, life becomes its own reckoning. Time is no longer a prelude to another existence but the entire span in which value can be created. The question that once haunted religion—what happens after death—gives way to one more urgent: what will we make of the days we have?

Mortality sharpens purpose. Knowing that existence ends invests every act with weight. The smallest kindness, the quietest generosity, gains significance precisely because it is temporary. When permanence disappears, presence becomes sacred. A shared meal, a truth spoken, a life guided toward kindness—each becomes a fragment of meaning built from limited time.

Philosophers and poets have long wrestled with this awareness. The Roman emperor Marcus Aurelius reminded himself that each breath could be the last, and virtue lay in acting justly while one could. Centuries later, the existentialists restated the same lesson in modern terms. Jean-Paul Sartre called it authenticity—the courage to define oneself through action rather than intention. The French writer and philosopher Albert Camus, known for his philosophy of the absurd, described it as rebellion against absurdity, the refusal to surrender purpose even when the universe offers none. Both saw mortality not as defeat but as discipline.

Psychological research supports this intuition. Studies of meaning and well-being indicate that people who confront mortality directly often report increased gratitude, clearer priorities, and greater concern for others. Awareness of finitude tends to shift attention away from accumulation and toward contribution. When time is understood as limited, significance is found less in what is owned and more in how one participates in the lives of others.

The significance of a life is not determined by its duration, but by its effects. Where religion once emphasized salvation through belief, secular understanding emphasizes continuity through influence. Teachers who cultivate curiosity, artists who change perception, and individuals who offer support during difficulty extend their impact beyond their own lifespan. Memory and example allow influence to persist, even when biological life ends.

Living with mortality in view is not morbid; it is clarifying. Limited time sharpens judgment about what matters and what does not. Status, possessions, and disputes lose urgency, while the consequences of care and neglect become more visible. Acts of integrity and compassion accumulate through their effects on others, shaping future behavior in ways that cannot be fully measured.

Mortality also reframes responsibility. In the absence of guaranteed cosmic correction, responsibility for harm and repair remains with those who cause or prevent it. Justice becomes a matter of present action rather than deferred judgment. Every choice leaves effects that persist beyond the moment in which it is made. To live responsibly is to recognize that future conditions depend on present decisions.

This recognition supports humility rather than despair. The universe may be indifferent, but human responses are not. Meaning does not require permanence; it requires consequence. Purpose may not be predetermined, but it can be created through relationships, understanding, and acts that reduce harm or increase possibility for others.

An honest assessment of a life therefore focuses not on what it acquires, but on what it contributes. Material success fades, reputations change, and physical markers disappear. What remains are patterns of understanding and care transmitted from one person to another. Social progress depends on this accumulation of influence across generations.

At death, there is no final accounting beyond the effects already set in motion. Accepting this without appeal does not diminish meaning; it clarifies it. The continuation that matters is carried forward in others.

Without eternity, purpose becomes a matter of authorship. Each life adds something to a shared human record. The relevant question is not how it concludes, but what it contributes while it is lived.

WHAT REMAINS TO BELIEVE IN

When I say I do not believe in God, people often ask, "Then what do you believe in?" The question assumes that disbelief leaves a void, that without the divine there can be only emptiness. But disbelief is not absence; it is rearrangement. It removes the ceiling so the world can widen.

I believe that truth, even when it wounds, is better than comfort built on pretense. Compassion needs no promise of reward to matter, and beauty loses nothing by being explained.

I believe in the small continuities that hold the human story together: the teacher who changes a life, the friend who stays through silence, the stranger who acts from empathy without recognition. And most of all, I believe in my wife, whose patience, unselfishness and steadiness remind me that meaning is built, not bestowed. These are not miracles; they are proofs of possibility.

There is also the unfinished project of understanding. Science does not close mystery; it expands it. Each discovery deepens wonder, and each correction refines humility. To learn is to participate in creation without pretending to command it. The frontier of knowledge is not a boundary but an invitation, reminding us that awareness itself is sacred work.

Meaning is constructed, not bestowed. It appears whenever effort becomes care, whenever awareness becomes responsibility. To build, to heal, to preserve, to love—these are acts of faith in the only sense that still earns the word. What once was prayer becomes participation. What once was worship becomes stewardship.

I believe in forgiveness, not as pardon from above but as patience among equals. It is the practice of choosing repair over resentment, dialogue over silence. Grace, in this light, is not supernatural; it is emotional intelligence made visible. To forgive is not to forget what was done but to insist that compassion remains possible after injury.

I believe that truth and tenderness are not opposites but partners. Honesty without kindness can wound, and kindness without honesty can deceive. To hold both together, to speak clearly and care deeply, is the work of maturity. Civilization itself depends on that balance.

I believe in the resilience of consciousness, the capacity to imagine better worlds and to build them, however briefly, before the light fades. If the cosmos is indifferent, that only magnifies the importance of tenderness within it. Our significance lies not in being noticed by the universe but in noticing one another.

Disbelief is not despair. It is the moment when the training wheels of certainty come off and the mind learns to balance on its own. The absence of divine oversight does not make life smaller; it gives it back to us in full scale. Each day becomes a sentence in a story we are still writing, a chance to add coherence where chaos once ruled.

So, when people ask what I believe in, I answer: in us, in the fragile, fallible, remarkable experiment of being human. In our ability to see the truth and still choose compassion. In our power to make meaning even when no one else will make it for us.

Doubt has never been faith's enemy; it has been its architect. Every era of disbelief has forced belief to evolve, reshaping the sacred to survive its own contradictions. In that sense, doubt is not destruction but refinement, the pressure that keeps reverence alive. The dialogue between belief and unbelief is the furnace in which new meanings are forged.

It is the skeptic who ensures that wonder endures. By questioning its claims, doubt prevents divinity from collapsing into dogma. The conversation between belief and inquiry keeps meaning alive and supple. Through that exchange, humanity's search for coherence becomes its truest form of prayer.

THE NEW SACRED

If wonder reveals what matters, the sacred determines what we are willing to protect. If the gods are gone, what remains to sanctify the world? The answer is what has always been here: awareness, connection, and care. The sacred did not vanish with belief; it changed direction. It moved from the heavens into the spaces between people, from temples of stone to the fragile continuity of life itself.

To call something sacred is to declare it worthy of protection. For millennia, that protection was reserved for the divine—texts, rituals, and hierarchies guarded by authority. In a secular age, reverence returns to its source: the human mind that first imagined it. The new sacred is not worship but attention. It is the willingness to see the extraordinary in the ordinary, to treat existence as inheritance rather than possession.

Science, art, and ethics become its modern devotions. The researcher examining the architecture of a cell, the artist uncovering beauty in imperfection, the citizen defending justice in a divided world—all practice reverence without theology. Their work honors the improbable fact of consciousness and the shared conditions that sustain it. Gratitude replaces prayer; preservation replaces praise.

Community, too, takes on a new holiness. Where religion once divided the saved from the lost, the new sacred unites those who care from those who do not. The dividing line is empathy. To protect a river, to feed the hungry, to seek truth amid noise—these are acts of worship in the language of reason. Holiness survives not as purity but as perseverance: the steady refusal to stop caring.

This revised sense of the sacred is grounded in an honest view of scale. It does not rely on promises of eternity or perfection. Fragility is not treated as a flaw, but as a condition that gives experiences their value. A sunrise does not require an observer to exist, and care does not require permanence to matter. Accepting limits allows for a form of awe based on participation rather than expectation of intervention. Mortality, understood this way, does not diminish meaning; it defines it.

Reverence, once oriented toward transcendence, becomes relational. It is expressed through interactions among living beings and through responsibilities carried across generations. Teaching empathy, preserving ecosystems, and documenting cultural or environmental change extend concern beyond the present moment. These actions form a record of values expressed in practice rather than belief. Each effort to preserve or protect contributes to the ongoing human task of sustaining what can endure.

To live within this understanding is to see that redemption, awe, and duty converge in a single gesture: care. The skeptic's prayer is action; the skeptic's hymn is curiosity. Our rituals are the choices that prevent harm, preserve beauty, and extend kindness into a future we will not see. What we call sacred now is the commitment to keep the world hospitable to life and truth—to act as though existence were a gift, even when we know it was not given.

Even unbelief plays a creative role in this renewal. As cultures question and reinterpret their inherited creeds, doubt becomes the mechanism by which moral imagination stays alive. Each challenge forces refinement; each act of disbelief invites reinvention. The persistence of questioning ensures that meaning remains open rather than frozen, evolving with us instead of against us.

The new sacred is not a creed but a practice: attention without illusion, reverence without hierarchy, devotion without reward. It invites humanity to see itself not as the center of creation but as its caretaker. The world does not need our worship; it needs our stewardship. In the end, what remains after God is what was always ours to begin with: the capacity to choose, to care, to create.

The silence that once followed the death of gods has become the silence in which responsibility begins. Nothing answers from beyond it. What remains is care—deliberate, imperfect, and human. That is where meaning now resides.

10

The Quiet That Remains

"Man is nothing else but what he makes of himself."

Jean-Paul Sartre

AFTER THE ANSWERS STOP

I once believed that doubt marked the end of belief—the point where meaning ran out. It felt like the moment after certainty ends, when nothing replaces it immediately. For years, I mistook that silence for loss. Now I understand it as presence, the kind that asks nothing and explains nothing. It is the sound the universe makes when it no longer needs to reassure you.

The night sky used to feel like a question waiting for an answer. I would look upward, half expecting something to look back. That reflex remains, though it no longer carries a name. The silence I once filled with prayer has become a space for attention. It holds everything that belief tried to hold but without the demand for response. It is neither empty nor cold. It is vast, indifferent, and alive with possibility.

What I used to call prayer has changed shape. Now it begins when the morning light first touches the window, or when the day ends and quiet spreads across the house. There is no kneeling, no invocation—only a pause long enough to notice being alive. The smallest sounds; my cats purr, the breathing of my wife sleeping nearby—become reminders that existence needs no audience to continue.

There are still moments when the old habit returns—during illness, close calls, or bad news that arrives unexpectedly. For a brief moment, I find myself thinking in terms I no longer accept. The reaction passes, but it has not disappeared entirely. I have come to understand that abandoning belief does not eliminate ingrained responses; it makes them visible. What matters is not that the reaction occurs, but that I no longer treat it as evidence.

For much of my youth, I believed that mystery proved divinity. The first cracks appeared long before adulthood, when questions began to outnumber answers. Now I see that mystery is simply the shape of what we do not yet understand. The quiet between thoughts, the stillness after grief, the pause before understanding are not absences but thresholds. The world is full of them, and they do not point beyond themselves. They point inward, to the mind that keeps searching.

Silence, I've learned, has its own kind of speech. It speaks in pattern and pulse, in the rhythm of wind through leaves and the slow patience of stars. It does not console or condemn; it simply continues. That continuation is its wisdom. The sacred was never in the voice that might answer, but in the act of listening itself.

There is a humility that comes from realizing the universe does not need to notice us to be complete. Yet within that indifference lies something almost tender: permission. We are free to care, to imagine, to build meaning not because we must, but because we can. The silence does not command; it allows.

What began as emptiness has become invitation. It no longer frightens me that the universe is indifferent. What frightens me more is how easily we can overlook its quiet generosity—the way it allows us, for a brief while, to notice that we are here at all.

INHERITANCE OF DOUBT

I did not invent my skepticism. I inherited it. Somewhere in the long chain of human thought, someone looked at lightning and wondered whether a hand had really thrown it. Someone watched an eclipse and questioned whether the gods had blinked. Those first moments of inquiry were not rebellions but acts of attention. They were the beginning of honesty.

Uncertainty is older than disbelief. It began as curiosity—the impulse to look closer when fear said to look away. The first people who challenged the voices of their priests or the movements of the stars passed that inheritance forward. Their hesitation became our legacy: a fragile courage refined through generations of minds unwilling to mistake reverence for truth. That inheritance does not dictate what we must conclude, only how honestly we must arrive there.

Socrates made a virtue of not knowing, turning ignorance into a tool for discovery. The Egyptian philosopher and mathematician Hypatia of Alexandria, one of the last great scholars of the ancient world, taught mathematics and astronomy in the fourth century and embodied this evolution of thought. She defended reason against the growing dogmatism of her time and was murdered by a mob that saw learning as blasphemy.[1] Her death revealed what happens when faith feels threatened by curiosity: the loss of both wisdom and compassion. Doubt may unsettle belief, but suppression destroys the civilization that depends on free minds.

Across centuries, every leap in understanding has begun with someone who would not bow to certainty. The astronomers who moved the Earth from the center of creation, the physicians who traced illness to causes rather than curses, the reformers who read sacred texts and saw not revelation but revision—all carried the same quiet conviction that truth should never depend on authority. Their courage made questioning a form of devotion, one aimed not at heaven but at reality itself.

Sometimes I imagine this lineage as a procession of small lanterns winding through history. Each thinker carries a light that burns only because someone earlier refused to let darkness mean silence. The line stretches backward through philosophers, poets, and nameless skeptics who whispered their misgivings in safer tones. We owe them more than memory; we owe them the freedom to keep asking.

To inherit this lineage is not to inherit despair. It is to belong to a tradition that values inquiry over obedience, clarity over comfort. Skepticism, at its best, is not destruction but stewardship—an act of care for the integrity of truth. It keeps curiosity honest. When the last temple crumbles, the questions will still remain, flickering in the minds of those who cannot stop looking.

To question well is to love the world enough to want a truer version of it. Doubt, in that sense, is devotion in another language. It is faith without fear—the willingness to see reality as it is, even when it contradicts

1. Dzielska, *Hypatia of Alexandria*, 84–102.

what we wish were true. The skeptic's gaze is not cynical; it is reverent toward fact, tender toward reason. Faith asks for surrender; questioning demands participation. Both begin with awe, but only one ends in understanding. Doubt, in this sense, is not an answer but a discipline—one that prepares the ground without determining what will grow from it.

After everything examined in these pages—the unanswered prayers, the failed wagers, the silence behind miracles, and the weight of inherited belief—the conclusion is not dramatic. It is simply honest.

The world looks exactly as it would if no personal, intervening God existed—yet for some, belief persists not because of evidence, but because of fear, habit, inheritance, and psychological need.

THE INCOHERENCE OF GOD

All of that honesty, all of that discipline of doubt, eventually brought me to a plain but unavoidable conclusion: there is no empirical evidence that convincingly demonstrates the existence of a supernatural, interventionist deity.

Doubt carries its own momentum. Once you inherit the courage to question, the next thing you discover is that the traditional idea of God begins to fracture under examination. I once assumed the concept was sturdy, but the more closely I looked, the less it held together. The attributes I had accepted for most of my life did not align. They strained against one another until the entire definition pulled apart.

This was the point at which my questions stopped circling and began to converge—not emotionally, but conceptually.

A timeless being cannot choose a moment to act because choice requires a sequence. If God exists outside time, then every decision must be fixed from eternity, including the act of creation itself. A decision that cannot be made cannot be described as free, yet the idea of a freely created universe is central to belief.

Omniscience introduces its own difficulty. If God knows everything that will happen, the future must already be settled. A settled future leaves no space for free will. And if God created the universe with full knowledge of every outcome, then nothing could have been otherwise.

The problem reaches deeper when morality enters the picture. Love requires vulnerability. A being that cannot suffer cannot love in any sense we recognize. The familiar stories of compassion lose their meaning when the one who cares cannot feel.

Omnipotence complicates things further. A being that can do anything cannot also be bound by its own nature. If God cannot create evil, power has limits. If God can create evil, perfection has limits. Unlimited power and moral perfection cannot both be true in the same definition.

None of these conflicts require advanced theology to see. The idea that seemed complete from a distance dissolves when examined at close range. This does not make spiritual longing foolish. It only shows that the classical portrait of God cannot survive its own description. Recognizing this does not remove meaning. It redirects it. It turns toward the world that remains, where clarity can be built on foundations that do not contradict themselves. From that moment on, the question was no longer whether belief could be repaired, but how meaning might be practiced without it. Letting go of that definition felt less like winning an argument than like closing a door I once expected never to shut.

THE EVERYDAY SACRED

The loss of belief did not erase wonder. It changed its direction. What once rose toward heaven now turns outward, toward the world that remains. The sacred is still here, scattered in small, unclaimed moments: the quiet before sunrise, the sound of rain on a roof, the kindness of someone who expects nothing in return. Reverence has shed its old vocabulary and found a new home in the ordinary.

You can see it in the way people pause before a painting, or in the hush that settles when a symphony begins. It appears when a scientist looks through a microscope and feels awe at the order beneath the chaos, or when a parent watches a sleeping child and feels gratitude that needs no address. These are not diminished forms of worship. They are what survive when meaning is stripped of superstition and left with its most human core: attention. They are not arguments about meaning, but expressions of it—ways of living that do not wait for metaphysical permission.

As Einstein once wrote, "I am satisfied with the mystery of the eternity of life and with the awareness and a glimpse of the marvelous structure of the existing world."[2]

2. Einstein, "What I Believe," 11.

His words captured what I had come to feel: that reverence does not require divinity. Wonder survives not in the promise of heaven, but in the elegance of what already exists.

The sacred has always been less about gods than about focus. To pay attention is to give something of yourself, to acknowledge that existence is not yours alone. When we look closely at a leaf, a star, or a face, we encounter a world that existed before us and will continue after. That recognition breeds humility, the oldest root of prayer. Wonder does not require belief; it requires awareness.

Even in a secular age, ritual persists. A person still lights a candle, not to summon spirits but to remember someone gone. I still do. When I strike the match, I'm not calling to heaven; I'm remembering my parents—my mother's quiet steadiness, her care for everyone around her, her unshakable belief in her family and faith; my father's toughness, his loyalty, the way he showed love less through words than through constancy. Their faces return, their voices, the ordinary grace of their presence. The flame doesn't promise reunion; it holds a kind of continuity, a small defiance against forgetting. Another walks each morning to the same bench in the park, not to commune with divinity but to listen to the wind. Someone plants a tree each year on a birthday or keeps an old photograph near the bed. These gestures carry the same impulse that once built cathedrals: the wish to make meaning visible. They remind us that reverence survives wherever gratitude takes form. What matters is not what these gestures signify, but that they continue to be enacted.

Art remains its purest expression. In galleries and concert halls, the ancient posture of reverence endures: silence, stillness, the quiet awe before something made by human hands yet greater than its maker. The artist becomes a priest of perception, revealing beauty where others saw only the ordinary. A brushstroke, a phrase, a chord—all remind us that transcendence can be built, not bestowed.

Science, too, participates in this renewal. Each experiment, each discovery, each long night of observation is a form of devotion to the real. When a researcher studies the structure of a cell or measures the distance of a star, it is not faith that drives them but wonder disciplined by patience. The sacred has always belonged to those who look closely.

What connects these expressions is attention. Attention leads to care, and care assigns value. The sacred is not limited to religious spaces or texts, but appears wherever awareness produces responsibility. It is present in the patience of a gardener, the compassion of a nurse, and the honesty of a teacher who refuses to simplify the truth. Each act of care contributes, in small but real ways, to the improvement of the world.

This recognition restores meaning without miracle. It tells us that awe is not proof of another realm but appreciation of this one. To notice beauty, to preserve what is fragile, to love without guarantee—these are gestures of faith in life itself. They replace the question "Is there something beyond?" with the answer "There is enough here."

The sacred, it turns out, never needed belief. It only needed witnesses. To live as one of them is to recognize that the world does not wait for permission to be holy. It simply waits to be seen.

HUMAN PATTERN

Humanity keeps repeating itself. Every generation imagines it has broken from the past, yet the same instincts reappear in new disguises. We still build systems that promise guidance and invent symbols to steady us when the world feels uncertain. Where temples once stood, we now have screens that glow through the night. Where prophets once spoke, we have commentators and influencers. The surface changes, but the pattern underneath endures: people searching for coherence in chaos. To recognize this pattern is not to judge it, but to understand the conditions under which belief repeatedly takes shape.

Anthropologists often describe religion as an adaptive behavior—a way to unite groups through shared story and purpose. Even when divine claims fall away, the structure persists. Communities still gather around rituals, shared narratives, and mutual ideals. Sports arenas, political movements, and cultural fandoms all echo the choreography of the sacred. The objects of devotion differ, but the human need to belong does not.

People who abandon formal religion often carry its architecture into new realms. Economics becomes a doctrine of salvation through growth. Nationalism promises redemption through unity. The marketplace, the movement, the brand—all acquire their saints and heresies.

Even reason can become rigid when it is no longer examined. The belief that every unanswered question must eventually be explained can turn inquiry into assumption rather than investigation. Knowledge is most reliable when it remains provisional and open to correction. When confidence hardens into certainty, reasoning loses its flexibility and begins to mirror the dogmatism it was meant to challenge. Claims treated as final are less likely to be revised, even in the face of new evidence.

Cognitive science offers a glimpse into why this repetition is inevitable. The brain favors pattern over chaos. It rewards prediction and punishes ambiguity. When events seem random, we invent connections because doing so calms us. Meaning is not only an idea; it is a neurological comfort. We are wired to prefer a flawed explanation to none at all. In that sense, belief is not an error but an adaptation—a strategy for surviving uncertainty.

To understand this impulse is not to dismiss it but to humanize it. The instinct to interpret, to link events into story, is what gave birth to both science and superstition. The same urge that created omens also created hypotheses. One turns mystery into myth; the other into method. What matters is not the presence of belief, but the discipline of revising it.

Viewed this way, human inquiry does not simply repeat itself, nor does it move in a straight line. People continue to ask enduring questions, but they do so with improved methods and expanded knowledge. Although the tools differ, the underlying aim is consistent: to make sense of what is not yet understood. What changes over time is not the impulse to seek meaning, but the framework used to pursue it. Progress lies less in abandoning belief than in reshaping it, shifting emphasis from certainty toward inquiry.

This rhythm of rediscovery is not a flaw; it is the evidence of our persistence. To search for order in a disorderly universe is the mind's most human act. Even when our explanations change, the yearning that drives them remains constant. We are creatures who cannot help but wonder what connects things. The danger lies only in forgetting that our answers are temporary.

The challenge, then, is to live with this understanding deliberately. Meaning must be created while recognizing that it remains open to revision. Systems such as religion, science, ideology, and art provide ways of interpreting experience, not complete representations of reality itself. When methods of understanding are treated as final truths, familiar mistakes reappear in new forms. When convictions are held with openness to correction, change becomes cumulative rather than repetitive.

Each generation must learn this balance anew. We inherit systems of thought as we inherit language, full of brilliance and blind spots. Our task is to speak them more clearly, to keep what clarifies and discard what confines. Progress is not measured by how far we move from the past, but by how honestly we confront the instincts that built it.

Perhaps that is the quiet triumph of the human pattern: not perfection, but awareness. We are capable of seeing our own loops, of recognizing the hands that built our gods, the minds that shaped our certainties. To live with that awareness is not cynicism but wisdom. It is what allows us to love our creations without kneeling before them.

In the end, to be human is to live between knowledge and need, clarity and craving. We are pattern-makers who must learn to see the pattern itself. The miracle is not that we repeat, but that we recognize the repetition and choose, again and again, to seek understanding anyway.

LIVING WITH UNCERTAINTY

This is where the argument ends and living begins. The final step in questioning is not despair but acceptance. Every search for ultimate truth ends where knowledge meets its limits, and what remains is how we live within that boundary. The goal was never to solve the mystery completely, only to face it without distortion. What remains unresolved is not the universe, but the responsibility of how one lives within it.

Science has shown that the universe runs on principles that need no permission to exist. Religion once gave those principles faces and names. Now we understand them as gravity, evolution, entropy, and time—forces indifferent to our hopes yet consistent in their law. The cosmos does not require belief to continue; it unfolds in silence, impartial and vast. Still, something in us longs to find a place within it.

Uncertainty once frightened me. I thought it meant ignorance or failure, a gap waiting to be filled. Now I see it as a form of belonging. To live without final answers is to live honestly in a world that never promised them. The absence of certainty is not emptiness; it is possibility. It leaves room for discovery, for humility, for awe unchained from explanation.

Philosophers have long wrestled with this condition. The Stoics taught that peace comes not from control but from consent—the willingness to align one's will with reality. The existentialists later extended that idea into freedom. Sartre wrote that we are condemned to choose, forever defining ourselves through decision in a universe that offers no blueprint. Camus imagined Sisyphus pushing his stone not in defeat, but in defiance, finding meaning in the act itself. They understood that certainty is a mirage and that the truer measure of a life is how one continues in its absence.

Living with uncertainty does not mean accepting confusion. It means approaching the world with careful attention rather than fear. One can observe nature without expecting guidance from it, and study reality without insisting that it confirm personal significance. This stance does not rely on revelation, but on clarity, and it values coherence over reassurance. The willingness to say "I do not know" is not a weakness, but the starting point of genuine understanding.

The natural world teaches this lesson every day. The tides move without audience, the stars burn without intention, and yet their constancy steadies us. When we accept that the universe owes us no explanation, its silence becomes eloquent. The task is not to fill it with answers but to listen deeply enough to hear its rhythm.

Meaning persists without revelation because it never depended on revelation alone. It arises from attention and from how people respond to the world as it is. When individuals learn, create, or care for one another, they express values that theology once framed as divine. The absence of a supernatural order does not remove morality; it places responsibility for it squarely within human judgment. What remains is a shared obligation to reduce harm and increase care where conditions allow otherwise.

When certainty is no longer the objective, a different kind of life becomes possible. People are freer to revise their views, to grow through correction, and to form connections without fear of doctrinal error. Belief gives way to inquiry, and ritual gives way to practice. Understanding becomes something developed over time rather than something received all at once. Questions about truth become inseparable from questions about conduct.

In this sense, doubt is not the negation of faith but its refinement. It represents a commitment to honesty over finality and to continued inquiry over premature conclusion. Truth is approached incrementally and provisionally, not possessed. Living with uncertainty means remaining open to revision while continuing to act responsibly.

If the idea of grace retains any meaning within a rational framework, it lies in the willingness to keep asking, the discipline of listening carefully, and the resolve to live without final assurances. Accepting the persistence of uncertainty is not resignation; it is an acknowledgment of the conditions under which understanding actually develops.

CLOSING REFLECTION

I began this search asking whether God could still matter in an age that measures everything. I end it knowing that the search itself was what mattered. Every question became a kind of prayer, not to the heavens but to the unknown within. Each doubt pulled back another layer of illusion, revealing not emptiness but a deeper kind of presence—awareness unguarded, unpromised, and real.

I often think of Bertrand Russell's reminder that the Christian God may exist, but so might the gods of Olympus, Egypt, or Babylon.[3] None is more probable than the rest; all lie beyond what we can know. That thought no longer feels dismissive to me; it simply restores proportion. It reminds me that reverence was never about proving which god was real, but about learning how to live meaningfully in a world where the answer may never come.

It was the same silence I had heard as a child, the one that followed prayer and asked more of me than any answer ever could.

When belief faded, I thought purpose would fade with it. I was wrong. What vanished was certainty, not significance. What dissolved was the idea that direction must descend from above. What remained was life itself—imperfect, brief, luminous. The world never needed our permission to be sacred; it only needed our attention. Reverence is not something given but something created, moment by moment, through care and truth.

We search for order because we are capable of imagining it. We create stories because we cannot bear to live without coherence. Perhaps that is our greatest inheritance—not belief but the capacity to seek, to build, to imagine better worlds from fragments of the one we have. The divine we once projected outward was a reflection of that same impulse within: the wish to understand, to love, to persist despite knowing the end.

The silence I once feared no longer felt unresolved. It no longer feels like the absence of an answer but the space in which answers can arise. It is the quiet that holds the pulse of life continuing. When I listen now, I hear it everywhere: the rhythm of trees in the wind, the breath of cities, the soft murmur of people doing their best to live decently in an indifferent universe. The sacred, I think, is not a presence to be found but a quality of attention to what already is.

3. Russell, *Why I Am Not a Christian*, 6–7.

If God was ever real, perhaps the truest miracle was this: that the universe learned to ask about itself. The gift was not revelation but freedom—the chance to see whether love, justice, and understanding could sustain themselves without supervision. That experiment continues in us. Every act of compassion, every moment of integrity, is another step in proving that it can.

Purpose is not a riddle waiting to be solved. It is a conversation between what we know and what we cannot, between the finite mind and the infinite horizon. It lives in the tension, not the resolution. To live well is to dwell in that tension with grace—to admit what we do not know while caring deeply for what we do. It is to build small certainties—love, art, kindness—within the vast field of uncertainty and to let those certainties be enough.

What follows belief may be better understood as maturity rather than loss. The sacred becomes a matter of choice rather than command. It appears wherever compassion outweighs fear, where truth is pursued without expectation of reward, and where one person responds to another with care. The significance lies not in being observed, but in the human capacity to observe, to recognize beauty, to experience empathy, and to choose what is good without coercion.

This is the quiet revelation that outlives belief: the universe is not required to give us purpose for us to shape it within ourselves. Consciousness, brief as it is, has the power to turn chaos into understanding and matter into memory. We are both the question and the answer, both the seeker and what is sought.

I do not know whether anything awaits beyond this life, and perhaps it no longer matters. Eternity was never the point. What matters is the moment of awareness itself—the fleeting miracle of being able to ask, to wonder, to feel. If there is eternity, it exists in that awareness, multiplied across every mind that has ever paused to say, even silently, this matters.

What endures is what we make together: the unfinished, imperfect beauty of human effort. The hands that reach, the minds that question, the hearts that keep choosing kindness even in the face of indifference. If there is redemption, it lies in those gestures. If there is salvation, it is in the willingness to keep creating value, knowing it could vanish and choosing it anyway.

The story of belief was never only about gods. It was about us—our need to belong to something larger, our longing to make sense of what exceeds us. We have not outgrown that longing; we have learned to hold it without illusion. To live without God is not to live without reverence. It is to see reverence everywhere: in knowledge honestly pursued, in compassion freely given, in the fragile persistence of hope.

The search itself was the purpose, and the silence that follows it is not empty but complete. The universe will continue long after we are gone, but while we are here, we can answer its silence with care. We can meet its indifference with love.

When I first began writing, I thought I was simply recording what belief left behind. But looking back, I see that these pages trace something different: how silence slowly became understanding, and how questioning revealed its own form of faithfulness.

Sometimes, on clear early mornings, I still catch a shooting star. For an instant the sky seems alive, as if creation were speaking in light. I know it's only a fragment of rock burning through the atmosphere, but that knowledge never robs it of wonder. Centuries ago, people saw omens in those streaks; gods in battle, souls ascending, messages flung across the dark. I see something quieter: chance made luminous. Perhaps that's what reverence has become—not a cry to the heavens, but a moment of astonishment at what needs no meaning to be beautiful.

If there is a final truth here, it is not one we were given. We were never promised significance. We created it ourselves. The shaping of value from uncertainty, the insistence on care in a world that offers no guarantees, is not consolation—it is responsibility.

That responsibility begins only when we stop waiting for answers from beyond ourselves.

This is the great silence: not a void where meaning disappears, but the condition in which it must be made. What remains after belief is not certainty, revelation, or command, but the obligation we carry forward—to act with care, to seek understanding, and to live as though what we do matters, even when nothing answers back.

Bibliography

Adams, Douglas. *The Salmon of Doubt*. New York: Harmony Books, 2002.

Alexander, David. *Star Trek Creator: The Authorized Biography of Gene Roddenberry*. New York: Penguin Books, 1994.

Aquinas, Thomas. *Summa Theologica*. Translated by the Fathers of the English Dominican Province. New York: Benziger Brothers, 1947 (orig. 1265–1274).

Aristotle. *Metaphysics*. Translated by W. D. Ross. Oxford: Clarendon Press, 1924.

———. *On the Heavens*. Translated by W. K. C. Guthrie. Cambridge, MA: Harvard University Press, 1939.

Armstrong, Karen. *A History of God*. New York: Ballantine Books, 1993.

Atran, Scott. *In Gods We Trust: The Evolutionary Landscape of Religion*. Oxford: Oxford University Press, 2002.

Asch, Solomon E. "Opinions and Social Pressure." *Scientific American* 193, no. 5 (1955): 31–35.

Atkins, Peter. *The Four Laws That Drive the Universe*. Oxford: Oxford University Press, 2007.

Aurelius, Marcus. *Meditations*. Translated by Gregory Hays. New York: Modern Library, 2002.

Augustine of Hippo. *Confessions*. Translated by Henry Chadwick. Oxford: Oxford University Press, 1991 (orig. c. 400 CE).

———. *Confessions*. Translated by R. S. Pine-Coffin. London: Penguin Classics, 1961.

———. *Enchiridion on Faith, Hope, and Charity*. Translated by J. F. Shaw. New York: Macmillan, 1955.

Azim, Shariff, and Ara Norenzayan. "God Is Watching You: Priming God Concepts Increases Prosocial Behavior in an Anonymous Economic Game." *Psychological Science* 18, no. 9 (2007): 803–9.

Baldwin, James. *The Fire Next Time*. New York: Dial Press, 1963.

Barrett, Stephen. *Healers and the Healing Process*. Buffalo, NY: Prometheus Books, 1987.

Barrett, Justin L. *Why Would Anyone Believe in God?* Walnut Creek, CA: AltaMira Press, 2004.

Benson, Herbert, et al. "Study of the Therapeutic Effects of Intercessory Prayer (STEP) in Cardiac Bypass Patients: A Multicenter Randomized Trial." *American Heart Journal* 151, no. 4 (2006): 934–42.

Bonhoeffer, Dietrich. *Letters and Papers from Prison*. Translated by Eberhard Bethge. New York: Touchstone, 1997.

Boyer, Pascal. *Religion Explained: The Evolutionary Origins of Religious Thought*. New York: Basic Books, 2001.

Brown, Raymond E. *An Introduction to the New Testament*. New York: Doubleday, 1997.

Bushman, Richard L. *Joseph Smith: Rough Stone Rolling*. New York: Knopf, 2005.

Camus, Albert. *The Myth of Sisyphus*. Translated by Justin O'Brien. New York: Vintage International, 1991 (orig. 1942).

———. *The Rebel*. Translated by Anthony Bower. New York: Vintage Books, 1956.

Carroll, Sean. *The Particle at the End of the Universe: How the Hunt for the Higgs Boson Leads Us to the Edge of a New World*. New York: Dutton, 2012.

Carter, Brandon. "Large Number Coincidences and the Anthropic Principle in Cosmology." In *Confrontation of Cosmological Theories with Observational Data*, edited by M. S. Longair, 291–98. Dordrecht: Reidel, 1974.

Clarke, Arthur C. *Profiles of the Future: An Inquiry into the Limits of the Possible*. New York: Harper & Row, 1962.

Clifford, William K. *Lectures and Essays*. London: Macmillan, 1879.

Confucius. *The Analects*. Translated by Arthur Waley. New York: Vintage Books, 1989.

Coyne, Jerry A. *Why Evolution Is True*. New York: Viking, 2009.

Dalley, Stephanie. *Myths from Mesopotamia: Creation, the Flood, Gilgamesh, and Others*. Oxford: Oxford University Press, 2000.

Darwin, Charles. *On the Origin of Species*. London: John Murray, 1859.

Dawkins, Richard. *The Blind Watchmaker*. New York: W. W. Norton, 1986.

———. *The God Delusion*. Boston: Houghton Mifflin, 2006.

d'Aquili, Eugene, and Andrew Newberg. *The Mystical Mind*. Minneapolis: Fortress Press, 1999.

De Beauvoir, Simone. *The Ethics of Ambiguity*. Translated by Bernard Frechtman. New York: Philosophical Library, 1948.

Dennett, Daniel C. *Darwin's Dangerous Idea*. New York: Simon & Schuster, 1995.

Donner, Fred M. *Muhammad and the Believers*. Cambridge, MA: Harvard University Press, 2010.

Drummond, Henry. *The Ascent of Man*. London: Hodder and Stoughton, 1894.

Durkheim, Émile. *The Elementary Forms of Religious Life*. Translated by Karen E. Fields. New York: Free Press, 1995.

Dzielska, Maria. *Hypatia of Alexandria*. Translated by F. Lyra. Cambridge, MA: Harvard University Press, 1995.

Easwaran, Eknath, trans. The Upanishads. Tomales, CA: Nilgiri Press, 2007.

Ehrman, Bart D. *Jesus, Interrupted: Revealing the Hidden Contradictions in the Bible (and Why We Don't Know About Them)*. New York: HarperOne, 2009.

Einstein, Albert. *Ideas and Opinions*. New York: Crown, 1954.

———. *The World as I See It*. New York: Philosophical Library, 1934.

———. "Religion and Science." In *Ideas and Opinions*, 36–44. New York: Crown, 1954.

Eisenberger, Naomi I., and Matthew D. Lieberman. "Why Rejection Hurts: A Common Neural Alarm System for Physical and Social Pain." *Trends in Cognitive Sciences* 8, no. 7 (2004): 294–300.

Eliot, George. *Middlemarch*. London: Blackwood and Sons, 1871–72.

Epicurus. *The Extant Remains*. Translated by Cyril Bailey. Oxford: Clarendon Press, 1926.

Eusebius of Caesarea. *Life of Constantine*. Translated by Averil Cameron and Stuart G. Hall. Oxford: Oxford University Press, 1999.

Festinger, Leon. *A Theory of Cognitive Dissonance*. Stanford, CA: Stanford University Press, 1957.

Flew, Antony. *Theology and Falsification*. London: Society for Philosophical Study, 1950.

———. "The Presumption of Atheism." In *God, Freedom and Immortality: A Critical Analysis*, 13–30. Buffalo, NY: Prometheus Books, 1984 (orig. 1976).

Foucault, Michel. *Discipline and Punish: The Birth of the Prison*. Translated by Alan Sheridan. New York: Vintage Books, 1977.

Francis. "Address to the Pontifical Academy of Sciences." Vatican City, October 27, 2014.

Friedman, Richard Elliott. *Who Wrote the Bible?* New York: HarperCollins, 1997.

Galilei, Galileo. *Dialogue Concerning the Two Chief World Systems*. Translated by Stillman Drake. Berkeley: University of California Press, 1953.

Gilgamesh. *The Epic of Gilgamesh*. Translated by Andrew George. London: Penguin Classics, 1999.

Goldstein, Rebecca. *Plato at the Googleplex: Why Philosophy Won't Go Away*. New York: Pantheon Books, 2014.

Granqvist, Pehr, et al. "Sensed Presence and Mystical Experiences Are Predicted by Suggestibility, Not by the Application of Transcranial Weak Complex Magnetic Fields." *Neuroscience Letters* 379, no. 1 (2005): 1–6.

Haleem, M. A. S. Abdel, trans. The Qur'an. Oxford: Oxford University Press, 2004.

Hawking, Stephen. *A Brief History of Time: From the Big Bang to Black Holes*. New York: Bantam Books, 1988.

Hick, John. *Evil and the God of Love*. New York: Harper & Row, 1966.

Hitchens, Christopher. *God Is Not Great*. New York: Twelve, 2007.

Hume, David. *An Enquiry Concerning Human Understanding*. Edited by Tom L. Beauchamp. Oxford: Oxford University Press, 1999 (orig. 1748).

———. *An Enquiry Concerning the Principles of Morals*. London: 1751.

———. *Dialogues Concerning Natural Religion*. Edited by J. C. A. Gaskin. Oxford: Oxford University Press, 1993 (orig. 1779).

Hypatia. "Fragments and Letters." In *Women Philosophers of the Early Modern Period*, edited by Margaret Atherton. Indianapolis: Hackett, 1994.

Hypatia of Alexandria. In Dzielska, Maria. *Hypatia of Alexandria*. Translated by F. Lyra. Cambridge, MA: Harvard University Press, 1995.

Ibsen, Henrik. *An Enemy of the People*. Translated by Eleanor Marx-Aveling. London: Walter Scott, 1889.

James, William. *The Varieties of Religious Experience*. New York: Longmans, Green, 1902.

———. *The Will to Believe and Other Essays in Popular Philosophy*. New York: Longmans, Green & Co., 1897.

Jumper, John, et al. "Highly Accurate Protein Structure Prediction with AlphaFold." *Nature* 596 (2021): 583–89.

Kahneman, Daniel, and Amos Tversky. "Prospect Theory: An Analysis of Decision under Risk." *Econometrica* 47, no. 2 (1979): 263–91.

Kant, Immanuel. *Critique of Pure Reason*. Translated by Norman Kemp Smith. New York: St. Martin's Press, 1965.

———. *Groundwork of the Metaphysics of Morals*. Translated and edited by Mary Gregor. Cambridge: Cambridge University Press, 1998 (orig. 1785).

Keats, John. *Selected Letters*. Edited by Robert Gittings. Oxford: Oxford University Press, 1970.

Kierkegaard, Søren. *Fear and Trembling*. Translated by Alastair Hannay. London: Penguin Classics, 1985 (orig. 1843).

Krauss, Lawrence M. *A Universe from Nothing: Why There Is Something Rather than Nothing*. New York: Free Press, 2012.

Kruglanski, Arie W. *Motivated Social Cognition: Principles of the Interface*. Mahwah, NJ: Lawrence Erlbaum Associates, 1996.

Lactantius. *On the Anger of God*. Translated by William Fletcher. Washington, DC: Catholic University of America Press, 1965.

Lao Tzu. *Tao Te Ching*. Translated by D. C. Lau. London: Penguin Classics, 1963.

Leibniz, Gottfried Wilhelm. *Theodicy: Essays on the Goodness of God, the Freedom of Man, and the Origin of Evil*. Translated by E. M. Huggard. La Salle, IL: Open Court, 1952.

Levack, Brian P. *The Witch-Hunt in Early Modern Europe*. 3rd ed. London: Routledge, 2006.

Lucretius. *On the Nature of Things*. Translated by A. E. Stallings. New York: Penguin Classics, 2007 (orig. c. 50 BCE).

MacCulloch, Diarmaid. *The Reformation: A History*. New York: Viking, 2004.

Mackie, J. L. *The Miracle of Theism: Arguments for and against the Existence of God*. Oxford: Clarendon Press, 1982.

Mark Twain (Samuel L. Clemens). *Letters from the Earth*. New York: Harper & Row, 1962.

Martin, Michael. *Atheism: A Philosophical Justification*. Philadelphia: Temple University Press, 1990.

McGrath, Alister E. "The God of the Gaps." In *Science and Religion: An Introduction*, 195–208. Oxford: Wiley-Blackwell, 2010.

Melzack, Ronald, and Patrick D. Wall. *The Challenge of Pain*. New York: Penguin Books, 1996.

Milgram, Stanley. *Obedience to Authority*. New York: Harper & Row, 1974.

Mill, John Stuart. *Utilitarianism*. London: Parker, Son, and Bourn, 1863.

Montaigne, Michel de. *The Complete Essays*. Translated by M. A. Screech. London: Penguin Classics, 1991.

Moore, R. I. *The Formation of a Persecuting Society: Authority and Deviance in Western Europe 950–250*. Oxford: Blackwell, 1987.

Newberg, Andrew B. *How God Changes Your Brain*. New York: Ballantine Books, 2009.

Newberg, Andrew, with Eugene d'Aquili and Vince Rause. *Why God Won't Go Away*. New York: Ballantine Books, 2001.

Nickell, Joe. *Looking for a Miracle: Weeping Icons, Relics, Stigmata, Visions & Healing Cures*. Amherst, NY: Prometheus Books, 1993.

Nightingale, Florence. *Notes on Nursing: What It Is, and What It Is Not*. London: Harrison, 1860.

Norenzayan, Ara. *Big Gods: How Religion Transformed Cooperation and Conflict*. Princeton: Princeton University Press, 2013.

Nussbaum, Martha C. *The Fragility of Goodness: Luck and Ethics in Greek Tragedy and Philosophy*. Cambridge: Cambridge University Press, 1986.

Ockham, William of. *Ockham's Razor: A Selection of Writings*. Edited by Philotheus Boehner. Indianapolis: Bobbs-Merrill, 1957 (orig. 14th cent.).

———. *Summa Logicae*. Translated by Michael J. Loux. Notre Dame, IN: University of Notre Dame Press, 1974.

Paine, Thomas. *The Age of Reason*. Philadelphia, 1794.

Paley, William. *Natural Theology; or, Evidences of the Existence and Attributes of the Deity*. London: R. Faulder, 1802.

Pascal, Blaise. *Pensées*. Translated by A. J. Krailsheimer. London: Penguin Classics, 1995 (orig. 1670).

Persinger, Michael A. *Neuropsychological Bases of God Beliefs*. New York: Praeger, 1987.

———. "The Tectonic Strain Theory as an Explanation for UFO Phenomena." *Perceptual and Motor Skills* 60, no. 3 (1985): 895–902.

Persinger, Michael A., and Paul Healey. "Experimental Facilitation of the Sensed Presence: Possible Contributions of the Right Hemisphere." *Journal of Nervous and Mental Disease* 191, no. 10 (2003): 683–93.

Pew Research Center. "Americans' Feelings About Religion." Washington, DC, 2019.

———. "America's Changing Religious Landscape." Washington, DC: Pew Research Center, 2017.

———. "Religious Upbringing and Views of God." Washington, DC, 2017.

———. *The Global Religious Landscape*. Washington, DC, 2012.

Popper, Karl. *The Open Society and Its Enemies*. Princeton: Princeton University Press, 1971.

Pseudo-Dionysius the Areopagite. *The Complete Works*. Translated by Colm Luibheid. New York: Paulist Press, 1987.

Ra, Christopher K., Jae Cho, Michael D. Stone, et al. "Association of Digital Media Use with Subsequent Symptoms of Attention-Deficit/Hyperactivity Disorder among Adolescents." *JAMA Pediatrics* 173 (2019) 207–15.

Rembrandt van Rijn. *Self-Portrait with Two Circles*. 1665–69. Kenwood House, London.

Rizzolatti, Giacomo, and Corrado Sinigaglia. *Mirrors in the Brain: How Our Minds Share Actions and Emotions*. Translated by Frances Anderson. Oxford: Oxford University Press, 2008.

Roth, Martha T. *Law Collections from Mesopotamia and Asia Minor*. 2nd ed. Atlanta: Scholars Press, 1997.

Rudd, Melanie, Jennifer Aaker, and Kathleen Vohs. "Awe Expands Perception of Time and Enhances Generosity." *Emotion* 12, no. 8 (2012): 1232–1240.

Russell, Bertrand. "Is There a God?" *Illustrated Magazine*, 1952. Reprinted in *The Collected Papers of Bertrand Russell*, vol. 11. London: George Allen & Unwin, 1983.

———. *The Problems of Philosophy*. London: Williams and Norgate, 1912.

———. *Why I Am Not a Christian*. London: George Allen & Unwin, 1927.

Sagan, Carl. *Cosmos*. New York: Random House, 1980.

———. *Pale Blue Dot: A Vision of the Human Future in Space*. New York: Random House, 1994.

———. *The Demon-Haunted World: Science as a Candle in the Dark*. New York: Random House, 1995.

Sartre, Jean-Paul. *Being and Nothingness*. Translated by Hazel E. Barnes. New York: Philosophical Library, 1956 (orig. 1943).

———. *Existentialism Is a Humanism*. Translated by Carol Macomber. New Haven: Yale University Press, 2007.

Shaw, George Bernard. *Androcles and the Lion*. London: Constable, 1916.

———. *The Quintessence of Ibsenism*. London: Constable, 1913.

Shermer, Michael. *The Believing Brain: From Ghosts and Gods to Politics and Conspiracies—How We Construct Beliefs and Reinforce Them as Truths*. New York: Times Books, 2011.

Schweitzer, Albert. *Civilization and Ethics*. Translated by C. T. Campion. London: A. & C. Black, 1923.

———. *Reverence for Life*. Translated by Reginald H. Fuller. New York: Harper & Brothers, 1969.

Scholem, Gershom. *Major Trends in Jewish Mysticism*. New York: Schocken Books, 1995.

Smart, Ninian. *The World's Religions*. Cambridge: Cambridge University Press, 1989.

Spinoza, Baruch. *Ethics*. Translated by Edwin Curley. London: Penguin Classics, 1996.

Taubenberger, Jeffery K., and David M. Morens. "1918 Influenza: The Mother of All Pandemics." *Emerging Infectious Diseases* 12, no. 1 (2006): 15–22.

Tegmark, Max. *Our Mathematical Universe*. New York: Knopf, 2014.

Twain, Mark. *Mark Twain's Notebook*. New York: Harper & Brothers, 1935.

Vinge, Vernor. "The Coming Technological Singularity: How to Survive in the Post-Human Era." In *Vision-21: Interdisciplinary Science and Engineering in the Era of Cyberspace*, 11–22. Washington, DC: NASA Conference Publication 10129, 1993.

Vogelsberger, Mark, et al. "Introducing the Illustris Project: Simulating the Coevolution of Dark and Visible Matter in the Universe." *Monthly Notices of the Royal Astronomical Society* 444, no. 2 (2014): 1518–47.

Voltaire. *Candide*. Translated by John Butt. London: Penguin Classics, 1947.

———. *Philosophical Dictionary*. Translated by Theodore Besterman. London: Penguin Classics, 1972.

———. *Poem on the Lisbon Disaster*. Translated by Tobias Smollett. London, 1756.

Weinberg, Steven. *Dreams of a Final Theory*. New York: Pantheon Books, 1992.

Wittgenstein, Ludwig. *Tractatus Logico-Philosophicus*. Translated by C. K. Ogden. London: Routledge & Kegan Paul, 1922.

Wollstonecraft, Mary. *A Vindication of the Rights of Woman*. London: J. Johnson, 1792.

World Health Organization. *World Malaria Report 2023*. Geneva: World Health Organization, 2023.

Zuckerman, Phil. *Living the Secular Life: New Answers to Old Questions*. New York: Penguin Books, 2014.

———. *Society Without God: What the Least Religious Nations Can Tell Us about Contentment*. New York: New York University Press, 2008.

www.ingramcontent.com/pod-product-compliance
Lightning Source LLC
LaVergne TN
LVHW050628100826
845148LV00011B/1772

9798385274925